Quality
Matters
in **Children's**
Services

Kinship Care

Fostering Effective Family and Friends Placements

- Elaine Farmer
- Sue Moyers

LEARNING RESOURCES
CENTRE

Havering College
of Further and Higher Education

Jessica Kingsley Publishers
London and Philadelphia

First published in 2008
by Jessica Kingsley Publishers
116 Pentonville Road
London N1 9JB, UK
and
400 Market Street, Suite 400
Philadelphia, PA 19106, USA

www.jkp.com

Library of Congress Cataloging in Publication Data

Farmer, Elaine.
   Kinship care : fostering effective family and friends placements / Elaine Farmer and Sue Moyers.
       p. cm. -- (Quality matters in children's services series)
   Includes bibliographical references.
   ISBN 978-1-84310-631-9 (pb : alk. paper) 1. Kinship care. 2. Foster home care. 3. Foster children--Services for. 4. Foster children--Family relationship. 5. Children--Legal status, laws, etc. I. Moyers, Sue, 1948- II. Title.
   HV873.F35 2008
   362.73'3--dc22

                                                                        2007047559

British Library Cataloguing in Publication Data
A CIP catalogue record for this book is available from the British Library

ISBN 978 1 84310 631 9

Printed and bound in Great Britain by
Athenaeum Press, Gateshead, Tyne and Wear

Kinship Care

Quality Matters in Children's Services

Series Editor: Mike Stein

Consultant Editor: Caroline Thomas

The provision of high quality children's services matters to those who use and provide children's services. This important series is the result of an extensive government funded research initiative into the *Quality Protects* programme which aimed to improve outcomes for vulnerable children, as well as transform the management and delivery of children's services. Focussing on current challenges in making every child matter, titles in the series are essential reading for all those working in the field.

also in the series

Child Protection, Domestic Violence and Parental Substance Misuse
Family Experiences and Effective Practice
Hedy Cleaver, Don Nicholson, Sukey Tarr and Deborah Cleaver
ISBN 978 1 84310 582 4

The Pursuit of Permanence
A Study of the English Child Care System
Ian Sinclair, Claire Baker, Jenny Lee and Ian Gibbs
ISBN 978 1 84310 595 4

of related interest

Nurturing Attachments
Supporting Children who are Fostered or Adopted
Kim S. Golding
ISBN 978 1 84310 614 2

Understanding Looked After Children
Psychology for Foster Care
Jeune Guishard-Pine, Suzanne McCall and Lloyd Hamilton
Foreword by Andrew Wiener
ISBN 978 1 84310 370 7

Big Steps for Little People
Parenting Your Adopted Child
Celia Foster
Forewords by David Howe and Daniel A. Hughes
ISBN 978 1 84310 620 3

Managing Children's Homes
Developing Effective Leadership in Small Organisations
Leslie Hicks, Ian Gibbs, Helen Weatherly and Sarah Byford
ISBN 978 1 84310 542 8
Costs and Effectiveness of Services for Children in Need series

Fostering Now
Messages from Research
Ian Sinclair
Foreword by Tom Jeffreys, Director General, Children, Families and Young People Directorate, DfES
ISBN 978 1 84310 362 2

Contents

List of Tables

Acknowledgements

The Department of Health initially funded this research and latterly the funding was taken over by the Department for Children, Schools and Families as part of the group of research projects funded under the *Quality Protects* initiative. We are very grateful for this assistance and would particularly like to thank our research liaison officers, Dr Caroline Thomas and Dr Carolyn Davies for their invaluable assistance and for thinking that it was important to find out more about kin placements.

We are extremely grateful to the four local authorities that allowed us access and introduced us to children and their kinship carers. In particular, their administrative staff made our lives considerably easier by being well organised and extremely efficient. Team managers and social workers made us welcome, facilitated the work and were very interested in what we were doing. All had a view about kinship care and provided us with a great deal of thought-provoking discussion, both formally in the interviews and informally as we worked alongside them. We are also indebted to the kin carers, children, young people and their parents who talked to us at length and shared their experiences with us.

Regular meetings with our Research Advisory Group were invaluable and we would like to thank Helen Jones and Sonia Heywood from the Department for Children, Schools and Families; David Berridge, Ian Sinclair, Mike Stein, David Quinton, Harriet Ward, Ian Gibbs and Joan Hunt, Cherie Talbot from the Fostering Network, Lynn Chesterman from the Grandparents Federation, Felicity Collier from the British Association for Adoption and Fostering and Robert Tapsfield from Family Rights Group for giving their valuable time to help us with this work.

We would particularly like to thank David Berridge and Ian Gibbs for reading the draft report on which this book is based and for their very helpful comments. Also invaluable were the comments made by Kate Thomas-Peter about the complex legislation that governed the placements.

We are very grateful to Pat Lees, our research support officer, who provided much needed help and support throughout the project until her retirement. We would also like to thank Carol Marks who provided an extremely efficient, fast and accurate transcription of the interview tapes.

We have tried to represent accurately the many different experiences and views of kinship care in this report and also convey some of the complexity of the issues. However, if there are any errors they are solely our responsibility.

Part I
The Study

Chapter 1

Background

Introduction

> I'm glad that I'm with my nan and granddad because I know that I'm not going to be going anywhere because they're settled down and they're happily married.

There is a long history in the UK, as in most countries, of children being cared for by relatives and other kin when their parents, for whatever reason, are unable to care for the children themselves. Most of these care-taking arrangements are made without the involvement of the child welfare system.

Where children's services are involved, government statistics show that there has been a steady rise in the numbers of children in care in England who are fostered with family and friends. The proportion increased from 6 per cent of looked after children in 1989 to 10 per cent in 1998 and 12 per cent in 2005 (Department of Health 1991 and 1999; Department for Education and Skills 2006). At the same time, a more hidden group of children cared for by kin, (which does not appear in these figures), are those supported outside the care system, through the use of residence or special guardianship orders or payments for children in need.

The increasing use of kin care, which in some local authorities may represent as much as 40 per cent or more of all foster placements, has not been matched by an increase in knowledge for practitioners and policy-makers about how well these placements work, what helps them to succeed or when they should not be used. It is these issues which this book addresses.

About this book

This book shows which children in which circumstances go to family and friends rather than unrelated foster carers, the progress they make and the outcomes for children in each kind of placement. Placement progress and the supports and services provided to children in these two settings are compared so that the implications for practice and policy can be drawn out.

In the rest of this opening chapter we sketch in the background to the study on which this book is based, and provide a brief review of the relevant literature. In Chapter 2 we turn to the design of the study and the research methods employed. Chapters 3 to 5 compare kinship care with unrelated foster care and consider how the placements were made, the backgrounds of the children and carers, the services provided, contact with parents, how children progressed and the outcomes of placements at the two-year follow-up. Chapters 6 to 9 look in depth at kin carers' experiences of looking after these children, including such issues as assessment, relationships with other family members and social workers, financial and other forms of support, the children's safety and the impact of caring for the children on the carers themselves. These chapters draw on detailed information from the case files and more particularly on interviews with kin carers, the children who live with them, their birth parents and social workers. The final chapter draws the findings together and considers their implication for policy and practice.

Definitions

The book focuses on those placements with family and friends that come to the attention of children's services and receive some help, irrespective of the legal status of the children. Thus, children supported under Section 17 of the Children Act 1989 or on residence orders are included, as well as kin who had been approved as foster carers (more information on the legal status and arrangements that cover the placements are given in Chapter 4). In this book family and friends are often referred to as 'kin' for the sake of simplicity – 'kin placements', 'kin care' or 'kinship care' therefore refer to placements with either family or friends. 'Unrelated', 'non-related', 'non-relative' or 'stranger' foster carers are the terms used for foster carers who are not related to the child or are not friends of the family. Placements with family include any placements with a family member other than the birth parents, such as grandparents, aunts, uncles, cousins or older siblings. Placements with friends include the friends of the child or of the parents, guardians, god-parents, step-parents, teachers or any other unrelated adult who has offered the child a home.

Earlier research on family and friends placements in the UK

Despite the exhortation in the Children Act 1989 to pursue placements with family and friends before considering stranger foster care for children, there has been little research into these placements in England, with the notable exception of the pioneering work of Broad and others (e.g. Broad 2001; Broad, Hayes and Rushforth 2001; Doolan, Nixon and Lawrence 2004; Flynn 2000; Greef 1999; Pitcher 2002). Nonetheless, most of these studies have been small projects and had limitations, particularly in terms of evaluating outcomes. Yet kin placements have the potential to help local authorities to meet the Every Child Matters outcomes and the earlier *Quality Protects* objectives (Department of Health 1998), for example by increasing placement choice, promoting attachment to carers, promoting placement stability and ensuring young people leaving care are not isolated as they enter adulthood. It is particularly surprising that so little research on family and friends placements has been conducted in this country, since as long ago as 1984 Rowe suggested that placement with relatives or friends might be beneficial for children (Rowe *et al.* 1984).

Subsequent research by Rowe and her colleagues (1989) showed that children placed with relatives were much more likely to be in long-term care than those in non-related foster care and these placements more often than others met their aims fully or in most respects. More recently, Sinclair, Gibbs and Wilson (2004; 2005a;) found, as part of a larger study of foster care, that the outcomes of kinship foster placements were similar to those with unrelated foster carers. Hunt (2001) found that the possibility of kinship placements was not 'routinely investigated' and cases could reach court before it had been explored. Other research has shown (Brandon *et al.* 1999; Packman and Hall 1998) that care with relatives is used in a minority of child protection cases at the outset of agency involvement.

The potential benefits of family and friends care

The potential benefits of placement within the extended family include placement in a familiar ethnic community, a greater sense of belonging (Mosek and Adler 2001) and security about identity, greater continuity and stability and that children anticipate staying with their carers into adulthood (Iglehart 1995). Young people in kinship care too are very positive about it (Broad *et al.* 2001) and, importantly, kin care may well be the first choice of both parent and child (Dubowitz 1994; Farmer and Owen 1995; Hegar and Scannapieco 1995; NFCA 1999; Rowe *et al.* 1984; Thornton 1987). Indeed, when 5000 young people were consulted about the Green Paper 'Care Matters: Transforming the Lives of Children and Young People in Care', three quarters said that 'it was really important to see if there are other relatives who could look after a child before they go into care' (DfES 2007, p.5).

Much research has demonstrated high levels of commitment by carers, the satisfaction they derive from caring and the strong bonds formed with children (see e.g. Altshuler 1999; Flynn 2001; Pitcher 1999; Tan 2000). In contrast, a Dutch and a New Zealand study found no difference in the quality of relationships or commitment between the two kinds of placement (Smith *et al.* 1999; Strijker, Zandberg and ven der Meulen 2003).

Government statistics on fostering in England suggest that a higher proportion of kin than stranger foster placements last for over two years (Department of Health 2001), whilst research suggests that children placed with kin have fewer moves both overall (Chipungu and Everett 1998) and before entering placement (Kosonen 1993; Rowe *et al.* 1984).

Continued contact with parents has been shown to be three times more likely than when children are placed with non-relative carers (Rowe *et al.* 1984) and links with the rest of the extended family may also be facilitated (see e.g. Brown, Cohon and Wheeler 2002). At the same time, research from the US suggests that, paradoxically, reunification with birth parents happens less frequently from placements with relatives or friends (Berrick *et al.* 1994; Dubowitz, Feigelman and Zuravin 1993; Scannapieco and Jackson 1996; Thornton 1991; Wulczyn and Goerge 1992; see also Rowe *et al.* 1989).

Potential problems and issues

Whilst there is likely to be more contact with parents and other relatives, contact difficulties have been shown to occur more often in kin than in stranger placements (see e.g. Cleaver 2000; Laws 2001; Malos and Bullard 1991; Rowe *et al.* 1984). We do not know how difficult it is for relative carers to protect children and to limit contact with parents if the safety of the child is compromised by contact, although in extreme cases this contact can lead to abuse or even death (Birmingham ACPC 2004; London Borough of Lambeth 1987). Similarly there is little research on the safety of kinship care, with American studies providing conflicting findings on whether there are more allegations of abuse in kinship than non-kin foster care (Benedict, Zuravin and Stallings 1996; Dubowitz *et al.* 1993). This book addresses these issues.

In addition, research has shown that placement with family and friends can lead to varying patterns of alliance between the agency, carers, child and parents, for example when an exclusive relationship between the carers and parents places the local authority on the sidelines or when a close alliance between the carers and authority actively excludes the parents (O'Brien 1999, 2000). However, we do not know how often these issues present serious obstacles in practice.

This links with some evidence of reluctance to use kinship care because it lessens social worker power and control; is seen as more difficult to work with partly because of the carers' prior relationship with the parents; placements are more difficult to supervise and practitioners lack confidence in their skills and knowledge in this area (Beeman and Boisen 1999; McFadden 1998; Portengen and van der Neut 1999). Moreover, some practitioners are wary of placing children with relatives for fear that the latter will display the same dysfunctional behaviour as the birth parents from whom the child was removed.

We need to know more too about the ability of grandparents to cope with looking after their grandchildren as they grow older and the potential challenges of adolescence emerge. The little evidence that exists is contradictory (Pitcher 1999; Richards 2001; Stokes and Greenstone 1981). Indeed, Stogdon (1999) sees ageism as a major obstacle to the use of kinship care in the UK.

Approval and assessment

In the UK kinship care has been grafted on to the existing system of children's services and one study found that of the ten local authorities considered, most did not include kin as part of their fostering services, with kin carers generally located under social work field services (Flynn 2000).

It is likely too that in the UK there may be a built-in disincentive to make such placements if the burden of approval of caregivers falls on overworked field or duty social workers with little experience of this kind of assessment (Waterhouse and Brocklesby 1999). On the other hand, where family placement workers are involved, it has been found that they often have reservations about the suitability of kin carers, partly related to standards of care but also reflecting their doubts about the cost-effectiveness of investing in this group of carers who will probably take no other children in the future (NFCA 2000).

There is a high level of uncertainty in some local authorities about how best to deal with these placements, with some evidence of a lack of written policy or practice documents (NFCA 2000; see also Mason et al. 2002). Moreover, there is considerable variation in how family and friends assessments are made and who undertakes them and many are, of necessity, made when the child is already in the placement (NFCA 2000; O'Brien 2000).

Behind these variations lies the thorny question about what standards should be expected of family and friend carers who may provide placements which are in a particular child's best interests, yet not meet the expectations held in relation to unrelated foster carers. Flynn (2002) argues that there should be flexibility on some criteria such as accommodation, health and age.

A number of differences between assessing kin and stranger foster carers have been noted, particularly that the child's placement is in the gift of the agency more clearly with stranger foster carers (O'Brien 2000), that kin carers may be shocked to find that they have to undergo an in-depth assessment (Waldman and Wheal 1999) and that good kin assessments may be more time-consuming than those for non-relative foster carers (Aldgate and McIntosh 2006; Laws 2001; Shlonsky and Berrick 2001).

Remuneration and support

A number of studies have shown that kin carers are disadvantaged because they receive fewer support services than other foster carers (see e.g. Broad, Hayes and Rushforth 2001; Doolan, Nixon and Lawrence 2004; Laws 2001; Richards 2001) even when they are approved as foster carers (see e.g. Rowe *et al.* 1984; Tan 2000; Waterhouse 2001) and they receive little training or preparation (Pitcher 1999; Waldman and Wheal 1999). On the other hand, a study in Ireland suggests that relative carers tend to view potential support as an attempt to monitor the child (O'Brien 2000). Tapsfield (2001) argues that there is a great deal of variation in the way that kinship carers are perceived and treated by local authorities, to the extent that some support whilst others undermine these placements.

The issue of the remuneration of kin carers is also linked to the vexed question of paying family members for what many think should be done out of a sense of kinship affection and obligation (O'Brien 2000). For all these reasons family and friends who look after children are likely to be variably supported and remunerated (Berrick, Barth and Needell 1994; NFCA 2000).

Profiles of children and carers

In the US and Canada, since the mid 1980s, pressures on child care agencies – because of increased reporting of child maltreatment and higher levels of parental drug misuse and HIV infection – have led to a large rise in the numbers of children being placed with the extended family (McFadden 1998). Figures show that kinship care accounts for a much higher proportion of care placements in the US than in the UK and this is also true in Australia and New Zealand (AIHW 2007; Connolly 2003; CWLA 2005; Mason *et al.* 2002; US DHSS 2000).

African-American and, to a lesser extent, Hispanic children are disproportionately represented among those cared for by relatives in the United States (Hegar and Scannapieco 1999). It has been suggested that the growth of family and friends placements in the UK may also prove to be greatest for black and minority ethnic children (Brandon *et al.* 1999; Broad 1999; Waterhouse 2001), although this book shows that this does not appear to be the case.

Many American studies suggest that compared with children in stranger care, children placed with family and friends carers have less troubled histories; are more likely to be placed because of neglect and parental substance misuse rather than abuse and display fewer difficulties prior to placement (Beeman, Kim and Bullerdick 2000; Chipungu and Everett 1998; Grogan-Kaylor 2000 and Iglehart 1994). This study explored whether or not this is also true in the UK and, as we will see, a different pattern emerged here.

Kin carers in the US are predominantly African-American or Hispanic, older, in poorer health, are less well educated, have lower incomes and comprise a higher number of families headed by a single woman than is the case with non-related carers (Dubowitz *et al.* 1993; Hegar and Scannapieco 1999; Iglehart 1994). The research, on which this book is based, found that kin carers in England have a somewhat different profile.

Gaps in the research

Much of the research on kinship care is from the US and there are real difficulties in transferring the findings to the UK with its different legislation, child care services, socio-economic pressures, history and culture. Indeed, the authors' findings show that there are considerable differences in the population of kin carers and children in this country and the US. At the same time the research in the UK is sparse. In particular, there are few studies that examine children's outcomes or compare children placed with kin with their counterparts in unrelated foster care.

Information is urgently needed about the effects on children of placements with kin in order to enable local authorities to make informed decisions about where best to place children. We need to know more about which children, in which circumstances are placed with kin; how well such children fare and how often such placements disrupt. Importantly, we do not know if children placed with kin do better or worse than other fostered children or whether there are specific differences in the characteristics of children who move to kin placements. Moreover, we do not know whether the factors that place an unrelated foster placement at greater risk of breakdown also operate in these placements. In addition, more information is needed about the supports provided, used and needed by relative and friend carers to enable placements to succeed. It is these gaps in our knowledge that this book addresses.

Chapter 2

The Design

Main aims of the research

Given the lack of national research on kinship care in the UK our objective was to provide a clear picture of how these placements are used, to examine the issues for the placed children, their birth parents, the carers and social workers and to compare the characteristics and outcomes of children placed in unrelated foster care placements.

The specific aims of the study were:

- to clarify the range and patterns of administrative and legal categories used for placements with kin in the local authorities in the study and their relationship with remuneration and support for caregivers

- to compare the characteristics of children placed with kin and unrelated foster carers

- to compare the quality of placements and outcomes for children placed with kin with those for children placed with unrelated foster carers and to examine which factors in which circumstances relate to the success of placements with kin

- to explore the particular features of placements with kin from the perspectives of the main participants and to consider in which situations such placements appear to be especially beneficial or detrimental and the kind of case management that is most effective.

Design of the study

The study was based on a cross-section of children who were living in kin and unrelated foster care placements on a set date.[1] This date was chosen so that the placements could be followed up for a period of two years from then.[2] (This is known as a 'catch-up prospective design'.) Before the sample selection date the children had already been in placement for varying periods of time, which were fairly similar for the two groups. Between a quarter and a third of the children had been in placement for under two years, half for between two and six years, whilst a fifth to over a quarter had lived with their carers for over six years (see Table 2.1).

Table 2.1 Length of time in the study placement before the sample was selected

Placement time	Kin placements[*] (Per cent) N = 141	Unrelated foster placements (Per cent) N = 128
Less than 2 years	23	31
2–6 years	49	50
6 years and over	28	19
	100	100

[*]Missing data on one case.

Four local authorities were selected which included southern, midlands and northern authorities. Three were urban areas or metropolitan districts with sizeable black and minority ethnic populations and one was a shire county which included two densely populated towns. They varied too in their levels of deprivation, with two authorities showing particularly high levels of deprivation. At the time, Department of Health figures (DoH 2000) showed that 17 per cent of children in foster care in England were placed with kin, with wide variations in different local authorities – from two with 40 per cent of their fostered children in kin foster care to others with none. In this sample, the highest using local authority placed 41 per cent of its fostered children with kin (higher than the proportion shown for it in government figures[3]), the next highest placed 26 per cent, whilst the other two were at around the national average with 19 per cent and 14 per cent of their fostered children going to kin foster placements.

Each local authority provided a list of all their children who were living in either a kin or unrelated foster placement during the month of July in our selection year. We encouraged them to include children with kin who were known to them because the carers were supported under the Section 17 children in need provisions or where the children were on residence orders as well as those in kinship foster care, although it is likely that the records on the first two groups of children were less robust.

We drew similar numbers of children in kinship care in each authority in order to represent practice in the four different areas. Two other considerations were introduced into the sampling: the first was to include all black and minority ethnic children (in both types of placement) in order that comparisons in relation to ethnicity could be made; an important consideration because of possible differences in the use of kin placements according to ethnicity. The second was stratification by age so that the proportions of children in each age grouping in the case file sample would reflect the age groupings of the full cohort of 2240 children from the four local authorities.

From the list of 2240 children provided, a sample of 270 children were selected in this way, just over half of whom (142, 53%) were placed with family or friends and just under half of whom (128, 47%) were with unrelated foster carers. Only one child from each family was included, although details about siblings were noted.

Case file review

Information was collected from the case files of these 270 children. This included demographic information; background histories and adversities experienced by the children; their placement histories, the supports and services provided and their progress with kin or with unrelated foster carers in the placement on which we focused (which we call the 'study placement'), as well as information about their development and behaviour. These data were noted on a schedule designed for the study on which we recorded 237 items of information.

Data on the study placement were examined in depth so that ratings of the quality of the placement for each child could be made on a number of dimensions, including those from the Assessment Framework (Department of Health, Department for Education and Employment and Home Office 2000) and from the Integrated Children's System (which drew on the Looking After Children dimensions). The information from the case file review was subsequently used to make comparisons between children and their outcomes in the two types of placement (kin care and unrelated foster care). In addition, a lengthy summary covering the whole progress of the case was completed on each child and these summaries were also analysed qualitatively, as we will see in Chapters 6 to 8.[4]

It should be noted that case file information has certain limitations. Some of these relate to data that are not routinely recorded on files (for example the reasons for some decisions, receipt of benefits and the ages of carers) and others to information that is found on some but not other files so that there may be missing data on particular issues. In addition, case file records are by definition the social workers' constructions of events. Nonetheless, we found them to be a rich source of information about the children, carers and placements and they allow access to the whole range of the population under study, which is not possible with interviews. This study aimed to capitalise on the strengths of these two sources of information.

Interviews

In the second stage of the study, our main source of information was from intensive semi-structured interviews undertaken with a sub-sample of kinship carers, the children they were looking after, their parents and their social workers. In addition, we used a small number of standardised measures relating to the children's behaviour and emotional well-being and the carers' health and stress. In all, 70 interviews were carried out relating to 35 cases (25% of the case file sample of kin carers): 32 with kin carers, 16 with children, six with parents and 16 with social workers. All interviews were audio taped and transcribed with the permission of the respondents and all identifiable information encrypted on computer to maintain their confidentiality. The carers, children and parents who took part in the interviews, were given a store voucher as a small token of thanks for the time they gave to the study.

Further details about the interviewees are given in Chapter 6 and 9.

CARER INTERVIEWS

When kin carers were in couples, both were interviewed where possible. They were asked about the child and the placement and the direct effects that the placement had had on their family and on relationships within the wider family network. Services and financial and legal issues were also discussed. If the placement had ended, they were asked about its ending and the child's subsequent movements.

Carers were also asked to complete two standardised questionnaires:

1. Strengths and Difficulties Questionnaire (Goodman 1994): this questionnaire asks about the emotional and behavioural development of children in different age groups.

2. General Health Questionnaire (Goldberg and Hillier 1979): this questionnaire asks about the health and well-being of carers.

CHILD INTERVIEWS

When their carers and social workers agreed, children over the age of seven years were asked if they were willing to be interviewed. If they gave consent, the interviews with them focused on: moving to live with kin, their placement with them, their normal routines, contact with other family members and relationships with social workers.

The interviews were interspersed with brief exercises and questionnaires that children either completed on their own, or with the help of the researcher. The exercises included:

- *Eco map* – this was a drawing of concentric circles with the child at the centre. Children were asked to write in the names of the people in their lives and to place them in one of the circles, depending on how close or distant they felt from them.

- *Important to me* – this exercise asks children to list the people who are most important to them.

- *Thoughts and feelings* (Stallard 2002). These exercises aimed to explore some of the things that made the children feel good or bad about themselves and their different feelings in different settings. They were: 'Things that make me feel good', 'Things that make me feel bad' and 'What feeling goes where'?

- *Childhood depression questionnaire* (Kovaks and Beck 1977), which was designed to identify depression in children.

PARENT INTERVIEWS

Interviews with parents covered topics such as the reasons for the placement, their relationships with kin carers, contact, their view of their child's development, support from children's services and their plans and hopes for the future.

SOCIAL WORKER INTERVIEWS

Social workers were asked about the child's history, the legal arrangements for the placement, assessment and approval of carers and planning for the placement. Aspects of the placement such as finance, support and contact issues were discussed, as well as what had happened to the child since the placement was made. Their attitudes towards kin placements in general were also explored.

Analyses

The case file material was coded and entered onto a computer database and analysed using SPSS for Windows. When correlations were examined to look for statistically significant associations chi-square or Fisher's exact test (two-tailed) were used and relationships were considered to be significant where $p < 0.05$, which indicates a relationship beyond the 5 per cent level of probability. Analysis of variance (ANOVA) techniques were used with interval variables to compare average values (means) between the two groups (e.g. length of time in the placement). It should be noted that exact levels of probability will be used sparingly in the text but any relationship described as significant or to which we draw attention should be assumed to be statistically significant unless stated otherwise.

Policy discussions

Interviews with managers and policy-makers were conducted in each of the four participating local authorities to clarify the range and patterns of administrative and legal categories used for kin placements and their relationship with financial and other support for the kin carers.

All four local authorities struggled to decide where to set the standards for assessments of kin carers (see also NFCA 2000) and whether the criteria for unrelated foster carers should be used for kin, especially in relation to previous convictions, some of which had been committed many years previously.[5] It was noted that children's guardians (Children and Family Court Advisory and Support Service workers) were instrumental in encouraging the use of kinship care and there was a growing awareness that such placements could be more successful than unrelated foster care and had the major advantage of continuity for children.

All the authorities saw contact with parents as being a difficult issue for kin carers to deal with effectively without the support of children's services, especially when parents had mental health difficulties, were drug users with disorganised life-styles or were violent and abusive. Local authority interviewees felt that kin carers were often reluctant to apply for residence orders (a situation in which social work involvement ceases) because they needed the support of children's services in managing difficult contact. None of the authorities provided kin carers with a family placement worker, although one had appointed two specialist kin workers within the family placements team to assess kin placements. However, by the time of the fieldwork these specialist workers had been re-allocated to adoption work, and in at least one other authority specialist kin workers were appointed after the study had ended (see Selwyn and Saunders 2006).

Financial arrangements for supporting kin placements varied considerably between the authorities. Initially, one study authority paid kin carers approximately two-thirds of the foster carer rate, which was a not unusual practice. However, during the study they revised their policy in response to the Munby judgement[6] and increased the allowance paid to kin carers to (more closely) match that paid to unrelated foster carers.

The administrative and legal categories used for such placements also varied considerably. Two of the authorities particularly often used Emergency Placement Regulation 38[7] for kin placements. Other arrangements for kin carers included the use of fostering, residence orders and private fostering regulations, whilst a number of kin carers only received financial support under the children in need arrangements (under Section 17 of the Children Act 1989). One authority had an explicit policy of encouraging carers to apply for residence orders from the outset, although others were active in doing so at a later stage.[8]

It was clear that in all four authorities, kin placements were increasingly being used, particularly as a means of managing the pressure on other foster placements, but that policies on kin care either did not exist or were being developed on an *ad hoc* basis (see also NFCA 2000, Waterhouse and Brocklesby 1998). There was also evidence that they were proving to be more complex than the local authorities had first envisaged.

In what follows the names and some of the details of the individuals who are described have been changed in order to preserve anonymity.

Summary

The study took place in four local authorities. The sample was made up of 270 children just over half of whom (53%, 142) were living with family or friends and just under half (47%, 128) with unrelated foster carers. They were selected from all the children living in such placements during the month of July in our selection year in our authorities. Placements had by then lasted for varying periods of time.

The case files of the 270 children were reviewed and their situations were followed up for two years from our selection date. Interviews were undertaken with a sub-sample of kinship carers (32), children (16), parents (6) and social workers (16).

Policy discussions in the authorities revealed that kin placements were increasingly being used as a means of managing the pressure on other foster placements, but that policies on kin care were being developed on an *ad hoc* basis and this was proving to be more complex than the local authorities had first envisaged. The administrative and legal categories used for kin placements and their accompanying financial arrangements varied considerably between the authorities.

Part II
Comparing Kinship and Non-kinship Foster Care

Part II

Chapter 3

Who Were the Carers
and Which Children Were
Placed with Them?

This chapter compares the characteristics of the children and their carers in the two types of placement (kin care and unrelated foster care) to examine whether there were any differences between the two groups. Children's previous experiences of adversity and their behavioural and emotional difficulties before the placements are compared, as well as their placement histories and previous social work involvement with their families. This information provides a deeper context for subsequent consideration of their placements and outcomes.

The characteristics of the kin carers

At the start of the placement, as shown in Table 3.1, the largest group of children placed with kin were with grandparents (45%), whilst 32 per cent lived with an aunt or uncle and 5 per cent with older siblings and adult cousins.

Maternal grandparents were the largest group (30%), followed by maternal aunts and uncles (22%). Paternal relatives, however, also provided a substantial amount of care for these children: with 15 per cent of paternal grandparents and some paternal aunts and uncles (10%) providing care. Two-thirds of the children were placed with maternal and a third with paternal relatives.

The ages of carers were not available from the files, but some of the grandparents, aunts and uncles were relatively young whilst others were more elderly.

Eighteen per cent of the children with kin lived with 'friends', that is other adults known to the child: seven with the parents of a child's friend and 18 with other adults known to the child (for example, an ex-school teacher, an ex-special

Table 3.1 Relationships between kin carers and children

Kin carer	Number	Per cent
Maternal grandparents	42	30
Paternal grandparents	22	15
Maternal aunts/uncles	31	22
Paternal aunts/uncles	15	10
Other relatives (5 with older siblings and 2 with cousins)	7	5
Other adults known to the child (e.g. ex-step-father, neighbour, friends of the family, ex-schoolteacher)	25	18
Total	142	100

school worker, a friend of the previous foster carers, a neighbour, the ex-wife of a father as well as friends of the family). Twenty-one children lived with a step-relative and most of these (19) lived with a grandparent whose partner was not the child's birth grandparent. Two children lived solely with a step-parent who had continued to care for the child when their relationship with the child's parents had ended.

How did the kin and non-relative carers compare?

When we compared the kin and non-relative carers we found that the kin carers were significantly more disadvantaged than the unrelated foster carers.

Lone carers

Although the majority of the carers in both groups were couples (73% of kin v. 86% of non-related foster carers), significantly more of the kin carers (27%) than the traditional foster carers (14%) were looking after the children alone.

As shown in Table 3.2 most of the lone kin carers were grandmothers (18) and aunts (8) but there were also four single older sisters and four other lone female friends. The five lone male carers were an ex-step-father, a grandfather and three uncles. (This pattern is more extreme in the US, where kin carers are pre-dominantly single grandmothers.) The issues associated with caring for children alone are discussed in detail in a later chapter.

Table 3.2 Lone kin carers

Lone carers	Number	Per cent
Maternal grandmothers	15	38
Maternal aunts	6	15
Older sisters	4	10
Female adults (e.g. ex-step-mother, family friend or neighbour)	4	10
Paternal grandmothers	3	8
Paternal aunts	2	5
Paternal uncles	2	5
Maternal uncles	1	3
Paternal grandfather	1	3
Male adult (ex-step-father)	1	3
Total	39	100

Financial hardship

The case files provided only partial information on the financial circumstances of the carers.[9] When this information was recorded, as many as 75 per cent of the kin carers were noted as experiencing financial difficulties, compared to only 13 per cent of the foster carers. Whilst it is likely that reports on file are slanted towards those situations where there are financial difficulties, it is notable that social workers so much more often noted hardship for kin carers. The interviews with kin carers also showed the gravity of the financial situation of many who were living in what has been described as 'state-sanctioned poverty' (Hegar and Scannapieco 1995).

Overcrowding

The level of overcrowding of each family in the study was rated by the researchers.[10] The files showed that over a third (35%) of the kin carers and children lived in overcrowded conditions at the start of the placement, compared to only 4 per cent of unrelated foster carers. In some instances the home was overcrowded at the start of the placement but this was later resolved, either by the kin carers themselves or with help from children's services and occasionally the housing department.

Health difficulties

We were able to obtain information from only half the case files about the health difficulties of the carers.[11] From the available data, kin carers of all ages had considerably more severe health problems than unrelated foster carers, with 31 per cent of kin carers having a disability or chronic illness (such as heart disease, high blood pressure or diabetes) compared with 17 per cent of unrelated foster carers. This difference was not quite significant but is probably an under-estimate of kin carers' health difficulties, as we discovered very serious health problems during the interviews with kin carers, some of which were underestimated by social workers.

In sum (as shown in Table 3.3), we found that the kin carers were significantly more disadvantaged than the non-related foster carers. Significantly more were lone carers (27% v. 14%), the majority of whom were lone women and they lived, at least initially, in overcrowded conditions (35% v. 4%). In addition, many more kin carers had a disability or chronic illness (31% v. 17%) and experienced financial hardship (75% v. 13%).

Table 3.3 The situation of the carers at the time of placement

	Children placed with kin (Per cent)	Children placed with unrelated foster carers (Per cent)	Level of significance
Lone carers	27	14	$p = 0.010$
Financial hardship	75	13	$p = 0.000$
Overcrowding	35	4	$p = < 0.001$
Severe health problems	31	17	NS

NS, not significant.

Kin carers in England compared to the US

Kin care is used very much more in the US than is currently the case in the UK. Placements with kin have been used extensively in the US since the mid-1980s and research estimates suggest that in some areas up to 60 per cent of children in care are placed with family members. As a result, research in this area in the US is far more extensive than in the UK and, as we have seen, findings suggest that kin carers in the US are predominantly older African-American or Hispanic, lone female carers who are poorly educated, in poor health and live in overcrowded conditions on an income below the poverty level (Dubovitz *et al.* 1993; Hegar and Scannapieco 1999; Iglehart 1994).

When we compared our findings on the situation in England with those from the US we found that our kin carers also experienced poor health, financial hardship and overcrowding. However, they differed in that (as we will see in a moment) the black and minority ethnic children in our sample were more likely to be placed with unrelated foster carers than with kin and, whilst some carers were single, most of the carers in both groups were in couple relationships, unlike in the US where kin carers are predominantly single grandmothers. These differences are important to note since we often rely on American research to inform our views on kinship care.

How did the children placed with kin and non-relative carers compare?

Given these differences between kin carers and unrelated foster carers, we were interested to explore whether the children in their care differed. We wondered, for example, whether kin carers look after children with fewer problems so that the more challenging children were placed with trained and experienced foster carers. Our findings showed that in practice there were very few differences between the children in these two kinds of placement. The following section examines these findings in more detail.

The characteristics of the children

As can be seen in Table 3.4, there were no significant differences between children in the two kinds of placement in terms of their gender or their age at the time that the case file sample was selected. Just over half the children in both groups were girls and more than half the children were over the age of ten at the time of selection in both groups. Similar proportions in each group had long-term health conditions or special educational needs. It was of particular interest to find that the proportion living in a kin placement with a sibling in either type of placement was almost the same (43% in kin care and 45% in non-related foster care) because it is sometimes argued that kin carers are particularly able to take sibling groups.

Table 3.4 Basic characteristics of the children

	Kin care N = 142		Unrelated foster care N = 128	
	Number	Per cent	Number	Per cent
Male	69	49	55	43
Female	73	51	73	57
Under 5 years at selection	23	16	23	18
5 to under 10 yrs at selection	39	28	38	30
10 to under 15 yrs at selection	59	41	53	41
15 years and older at selection	21	15	14	11
Long-term health condition	59	42	64	50
Special educational needs	33	23	36	28
Children placed with at least one sibling in the placement	61	43	58	45
Siblings at home with parents	26	18	31	24
Siblings in care	87	61	89	70
Siblings adopted	12	8	17	13

Ethnicity

At the time that we selected our sample, national statistics showed that people with black and minority ethnic backgrounds represented 8 per cent of the population of England but 18 per cent of the looked after population. The proportion of black and minority ethnic children in the case file sample was 20 per cent (see Chapter 2 for selection of the sample).

Against expectations, and as can be seen in Table 3.5, we found that children from black and minority ethnic backgrounds in our four local authorities were significantly more likely to be placed with unrelated foster carers than with kin. (This had also been true when we looked at all the placements in the four authorities before drawing our sample.) This contrasts with the expectations of researchers that the growth of family and friends placements in England would be greatest for black children (Brandon *et al.* 1999; Broad 1999; Waterhouse 2001), and with the situation in the US where African-American and Hispanic children are disproportionately represented among those cared for by kin (see e.g. Hegar and Scannapieco 1999).

It may be that some local authorities with very high numbers of black and minority ethnic children and pro-kin policies do use kin care more for black and minority ethnic children (see e.g. Broad *et al.* 2001), but this was not the case in the local authorities that took part in this study. It is also possible that black and minority ethnic relatives care for considerable numbers of children without having contact with local authorities and without any corresponding financial or other support. The findings later in this book that some kin had to press their case hard in order to make contact with children's services and then be allowed to care for a child from their family network might be relevant if black and minority ethnic relatives found it harder to do this or did not wish to have such formal contact with statutory services. Also we found that for some black and minority ethnic children the extended family lived overseas and had little or no contact with the children.

Table 3.5 Children's ethnicity

Children's ethnicity	Kin placements		Unrelated foster placements	
	Number	Per cent	Number	Per cent
White British	120	85	95	74
Other ethnicity	22	15	33	26
Total	142	100	128	100

Significance $p < 0.05$ (Fisher's exact test, $p = 0.049$).

Nonetheless and as might be expected, significantly more of the children who were placed with kin (88%) than those in non-related foster care (78%) were living with carers who had the same or a similar ethnic background to the children's parents, whilst a considerably higher proportion of non-related carers (10%) had no ethnic similarity with the children they looked after than was the case in kinship care (1%). The proportions with the same heritage as only one of the children's parents were very similar. These were usually children of mixed ethnicity whose carers, even when they were relatives, represented only a part of the child's ethnic inheritance (see Table 3.6).

Table 3.6 Matched ethnicity

	Kin placements		Unrelated foster placements	
	Number	Per cent	Number	Per cent
Matched ethnicity	117	88	63	78
Same heritage as one parent	15	11	10	12
No similarity in ethnicity	1	1	8	10
Total	133	100	81	100
Missing information	9		47	

Significance $p < 0.01$ (chi-square 10.637, df = 2, $p < 0.01$).

Jay, for instance, was a 7-year-old girl who was placed with her white maternal grandmother and step-grandfather. Her mother was white British and her father African-Caribbean. She had not seen her father since he left when she was nine months old and her paternal grandparents did not live in England. Jay's younger half-sister, Carrie, was white and Jay's step-father was described as hating black people. Carrie returned to live with their mother and step-father and Jay could not understand why Carrie could go home to their mother and she could not. At school she drew a sad face and wrote that she wanted a white face like everyone else and long blond hair. She had no contact with any member of her African-Caribbean family, despite attempts by the social worker to engage one of her paternal uncles and his wife.

Children's experiences of adversity before placement

The experiences of the children before they were placed with their carers (in the placements on which we focused in the study) were explored to look for differences between the two groups. Children's experiences were grouped into parental and child-related adversities. The former were parental circumstances that were likely to have an impact on the child and included: the death of one or both parents; psychiatric difficulties; physical disability or illness; addiction to drugs or alcohol; multiple sexual partners; offending behaviour; previously looked after by children's services; parental learning difficulties or whether either or both parents were sexually abused as a child.

Child-related adversities included: pre-natal exposure to drugs or alcohol; previous failed adoptive placements; multiple separations from their main care-giver; experience of many changes in the composition of the family household; child protection registration; physical or sexual abuse of the child or siblings; neglect of the child; violence between parents or children in the home; bullying or rejection of the child; health difficulties (including disability) and special educational needs.

The average number of all adverse experiences for children living with kin was 7.85 compared with 8.24 for the children living with unrelated foster carers and, as can be seen in Table 3.7, the average number of parental adversities and child-related adversities was also very similar.

Table 3.7 Total numbers of adversities prior to placement

	Children placed with kin (Mean)	Children placed with unrelated foster carers (Mean)
Parental adversities	1.97	1.95
Child-related adversities	5.88	6.29
Total adversities	7.85	8.24

Parental adversities

When we looked in more detail at the specific parental adversities that children had experienced, only one was significantly different for the two groups of children. When one or both of the children's parents had been in care themselves, their children were significantly more likely to be placed with unrelated foster carers than with kin. Twenty-three per cent were placed with traditional foster carers, whilst only 13 per cent were placed with kin. This suggests that in many instances, the relatives of these children were either unavailable or were considered to be unsuitable to care for the children.

As can be seen in Table 3.8, apart from this issue, the parent-related adversities for children in the two groups were at remarkably similar levels. Similar proportions of children in each group, for example, had been living with parents with mental health problems (44% with kin v. 45% in non-related care), parents who had had multiple partners (32% v. 34%) or who had learning difficulties (9% v. 8%). The proportion of parents who had misused drugs and alcohol was slightly but not significantly higher for children in kin than unrelated foster care (60% v. 51%).

Table 3.8 Parental adversities prior to placement

Parental adversity	Children placed with kin (Per cent)	Children placed with non-related foster carers (Per cent)	Level of significance
Death of parents	13	14	–
Parents with learning difficulties	9	8	–
Parental disability or serious illness	15	18	–
Parental mental health problems	44	45	–
Parental alcohol and drugs misuse	60	51	–
Parental drugs misuse only	41	33	–
Pre-natal exposure to drugs	11	8	–
Multiple sexual partners or parental involvement in prostitution	32	34	–
Parents convicted of offences	42	44	–
Parents in care as child	13	23	$p = 0.035$

The younger the children the more likely they were to have parents who misused drugs – showing, not surprisingly, that parental drug use has increased as a reason for children entering care over recent years. We also found that local authority 3 (LA3) had a significantly higher incidence of children in the study (68%) whose parents misused drugs and alcohol, compared to that in the other authorities (56% in LA2, 51% in LA1 and 43% in LA4 ($p < 0.05$)). This was also the authority which showed the highest rate of the use of kin placements and the highest rates of deprivation.

Child-related adversities

When child-related adversities were examined, again there was only one area where there was a significant difference between the groups. More children with multiple health difficulties (23%) were placed with unrelated foster carers than with kin (9%), as shown in Table 3.9.

Table 3.9 Child-related adversities prior to placement

Child-related adversity	Children placed with kin (Per cent)	Children placed with unrelated foster carers (Per cent)	Level of significance
Multiple separations from main caregiver	59	64	–
On Child Protection Register when moved to placement	70	72	–
Physically abused	35	38	–
Neglected	68	61	–
Sexual abuse (actual or suspected)	24	27	–
Sexual abuse (actual or suspected) to a sibling	13	14	–
Exposed to sexual activity or pornographic material	17	11	–
Domestic violence	52	52	–
Exposed to violence from another adult in the home	20	18	–
Violence between siblings	18	20	–
Bullied by peers	17	23	–
Singled out for rejection/scapegoated	22	26	–
Previous failed adoption	0.7	4	–
Child had multiple health difficulties	9	23	$p = 0.008$

Almost three-quarters of the children in both groups were on the Child Protection Register (under similar registration categories) when they moved into the study placement. Similar proportions had been separated from their parents on a number of occasions and rates of abuse and neglect showed little difference. In relation to sexual abuse, perpetrator patterns were the same, with the most frequent perpetrators of sexual abuse of the children and their siblings being the child's father in both groups (32% in both), and step-fathers (12% in both). Interestingly, there were no differences in whether children were placed with maternal or paternal relatives in relation to who had abused the child.

Six (2%) of the children in the study had already experienced an adoptive placement that had failed and five of them had subsequently been placed with unrelated foster carers rather than kin. This may be because if there had been a suitable carer within the extended family network, they would have been placed with kin initially instead of being adopted out of the family. This difference fell short of statistical significance.

Over half of the children in both groups (52%) had experienced violence between their parents during their childhood. Most of the domestic violence witnessed by children was from a male partner towards the mother (82% for kin-placed children and 88% for those with unrelated carers). The remainder of the children had experienced violence between both parents and in two cases the woman had been the aggressor.

Health conditions that had possible long-term consequences for children were recorded when mentioned on the case files but transitory conditions, such as influenza or measles, were not. The proportion of children in the whole sample who had a long-term health condition (42%) was similar to that in other studies of looked after children (see e.g. Ward *et al.* 2002). There were, however, some differences in how these were distributed in the two groups.

Children with respiratory difficulties, such as asthma, were more likely to live with kin (11%), than with non-related foster carers (4%). On the other hand, more of the children with multiple health difficulties lived with unrelated foster carers (23%) than with kin (9%) (see also Hunt, Lutman and Waterhouse 2007). It may be that kin carers were less able or willing to offer the care needed by some of these children, or that social workers were more inclined to place these children with specially trained and equipped foster carers. In spite of this difference, carers in both groups were looking after children with serious health difficulties, some of which resulted from their past experiences with parents. The following vignettes give some idea of the types of difficulty with which some of these children and their carers were coping.

> Eric, who had a number of health problems, lived with unrelated foster carers. He had epilepsy, a left hemiplegia (paralysis of the left side of his body), asthma and a sight defect.

Rita was 13 and lived with her aunt and uncle. She had suffered brain damage as a result of previous non-accidental injuries and had learning difficulties and physical and mobility problems, poor balance and co-ordination and poor motor and fine motor skills. This meant that she had difficulties in walking, climbing stairs and was unable to dress herself. She also had speech difficulties and problems with her eyesight.

In summary, when both parental and child-related adversities are considered, children were more likely to be placed with unrelated foster carers if they suffered from multiple health difficulties or if their parents had themselves been in care. Otherwise the patterns of past adversities for the two groups of children were remarkably similar.

Children's past emotional, behavioural and other difficulties
Previous emotional and behavioural difficulties

Children's emotional and behavioural difficulties before the study placement were sub-divided into (a) emotional difficulties; (b) conduct problems; (c) hyper-activity and (d) sexualised behaviour, and reference in the children's case files to any of these problems was noted. In all, information was collected on 30 behaviours covering these four areas and no differences were found between the total numbers of such behaviours recorded on children in the two types of placement.

When we looked at these in more detail, however, we found that in a few areas there were significant differences between the two groups. Table 3.10 shows children's emotional and behavioural difficulties before the study placement and highlights those few that were at different levels in the two groups.

Before the study placement was made three-quarters (75%) of children placed with kin and 73 per cent with non-related foster carers had experienced three or fewer emotional difficulties (that is, broadly, signs and symptoms that suggest anxiety, depression and stress), whilst 25 per cent in kin care and 27 per cent in unrelated foster care had demonstrated four or more of these behaviours. However, when all these problems were counted, children placed with unrelated foster carers were reported to have shown significantly higher levels of emotional difficulties overall (one-way analysis of variance $F = 2.472$, $p < 0.05$).

In addition, children who were placed in unrelated foster care had been noted to have shown more suspicion of other people and also more 'emotional distress' before the study placement. (Signs of 'emotional distress' were recorded when there was a comment on the case files about a child's distress, such as when

Table 3.10 Children's past emotional and behavioural difficulties

Previous difficulty	Children placed with kin (Per cent)	Children placed with unrelated foster carers (Per cent)	Level of significance
Previous emotional difficulties			
Miserable or depressed	34	44	–
Shyness/lacking confidence	32	38	–
Enuresis (wetting)	23	26	–
Fears	16	21	–
Eating difficulties	15	20	–
Soiling	12	14	–
Self-harm	11	16	–
Aches and pains	4	9	–
Drug or alcohol misuse	4	2	–
Emotional distress[*]	47	59	$p < 0.05$
Over-suspicious of people[**]	4	14	$p = < 0.01$
Previous conduct problems			
Conduct problems at home	45	54	–
Conduct problems outside the home	41	45	–
Defiant or uncooperative at home	31	38	–
Violence towards a parent	12	11	–
Aggression towards another carer	4	1	–
Defiant or uncooperative at school	27	30	–
Fighting with peers	13	16	–
Truanting from school	17	14	–
Exclusion or suspension from school	18	13	–
Bullying other children	17	23	–
Offending behaviour	8	7	–
Stealing or breaking things belonging to others[***]	11	23	$p = < 0.01$

[*]Significance $p < 0.05$ (chi-square 4.017, df = 1, $p < 0.05$).
[**]Significance $p < 0.01$ (Fisher's exact test, $p = 0.005$)
[***]Significance $p < 0.01$ (Fisher's exact test, $p = 0.009$).

there was reference to a child cringing in a corner, a baby or toddler crying constantly or a child who constantly sought attention.)

The findings that children with unrelated foster carers had shown more emotional difficulties may be a real difference or it may be because social workers had more information about the children who went on to be placed with unrelated carers since they had more often been in previous non-relative foster placements and had spent longer in care, as we will see later in this chapter.

Previous conduct problems

Behavioural problems, again, were not very different for the two groups of children. Nearly half the children living with kin (45%) and just over half (54%) of those in unrelated foster care had shown behavioural difficulties in the home before the study placement, and problem behaviour outside the home had been noted for similar proportions in kin care (41%) and unrelated foster placements (45%) (see Table 3.10).

The only conduct problem that differed significantly between the two groups of children was stealing or breaking the property of others: fewer children placed with kin had been reported to have stolen or broken things (11% in kin care and 23% in unrelated foster placements).

There were no differences between the two groups in the total numbers of conduct problems before the study placement. It is clear then that kin carers look after children who have remarkably similar childhood experiences and demonstrate almost the same levels of conduct problems before their study placements as the children looked after by unrelated foster carers.

Previous hyperactivity or sexualised behaviour

As can be seen in Table 3.11 there were no significant differences between the levels of concentration difficulties, hyperactivity or sexualised behaviour between the two groups of children. It is worth noting that children with symptoms of hyperactivity, restlessness or lack of concentration were highly likely to have shown many other types of difficult behaviour before the study placement.[12]

Similar proportions of children in the two kinds of placement showed inappropriate sexualised behaviour and such behaviour occurred most often, as might be expected, when children or their siblings had been sexually abused, exposed to sexual activity or pornographic material or when their parent/s were known to have been sexually abused as children. Slightly more children in unrelated care had previously sexually abused another child or been involved in relationships with much older children or adults which placed them at risk, but the differences were not significant.

Table 3.11 Children's previous hyperactivity, concentration difficulties and sexualised behaviour

Previous difficulty	Children placed with kin (Per cent)	Children placed with unrelated foster carers (Per cent)
Previous difficulties with concentration or hyperactivity		
Diagnosed hyperactivity disorder, e.g. ADHD	3	4
Found it hard to concentrate	31	32
Restless	15	15
Sexualised behaviour		
Inappropriate sexualised behaviour	16	19
Sexually abused another child	3	8
Formed relationship/s which placed child at sexual risk	5	10
Previous involvement in exploitative relationship	4	7

Placement patterns

Main carers during childhood

Of the children placed with kin, as many as two-fifths (42%) had spent most of their childhood with their grandparents, aunts and uncles or with other relatives. Over half (55%) prior to placement had lived mostly with one or both parents whilst just 3 per cent had spent most of their time with unrelated foster carers.

A completely different pattern emerged for children placed with unrelated foster carers. Compared to kin-placed children, more of the children in unrelated foster placements had spent most of their lives thus far with one or both parents (71%), whilst the proportion who had lived for much of the time with stranger foster carers was much higher (25%). Very few (2%) had previously mostly lived with kin (see Table 3.12).

Table 3.12 Main carers during childhood before the study placement

Main carers during childhood	Study placement – Children placed with:			
	Kin		Unrelated foster carers	
	Number	Per cent	Number	Per cent
One parent (with or without partner)	48	34	49	38
Grandparents	35	25	3	2
Both parents	30	21	42	33
Aunts and uncles	21	15	0	0
Non-related foster carers	4	3	32	25
Other kin	2	1	0	0
Other known adult	2	1	0	0
Residential/secure unit	0	0	1	1
Other	0	0	1	1
Total	142	100	128	100

Significance $p < 0.001$ (chi-square $= 89.053$, df $= 14$, $p < 0.001$).

The carers immediately before the study placement

In spite of these differences in whom the children had lived with for most of their lives, by the time of the study placement the differences in where they were living immediately before the study placement were fairly small, as can be seen in Table 3.13. Whilst more children were already living with kin (14% as compared with 7% for unrelated care) the proportions in foster or residential care were similar.

Table 3.13 Placements immediately before the study placement

Placement immediately before the study placement	Kin placements (Per cent) N = 142	Unrelated foster placements (Per cent) N = 128
One or both parents/parent figures	43	53
Parent and grandparents together	2	–
Relative or friend	12	7
Foster placement	35	31
Residential or secure unit or hospital	8	9
Total	100	100

Previous social work involvement with the child's family

Children's services had been involved with the children and their families before the placement for similar lengths of time in the two groups. The average duration of children's services involvement was 89 months for children placed with kin and 87 months for children in foster care (approximately 7 years).

We also investigated the extent of social work intervention prior to the study placement that might have prevented the child's entry to care. Fairly similar proportions of the birth families (19% of the birth families of children placed with kin and 23% in non-related foster care) had had extensive social work assistance before the study placement. A third in each group (32% in kin care and 34% in non-related care) had received some assistance; a smaller proportion (18% in kin care and 13% in unrelated care) had had a little, whilst 31 per cent in both groups had had no social work support before the study placement. The type of support included extensive 24-hour support for a mother with severe learning disabilities to enable her to care for her baby; nursery places for children and the provision of counselling for parents.

In sum, children's services departments had provided services for 69 per cent of the children in both groups before the placement on which we focused. This will be important when we consider later the administrative and legal classifications used for the placements.

Reasons for substitute care

Detailed information was collected about the family difficulties that preceded the children's moves from their parents. A possible three areas of difficulty were recorded for each child's family because although the primary reason for removing a child may be that he or she is seriously neglected, the neglect might be a result of unstable parental mental health, which in turn might be linked with parental drug or alcohol misuse. We were not trying to establish causal links between these factors but were attempting to get a detailed picture of precipitating factors.

Table 3.14 shows that there was no significant difference between the primary reasons for entry to care for the two groups of children, and this was also true for the secondary and tertiary reasons for children being separated from their parents.

Table 3.14 Primary reasons for children entering care

Reasons for entry to care	Primary reason for care	
	Kin care (Per cent) N = 140	Unrelated foster care (Per cent) N = 125
Neglect	29	29
Abuse of the child and/or siblings	18	22
Parents unable to care	21	16
Parental drug or alcohol abuse	14	10
Parental mental health difficulties	8	10
Child's behaviour	2	6
General concern for child	4	2
Other	2	2
Relationship breakdown	2	1
Request of young people	0	2
Total	100	100

Previous attempts to return children to their parents

There was a small but not significant difference between the two groups of children in whether attempts had previously been made to return children to their parents. Reunification had been attempted more often for the children placed with unrelated foster carers (39%) than for those living with kin (28%) in the study placement (see also e.g. Berrick *et al.* 1994; Rowe *et al.* 1989; Scannapieco and Jackson 1996).

Previous placements

There was some movement by children between the two types of placement before the study placement began. As many as 86 per cent of children living with kin had had at least one previous kin placement, compared to only 20 per cent of children placed with unrelated foster carers. There was a similar pattern (though not so dramatic) for children living with unrelated foster carers. Almost all (98%) of the children living with unrelated foster carers had previously lived with unrelated foster carers, compared to only just over half (51%) of the children living with kin (see Table 3.15). This finding chimes with that of other studies which have found that children in kinship care have had fewer previous placements in care (see e.g. Lernihan and Kelly 2006.)

In a few instances children had previously lived with non-related foster carers before relatives became aware of what was happening in the birth family, especially if the child's parents had moved away from their home area and been unwilling to let the wider family know of their difficulties. However, in other cases where children were not already living with kin when children's services became involved, children were placed temporarily with unrelated foster carers whilst assessments were made of kin who might be suitable as long-term carers for the child.

Jake, for instance, was a nine-year-old boy who was placed with an unrelated foster carer at the time of selection. His parents were serious drug users and had been imprisoned and he had lived with his paternal grandmother on two occasions but moved to an unrelated foster carer when she died. He lived with three different foster carers (one of whom was the study placement) before being placed with his maternal grandmother after she had been assessed as being a suitable carer for Jake.

It also became clear that if the placement ended, children in both types of placement were more likely to move to a similar rather than a dissimilar placement: those with kin were more likely to move to other kin and children with unrelated foster carers were likely to move on to other unrelated foster carers (see Table 3.16).

We found that once relatives cared for a child, the family looked first to other kin to take on the child if their present carer was no longer able to continue. Indeed, quite often the family had made contingency plans as to which relative would take over care if needed.

Table 3.15 Previous placements with kin and non-related foster carers

| | Study placement | | | |
| | Kin | | Unrelated foster carers | |
	Number	Per cent	Number	Per cent
Previous kin placements[*]				
No previous kin placement	20	14	103	80
At least one previous kin placement	122	86	25	20
Total	142	100	128	100
Previous unrelated foster placements[**]				
No previous unrelated foster placements	69	49	2	2
At least one previous unrelated foster placements	73	51	126	98
Total	142	100	128	100

[*]Significance $p = 0.000$ (Fisher's exact test, $p = 0.000$).
[**]Significance $p = 0.000$ (Fisher's exact test, $p = 0.000$).

Table 3.16 Subsequent placements with kin and non-related foster carers

| | Study placement – Children placed with: | | | |
| | Kin | | Unrelated foster cares | |
	Number	Per cent	Number	Per cent
Subsequent kin placements[*]				
No subsequent kin placements	130	92	125	98
At least one subsequent kin placement	12	8	3	2
Total	142	100	128	100
Subsequent non-related foster placements[**]				
No subsequent unrelated placements	131	92	105	82
At least one subsequent unrelated placement	11	8	23	18
Total	142	100	128	100

[*]Significance $p < 0.05$ (Fisher's exact test, $p = 0.034$).
[**]Significance $p < 0.05$ (Fisher's exact test, $p = 0.016$).

In contrast, children with stranger foster carers usually continued to move to other stranger foster placements. While this could mean that some children have fewer available or willing kin, it may also mean that less effort is made for children with unrelated foster carers to locate kin if the placement ends.

Length of time the children were looked after before the study placement

One important difference to emerge was that children who were placed with unrelated foster carers had spent significantly more time in care than had the children looked after by kin (ANOVA $p < 0.05$). Children placed with family or friends had previously spent a cumulative average of 11 months in care, compared to 16 months for those children in unrelated foster placements. As we have seen, the children placed with kin had often spent previous periods – or indeed the majority of their lives – with a relative or friend.

In the next chapter we will examine how placements were made and how they progressed.

Summary

In summary, the relatives who most often took on the care of the children were grandparents and, although most were maternal grandparents, a proportion of paternal grandparents became the primary carers for their grandchildren. Aunts and uncles were the next largest group to take on this role, often increasing their family size substantially in order to do so. A surprising number of ex-step-parents, friends of the family, neighbours, ex-residential workers, teachers and others also stepped in to care for the children when they needed a stable home.

The carers in both groups were predominantly couples but kin carers were more likely to be caring alone than their unrelated foster carer counterparts. More of the kin carers had health difficulties, which is not surprising given that many of them were the children's grandparents, and they were much more likely to be living in overcrowded conditions and to have financial difficulties. In short, kin carers were significantly more disadvantaged than unrelated foster carers.

In contrast, the children in the two types of placement were very similar in terms of their characteristics such as age, gender and placement with siblings. However, black and minority ethnic children were more likely to be placed with unrelated foster carers than with kin, in contrast to the findings of research in the US.

Adverse experiences before the study placement were also extremely similar, except that children were more likely to be placed with unrelated foster carers if they had multiple health difficulties or if the children's parents had themselves been in care.

There were also few differences in the behavioural and emotional problems that the two groups of children had displayed before the study placement, except that children placed with kin had shown less evidence of emotional difficulties and slightly less unhappiness before the study placement than children placed with unrelated foster carers. It is possible that this is related to the fact that kin-placed children had spent less time in care and so fewer emotional problems had been recorded for them. On the other hand, children placed with kin had spent longer periods with relatives and friends before the study placement – indeed, a considerable proportion had spent the majority of their lives with kin.

Routes into care and placement patterns differed between the two groups of children. Children placed with kin were significantly more likely to have experienced previous kin placements, sometimes with the same carers and sometimes with different members of the family. Families were also more likely to consider other members of the family as carers if, for some reason, the present carers were unable to continue to care for the child. Children placed with unrelated foster carers on the other hand were more likely to have had previous placements with unrelated foster carers and, if the non-related placement on which the study focused broke down, to move to another unrelated foster placement. This may be because there were no suitable family members to care for them or might be because social workers did not look actively for suitable kin carers for these children at this stage.

Compared with those with unrelated foster carers, children placed with kin:

- had spent less time in care before being placed with their kin carer
- were more likely to have experienced both types of placement, that is kin and unrelated foster placements
- were less often from a black and minority ethnic group
- their main carer so far had more often been a family member
- they were less likely to have shown emotional distress or misery before the study placement
- were less likely to have multiple health difficulties and
- were less likely to have parents who had been in care themselves as children.

Compared with unrelated foster carers, kin carers more often:

- had the same or similar ethnic background as the children

- were lone carers
- lived in overcrowded conditions at the start of the placement
- experienced financial hardship
- had a chronic illness or disability.

Now that the characteristics of the children and carers before the placement have been considered, the next chapter examines the placements themselves.

Chapter 4

Placement Making and Progress

In this chapter we look at the arrangements under which placements were made, assessments of kin carers and their commitment to the children. This chapter also covers the support offered by children's services, strain on carers, contact and placement progress.

Who instigated the study placement?

First, we consider how the placements came about. Most (86%) of the placements with kin were made because kin offered to look after the children. In addition, 9 per cent of the children initiated the placement themselves, as did one parent. It was interesting to note how rarely social workers initiated the kin placements in the first instance and this happened in just five cases (4%), although the case files might have under-reported their efforts. We examine this issue in more depth later.

Of the placements with unrelated foster carers, there was evidence that a placement with a relative had been considered in fewer than half the placements (43%), despite the Children Act 1989 stating that family members should be sought as potential long-term carers before unrelated foster carers.

Placement arrangements

When the sample was selected, 69 per cent of the children in each group were on care or interim care orders. Just two children were on residence orders, although such orders had been applied for in respect of another four. A quarter of children with kin and 30 per cent with unrelated carers were accommodated or cared for under informal arrangements (see Table 4.1).

Table 4.1 Legal orders when the sample was selected

Legal orders	Study placement	
	Kin carers (Per cent) N = 142	Unrelated foster carers (Per cent) N = 128
Care Order or Interim Care Order	69	69
Emergency or Police Protection Order	2	0
Remanded to care	0	1
Residence order in place or applied for	4	
No order	25	30
Total	100	100

All the children looked after by non-relative foster carers were fostered. There was, however, much more variety in the arrangements made for children placed with family and friends. A third of these children were placed with carers who had been approved as foster carers for that particular child, whilst well over half (56%) of the placements with kin had originally been made under Emergency Placement Regulations (now Regulation 38 of the Fostering Regulations 2002). Most of the remaining 10 per cent of the children were supported as children in need (under Section 17 of the Children Act 1989), were in placements made under the Private Fostering Regulations or were on residence orders (see Table 4.2).

The use of Emergency Placement Regulation 38[13]

Emergency Placement Regulation 38 (then Regulation 11) was commonly used. It allows that, in an emergency, a child can be placed with kin and was intended for use in exceptional and unforeseen circumstances and not where contingency plans could have been made. Kin carers have to be interviewed immediately and placements under these regulations can last no longer than six weeks.

The use of this regulation raised two issues. The first was whether the situation was an emergency. In 16 per cent of the cases where a Regulation 38 placement was made, this was the first encounter between children's services and the family so an emergency placement was clearly justified. However, in over half of the cases (55%), children's services had been involved with the children and their families for some time (between 8 months and 16 years) when the placement

Table 4.2 The initial arrangements covering the placements

Placement regulations	Kin		Unrelated foster carers	
	Number	Per cent	Number	Per cent
Fostering Regulations	38	34	128	100
Emergency fostering Regulation 38 (then Regulation 11)	63	56		
Residence Orders	2	2		
Private Fostering Regulations	2	2		
Children in Need (Section 17)	4	3		
Other (e.g. shared care)	4	3		
Total	113	100	128	100

Significance $p < 0.001$ (chi-square = 237.016, df = 7, $p < 0.001$).
Information was missing on 29 kin placements.

started, so that in theory contingency plans that included assessments of kin as potential carers might have prevented the use of emergency regulations in some cases.

The second issue is what action had been taken before the six-week period expired. We found that in 44 per cent of the cases the carers were assessed and approved as foster carers within the six-week period after the emergency placement was made, whilst for a few children residence orders were completed (4) or other arrangements made (5). However, in 41 per cent of cases (25) no other arrangements had been made so these placements appeared to be illegal after the six-week period. As an example, one nine-year-old girl was in placement under emergency placement regulations for three years before a residence order was made.

In another of these cases, Paul was placed with his maternal grandmother at the age of eight months under emergency placement regulations. He lived with his grandmother for 11 months and there was no concern about the placement until there was a change of social worker. It became clear that the placement conditions were unsatisfactory and that no assessment or approval of the placement had previously been carried out. The home was dirty and unsafe, unauthorised people were visiting the house and Paul was often left in the care of his 15-year-old relative. There were difficulties in the relationship

> between the grandmother and Paul's parents, who were concerned about the care Paul was receiving. They were particularly concerned because Paul was not developing and had speech difficulties. It became apparent on assessment that he was left in his pram on his own for much of the time and had little stimulation. The new social worker moved him to an unrelated foster carer, with whom he lived for a month, before returning to his parents' care.

By the end of the follow-up period 63 per cent (40) of the Regulation 38 carers had been assessed and approved as foster carers for the children they were looking after, although this had sometimes only occurred after the child had been living in the placement for many months and sometimes years. Occasionally, the need for assessment and approval was identified when a new social worker was allocated to the case.

Residence orders[14]

At the beginning of the placements, only two of the children were cared for under residence orders, although a considerable number of other carers later obtained residence orders either on their own initiative or with the active encouragement of (and, in some cases, pressure from) social workers to do so. Indeed, one of the local authorities had an explicit policy of encouraging kin to apply for residence orders as early as possible. A residence order settles the day-to-day living arrangements for the child, confers parental responsibility on the carers (although it is shared with the parent), any existing care order ceases and children's services no longer remain involved. Residence orders generally ended when young people reached the age of 16 (although the Adoption and Children Act 2002 has allowed their extension to the age of 18 at the request of the applicant for the residence order, and legislation is now planned to raise the age at which all residence orders end to 18 (DfES 2007)). Payment of residence order allowances by local authorities is discretionary and may be means-tested. Other issues concerning residence orders are discussed later in the book.

Private fostering[15]

Two children were classified under private fostering arrangements because the local authority argued that, in one case, the young person herself had sought the placement with friends and in the other the child's mother had made the placement. The local authority therefore considered these as private arrangements for which they had no responsibility.

Josie (aged 14) was cared for under a private fostering arrangement because she had sought the placement with friends after her father died and her mother, who had learning disabilities, went to live with a relative who, Josie said, was violent towards her mother and herself. Children's services had been involved with the family for many years because there were concerns about the ability of the parents to care adequately for the children. Fifteen pounds per week clothing allowance was offered to Josie's carers because children's services argued that, because this was a private fostering arrangement, they were not obliged to offer anything more.

Assessments

Over a third (36%) of the kin carers were assessed before the children moved into the family. However, in two-thirds (64%) of the placements with kin the suitability of the carers was either assessed when the child was already living in the placement or there was no evidence of an assessment having been carried out.

As we have seen, in some cases assessments were not conducted until many months after the placement was made. In yet others, because an application for a residence order was in progress no assessment of the carers had been undertaken but if the residence order application was then not followed through, the arrangements for the children might never be concluded.

Stewart was placed with his father's ex-wife and she initially agreed to apply for a residence order. Three years later, someone within children's services questioned why they were involved and it became apparent that they were paying a fostering allowance but that no assessment had ever been carried out. There were no other legal orders and, four years after the placement began, the situation seemed to be in limbo.

In some instances, the social worker did not feel that the family met the standards for approval as foster carers and suggested that they apply for a residence order instead. This raises another important issue, which will be discussed later, about the standards that are appropriate for kin carers:

Leonie was an eight-year-old girl, whose grandmother had taken major responsibility for her care until her death when Leonie was six. She was placed with an uncle and aunt pending assessment. However, the assessment raised concerns, because in the past her uncle had had convictions for assault. A medical report said that the carers had physical and mental health difficulties and that there had also been problems with their own children. For these reasons, children's services did not approve them as kin carers but told the carers that they would support them in an application for a residence order because Leonie was settled with them. It was felt that the high commitment of the carers to Leonie outweighed the potential difficulties.

Plans for the placements

Plans for the children differed significantly between the two groups. The plan for the majority (93%) of the children in kin placements was for a long-term home until they reached adulthood. The placement was intended as a short-term arrangement for only 3 per cent of the children with kin, whilst there was a plan for adoption out of the family for only one child, who was living with her grand-mother.

In contrast, rather fewer (61%) of the unrelated foster placements were planned as long-term placements for the child, whilst more (21%) were planned as short-term placements and 12 per cent of the children were being prepared for adoption. Plans for reunification with parents were few and had been made for only 2 per cent of the children in each group (see Table 4.3).

About the placements

Proximity to the children's family home and changes of school

Significantly more of the kin placements were close to the family home, with 65 per cent of kin placements near the parental home, compared to 46 per cent of unrelated foster placements.

Children placed with non-related foster carers were significantly more likely to change school when they moved into their placement than were children placed with kin (38% with kin did so as compared with 51% with non-related foster carers), probably in part because fewer were still close to their original school. It was interesting to find that a change of school at the beginning of the placement was linked to good school attendance in both types of placement. This suggests that a change of school provides some children with a chance to start

Table 4.3 Plans for children in the study placements

	Kin placements (Per cent) N = 139	Unrelated foster placements (Per cent) N = 127
Long-term home	93	61
Short-term placement	3	21
Preparation for adoption	1	12
Preparation for another placement	0	1
Preparation for independence	0	1.5
Reunification with parents	2	2
Other	1	1.5
Total	100	100

Significance $p < 0.001$ (chi-square $= 41.918$, df $= 6$, $p < 0.001$).

afresh, even though changes of school are also associated with disruption to the continuity of children's education and friendships.

Children's friendships

Well over half the children in both groups (59% in kin placements and 56% in unrelated foster placements) had some casual and some close friends, which was

Steven, for instance, was ten years old and living with his uncle at the time of selection. Previously he had been neglected by his parents and used as a scapegoat for the ills of his birth family. He had spent most of his weekends with his paternal grandmother, with whom he was close, but she died when he was eight and, from this time, Steven's parents began to request accommodation for him. Since then, he had moved between various members of his family, residential units and unrelated foster carers. His study placement with his uncle survived for two months only and between the ending of that placement and the follow-up, he had had five placements – one with his maternal grandmother where he remained for nine months, two in different residential units and two with unrelated foster carers (including one agency foster carer). A psychologist described him as a quiet, introverted boy who was very vulnerable, isolated and had no friends.

Kevin was 16 and living with his maternal grandmother but had stopped attending school at the age of 14 because he said that the work was too boring and easy. Nothing seemed to have been done to remedy this situation and his older brother, who had done exactly the same thing, had set a precedent. One of his teachers described him as 'a loner who keeps his peers at arms' length'. He was also described as a shy boy who spent most of his time at home on his computer and PlayStation.

the optimal situation. Unfortunately, 22 children in kin care and 23 in unrelated foster placements had difficulties in making or sustaining friendships and a small group of children, 6 children in kin care and 11 in unrelated foster care, were said to have no friends at all.

Siblings and other children in the placements

We were interested not only in children's friendships but also in their relationships with other children in the placements. However, information about other children in the family was sometimes difficult to obtain from the case files, especially for children living with unrelated foster carers.

PLACEMENT WITH SIBLINGS

More than 80 per cent of the children in both groups had brothers and sisters (full, half or step-siblings). As we saw, similar proportions of children in both groups were initially placed with brothers and sisters (53% of those with siblings in kin care and 51% of those with siblings in unrelated foster care). Although kin placements are often said to provide an opportunity to keep siblings together, there was no significant difference in the numbers of siblings placed together in the two types of placement (see Table 4.4).

WERE CHILDREN ALONE OR PLACED WITH OTHER CHILDREN?

There was however a significant difference between the two groups in whether or not children were likely to be the only child in the home at the time of sample selection. In kin placements almost a fifth (18%) of the children lived alone with their carers, compared with only 3 per cent of the children placed with unrelated foster carers. For a few children with kin this led to feelings of isolation and loneliness, as we will see later.

However, for most of the children living with kin there were other children under the age of 18 in the family. As shown in Table 4.4, 43 per cent of the

Table 4.4 Children placed with siblings at the start of the study placement

	Kin placements (Per cent) N = 142	Unrelated foster placements (Per cent) N = 127[*]
Child has no siblings	18	12
Child has siblings but was not placed with them	39	42
Child was placed with one sibling	26	29
Child was placed with two siblings	10	13
Child was placed with three siblings	5	3
Child was placed with four siblings	1	1
Child was placed with five siblings	1	
Total	100	100

[*]Missing data on one child.

children placed with kin lived with one or more of their brothers and sisters, whilst 37 per cent shared the house with the kin carers' own children. A few of the grandparents had their own children at home, whereas this was the case for most of the families of aunts and uncles and for some of the friends. In addition, 11 per cent of the kin homes also included the carers' adult children. The majority of children in kin placements were therefore living with other children, either with their siblings, cousins, nephews or nieces or adult friends' children.

RELATIONSHIPS WITH OTHER CHILDREN IN THE PLACEMENTS

Most children appeared to be close to at least one of their carers. From the small number of cases where we could get the relevant information, there were more reports that children living with kin were close to their carers' children, which is not surprising as they were often their cousins and younger aunts and uncles. On the other hand, more children living with unrelated foster carers were noted to be close to a sibling. These might be real differences or they might relate to the kinds of relationships that social workers were likely to note on file. A small number of children in each group were noted to have difficult relationships with either siblings or with the carers' children.

Children's services and other agency support

Children's social workers

When the sample was selected, most of the children with kin (87%) and unrelated foster carers (92%) had an allocated social worker. Similar proportions of the children in kin (70%) and unrelated care placements (76%) received regular visits from their social workers. However, slightly more (23%) of the children placed with kin were visited infrequently (less often than every 3 months) than those in stranger foster placements (16%). Visits to the carers followed a very similar pattern.

Family placement workers[16]

We found that the majority of non-related foster carers for whom we had information, had a family placement (or link) worker (96%), whilst very few of the kin carers (6%) had this support. The few kin carers who were allocated a family placement worker were those who were considered by social workers to be in exceptional need of extra support and were also offered other forms of assistance.

Services arranged for children

Similar proportions of children in the two groups were either receiving or awaiting mental health services. This was true for 28 per cent of the children placed with kin and for 29 per cent of the children placed with unrelated foster carers.

Moreover, the proportion of children with statements of special educational need in each group was similar: 22 per cent in kin care and 26 per cent in unrelated foster care. In addition, fairly similar proportions of children in each setting received additional educational services (31% of the children with kin and 38% of the children in unrelated foster care).

Services arranged for carers

Additional support for carers was also similar for the two groups: 20 per cent of the kin carers and 21 per cent of unrelated foster carers received specific help arranged by children's services to help support the placements, including nursery places, respite care, transport to school and occasionally, access to staff counselling services.

Overall children's services and other support

A judgement of the overall level of support and services (excluding financial support)[17] provided to the carers and children in each placement, was made by the researchers using all the information recorded on the case files. However, in a considerable number of unrelated foster care cases there was insufficient information on which to make this rating. In terms of the cases on which there were data, significantly fewer kin carers (31%) were rated as being well or fairly well supported by children's services, than was the case for unrelated foster carers (53%). This meant that 69 per cent of kin carers had little or no support, whilst this was also true for 47 per cent of the unrelated foster carers (see Table 4.5).

Table 4.5 Researcher ratings of children's services and other agency support

	Kin placement (Per cent) N = 120[*]	Unrelated foster placements (Per cent) N = 77[*]
Well or fairly well supported	31	53
Little or no support	69	47
Total	100	100

[*]Insufficient information on which to rate the remainder of placements.
Significance $p = 0.003$ (Fisher's exact test, $p = 0.003$).

Strain on carers and their commitment

Carers struggling to cope

Significantly more of the kin carers (45%) were clearly struggling to cope with the children in their care than was the case with the unrelated carers (30%). When carers had problems in managing, the main difficulty they faced was the children's behaviour. Kin carers were especially likely to struggle to cope when children were not attending school regularly, although this was not the case with the unrelated foster carers. However, not surprisingly, for both groups, having difficulty in coping was associated with looking after children who were considered to be beyond the carers' control.

Other issues that were at the heart of such difficulties in coping were problems related to the carers' health or age or in their relationships with the children's parents as well as lack of the particular parenting skills that the child needed, as can be seen Table 4.6. The minor differences between the two groups were not significant. The similar levels of problems in relation to the carers' health and age and in relationships with the children's parents for the two sets of carers may show higher levels than expected for unrelated foster carers or may reflect under-reporting of these difficulties for kin.

Table 4.6 The main difficulty in the study placements when carers were struggling to cope

	Kin placements		Unrelated foster placements	
	Number	Per cent	Number	Per cent
Difficult child behaviour	33	52	25	68
Problems with carers' health or age	8	12	4	11
Problematic relationships between the carers and parents	7	11	3	8
Lack of needed parenting skills	9	14	3	8
Other difficulties	7	11	2	5
Sub-total	64	100	37	100
Carers not struggling to cope	78	91		
Total	142	128		

We found that social workers visited carers who were struggling to cope in both types of placement significantly more regularly than carers who were not strained. In kin care, 59 per cent of the strained kin carers were visited monthly or more often (as were 65% of unrelated carers). However, 29 per cent of the kin carers and 14 per cent of the unrelated foster carers who showed clear signs of strain received visits from children's social workers less often than every two months. In addition to help from family placement workers, unrelated foster carers usually also had access to foster carer support groups and training courses, which were not generally available to kin carers. The fact that some of the kin carers had serious health difficulties[18] and were elderly added to the strain on them.

Commitment of carers

When there was evidence on children's case files that the carers demonstrated particularly high commitment to the child this was noted. These carers were described as putting the needs of the children before their own and being determined not to give up even when problems arose, for example when children showed very difficult behaviour. In short, highly committed carers were motivated to be in an enduring relationship with the children (Lindheim and Dozier 2007).

There were no differences in levels of commitment in relation to children's gender, ethnicity, age or disability. However, there was a significant difference in commitment between the two types of placement, with kin carers significantly more often demonstrating a particularly high level of commitment to the children in their care as compared with unrelated foster carers. Sixty-three per cent of kin carers demonstrated a high level of commitment to the children they looked after, compared with 31 per cent of unrelated foster carers. Of course, this difference is partly to be expected since kin carers elect to care for a particular child or children who are related or known to them whilst stranger foster carers do not. In addition, more of the kin carers were looking after children in what were always intended to be long-term placements. As we will see later, the commitment of kin carers in particular appeared to be an important factor contributing to the stability of placements.

Contact between children and family members
Face-to-face contact with family members

Similar proportions of children had direct contact with their birth mothers in the two kinds of placement (63% of those in kin care and 56% in unrelated foster care). However, children significantly more often saw their mothers if they were placed with maternal relatives (74% did so) than if they were with paternal kin (58%) or with friends (39%) (see Table 4.7).

Table 4.7 Direct contact with mothers by type of kin placement

| | Contact with mother | | |
	Yes (Per cent) N = 89	No (Per cent) N = 53	Total (Per cent)
Placed with maternal relatives	74	26	100
Placed with paternal relatives	58	42	100
Placed with friends	39	61	100

Significance $p < 0.005$ (chi-square $= 11.299$, df $= 2$, $p < 0.005$).

Nearly twice as many children in kin care saw their birth fathers (43%) as did those in non-related foster care (26%). Clearly placements with kin facilitated contact with fathers and this was in large part because some of the children were living with paternal relatives. Indeed, children much more often saw their fathers if they were placed with paternal relatives (75% did so) than if they lived with maternal kin (27%) or friends (39%). Of course, good relationships between children and their fathers might also mean that children were more likely to have been placed with paternal relatives in the first place (see Table 4.8).

Table 4.8 Direct contact with fathers by type of kin placement

	Contact with father		
	Yes (Per cent) N = 61	No (Per cent) N = 81	Total (Per cent)
Placed with maternal relatives	27	73	100
Placed with paternal relatives	75	25	100
Placed with friends	39	61	100

Significance $p < 0.001$ (chi-square = 24.578, df = 2, $p < 0.001$).

It was interesting to find that whilst only 18 per cent of the children with kin had no contact with either of their parents, this was the case for as many as 38 per cent of those with unrelated foster carers. This does suggest that more children in stranger care are completely detached from parental networks and the higher rates of death and prohibition on contact for those in unrelated care (16% as compared with 8% with kin) provide only part of the reason for this.

Similar proportions of children living with kin (61%) as in unrelated care (62%) were either living with siblings or had regular contact with them and this was also true for contact with maternal grandparents (38% in kin care and 35% in unrelated foster care). Contact with paternal grandparents was also at fairly similar levels, although slightly higher in kin care (22%) than unrelated foster care (15%).

In contrast, many more children in kin placements maintained contact with their aunts, uncles and cousins than was the case for children in non-related foster care. Similarly, more children in kin care (42%) had contact with some of these close relatives but not with others than did their peers in stranger care (21%). Again, no doubt this was because of the day-to-day meetings between close family members when children lived with kin (see Table 4.9).

Children in each group had some direct contact with other important adults (11% kin v. 12% in unrelated care), whilst contact by letter, emails, telephone or cards with parents and relatives were at similar levels in the two kinds of placement (41% of children in kin care and 45% in unrelated foster care). Most of this contact was by telephone.

Table 4.9 Direct contact with aunts, uncles and cousins

	Kin placements (Per cent) N = 120	Unrelated foster placements (Per cent) N = 128
Contact with all aunts, uncles and cousins	23	5
Contact with some aunts, uncles and cousins but not with others	42	21
No contact with aunts and uncles	35	71
Contact with aunts and uncles not allowed	–	1.5
No aunts, uncles or cousins	–	1.5
Total	100	100

Significance $p < 0.001$ (chi-square = 42.587, df = 4, $p < 0.001$).

The management of difficult contact

There was a court order or local authority ruling preventing contact with a named individual in slightly more placements with unrelated foster carers (20% in kin care and 29% in unrelated foster care) and difficulties in relation to contact for similar proportions in each type of placement (62% of children in kin care and 66% in unrelated foster care). Child protection issues arose or concerns were raised about the child's safety during contact for similar proportions of children in the two groups (39% with kin and 31% with stranger foster carers), although children with unrelated carers were considerably more often at risk from more than one family member (48%) than was the case with kin-placed children (16%).

However, difficulties between carers and family members were very much more common for kin carers and were evident in over half (54%) of the kin cases, as compared with only 16 per cent of unrelated foster carers. In spite of these much higher levels of difficulty with the children's parents (and sometimes other relatives), kin carers were much more often given the task of supervising contact than unrelated foster carers (43% as compared with 16%), whilst social work staff supervised many fewer kin placements (25% v. 55% in unrelated foster care). In all, there was supervised contact for about half the children in each group (47% in kin care and 56% in unrelated foster care) (see Table 4.10).

Table 4.10 Supervision of contact

Contact supervision	Kin placements		Unrelated foster placements	
	Number	Per cent	Number	Per cent
Social worker/assistant	17	25	38	55
Carer	29	43	11	16
Other (e.g. family centre)	21	31	20	29
	67	100	70	100

Significance $p < 0.001$ (chi-square 48.024, df = 3, $p < 0.001$).

The interviews with carers, which are discussed later, showed that managing contact was often a particularly difficult issue for the kin carers and was one of the main reasons that they gave for wanting the continued involvement of children's services.

Children's progress

Children's progress by the time of the follow-up was considered using the outcome ratings from the 'Looking After Children: Assessment and Action Records' (Department of Health 1995), now incorporated into the Integrated Children's System (Department of Health 2003), and a researcher rating about changes in children's behaviour during the placement was made using all the available information on the files.[19]

Whilst information about the children's health, education and emotional and behavioural development was recorded on most of the children's files, details about their self-esteem and social behaviour were only recorded on half of the files in each group. Occasionally, social work practitioners also presented a somewhat rosy view, which contrasted with evidence from another professional with closer day-to-day contact with the children. For example, social workers sometimes stated that children were doing well in school and making friends, but there was contrary evidence from school reports that children were having difficulties with school work and peer relationships and in such instances the school's evidence was given greater weight.

The children's progress on these dimensions was remarkably similar in the two groups, as can be seen in Table 4.11.

Table 4.11 Children's progress by the end of the follow-up period

'Looking After Children' developmental dimensions	Kin placements (Per cent)	Unrelated foster placements (Per cent)
Normally healthy and well	93	86
Performing below ability	52	48
Attending school regularly	87	94
School attendance improved during the placement	48	39
Children had a positive view of themselves	75	69
Social behaviour acceptable to adults and other children	80	80
Emotional and behavioural difficulties	66	71
Improvement in behaviour	77	77

Health

As can be seen, most children in both groups were considered to be normally healthy and well. Whilst slightly fewer (6%, 9) children in kin care than in unrelated foster placements (12%, 15) were 'sometimes ill' this difference was not significant and just two children in both groups were 'frequently ill'.

Education

About half the children in each group were thought to be performing below their ability (52% kin care and 48% unrelated foster care). This is very similar to the rates given by Skuse, Macdonald and Ward (1999) who found that on their SATs results 54 per cent of looked after children were below the expected level in English as were 53 per cent in Mathematics.[20]

Most children in both groups attended school regularly too and attendance levels did not differ significantly by age. Thirteen per cent (18) of children in kin and six per cent (8) in unrelated foster placements were not regular attendees at the time of our follow-up but this difference was not significant. School attendance improved for 48 per cent of those in kin placements and for 39 per cent in unrelated foster placements. However, the school attendance of five children in kin care and one child in unrelated foster care deteriorated during the placement.

Self-esteem and social behaviour

Based on more limited information, there appeared to be little difference in children's levels of self-confidence or social behaviour between the children in the two groups.

Emotional and behavioural progress

Two-thirds of the children had emotional or behavioural difficulties ranging from minor to severe and for over half the children in both groups (52%) these were at a level that, in the researchers' view, required some remedial help. This included 25 per cent of children with kin and 28 per cent of those with unrelated foster carers who had problems that were considered serious enough to require specialist input. Only about a third of the children had no emotional or behavioural difficulties (see Table 4.12).

Table 4.12 Children's emotional and behavioural difficulties during the placements

	Kin placements[*] (Per cent) N – 123	Unrelated foster placements (Per cent) N = 121
No emotional or behavioural difficulties	34	29
Minor emotional or behavioural difficulties	14	19
Moderate emotional or behavioural difficulties requiring some help or remedial action	27	24
Severe emotional or behavioural difficulties requiring specialist input	25	28
Total	100	100

[*] Missing information on 19 children in kin care and 7 in unrelated placements.

Children with the more severe difficulties in both groups were most likely to receive a service. However, over half the children in kin care with moderate or severe problems (56%, 35) were not receiving any help, whilst this was also true for 50% (31) of the children with this level of difficulty in unrelated care (see Table 4.13).

This deficit might be due to the general shortage of psychological services for children, since children in both groups were equally disadvantaged and, of course, occasionally adolescents would have refused offers of help. However, given the link between emotional and behavioural difficulties and poorer long-term outcomes for children and their placements, this lack of service is of considerable concern.

Table 4.13 How far help was provided for children with emotional and behavioural problems

	Kin placements		Unrelated foster placements	
	Number	Per cent	Number	Per cent
Children with minor problems receiving help	5	7	4	5
Children with minor problems not receiving help	9	12	19	22
Children with moderate problems receiving help	11	14	10	12
Children with moderate problems not receiving help	21	28	18	21
Children with serious problems receiving help	16	21	21	25
Children with serious problems not receiving help	14	18	13	15
Total	76	100	85	100
Missing information	24		8	

Information about emotional and behavioural change was recorded on 60 per cent of the children's case files. Very similar rates of change were found in the two groups and also as between boys and girls. There were improvements for 77 per cent of children in both groups, whilst deterioration was noted for six children in kin placements and three children in unrelated foster care (see Table 4.14).

Table 4.14 Behavioural or emotional change during the placement

	Kin placements (Per cent) N = 80	Unrelated foster placements (Per cent) N = 83
Improvement in behaviour	77	77
Deterioration in behaviour	8	4
Improvement in some respects and deterioration in others	15	19
Total	100	100

How often did placements end and why?

By follow-up almost three-quarters (72%) of the children placed with kin remained in placement, compared to only just over half (57%) of those with non-related foster carers. A major reason for this difference is that placements with unrelated foster carers were quite often a prelude to another kind of placement, whilst this was rarely the case with the kin placements. For example, as we have seen, there had been plans for a move to another placement for over a third of the children with stranger foster carers but for few with kin.

As can be seen in Table 4.15, the placements of a similar proportion of children in each type of care disrupted (18% and 17%), but significantly more of those in unrelated care had planned endings, when children moved on to other placements such as long-term foster care or adoption or were reunited with their parents. When placements disrupted, the reasons for this were broadly similar in the two groups, with most disrupting because of the children's behaviour, a relationship breakdown with the carers or other children in the family, the child requesting a move or, much more rarely, because the carer could no longer continue because of their health.

Table 4.15 Planned placement endings and disruptions

Placement endings or continuation	Kin placements		Unrelated foster placements	
	Number	Per cent	Number	Per cent
Disruption	25	18	20	17
Planned move	14	10	32	26
Continuing	102	72	69	57
Total	141	100	121	100

Significance $p < 0.005$ (chi-square $= 12.514$, df $= 2$, $p = 0.002$).

Whether placements disrupted is one of the two kinds of outcomes for children that we move on to consider in the next chapter.

Summary

Consideration of a kin placement

There was evidence that, despite the Children Act (1989) encouraging social workers to look for suitable family or friends carers before placing children with unrelated foster carers, kin were not considered for over half the children in this study. Indeed most kin placements were made because relatives or friends put themselves forward as carers.

Assessments and standards for approval

Over two-thirds of the children in each group were on care or interim care orders. Despite the fact that social workers had often been working with the study children and their families for long periods, many of the study placements were made under emergency placement regulations. Assessments of placements, even when the child was subject to a care order and on the child protection register, were often delayed for many months or years. This could leave children in potentially risky situations. In some instances, social workers felt that the carers did not meet the standards for approval as foster carers, and such carers were instead encouraged to apply for residence orders.

Plans

Whilst the initial plan for most (93%) of the children in kin placements was for a long-term home, this was only true for three-fifths (61%) of the unrelated foster placements, where a substantial minority of placements were intended to be short-term awaiting a move to long-term foster care or adoption.

Placements

More of the children in kin placements were the only child in the household and, as we shall see later, this meant that some were isolated from their peers. Nevertheless, the majority of the children in both groups were placed in families where there were other children, and similar proportions of children in both groups were initially placed with their brothers or sisters.

Support from children's services

Levels of social work visits to children and carers were slightly, but not significantly, lower to kin carers. In addition, kin carers did not have family placement workers or access to training courses, carer groups or other kin carers. They were further disadvantaged by not knowing how children's services departments operated. Overall, significantly fewer kin than unrelated foster carers were rated by the researchers as having adequate support from children's services. In spite of this, the children in the two groups received similar levels of mental health and additional educational services.

Strain on carers, support and commitment

Kin carers were more likely than unrelated foster carers to be struggling to cope with caring for the additional children in the family, and for some of the grand-parents the physical effort of looking after children was a challenge, especially when they were also struggling with financial difficulties and difficult behaviour as well as their own feelings about the situations that had led to the children moving to their care.

Despite these difficulties, the kin carers in the sample were more likely to have a very high level of commitment to the children they looked after than were unrelated foster carers.

Contact

Kin carers were much more likely than unrelated foster carers to have difficult relationships with the parents of the children (who might also live nearby), and in some cases with other members of the extended family. Volatile inter-familial conflicts or concerns about the safety of children meant that contact was a diffi-cult issue for some of the kin carers. Many carers wanted the protection of care orders and the involvement of children's services to maintain adequate bound-aries around contact between the children, their parents and/or other members of the family. Nonetheless, social work supervision of contact was at much lower levels than in unrelated foster care. At the same time, it was notable that children who were placed with relatives were much more likely to maintain contact with others in their extended family – especially aunts, uncles and cousins. Unsurprisingly, children placed with paternal relatives were more likely to maintain contact with their fathers and those placed with maternal relatives were more likely to maintain contact with their mothers.

Progress

At the time of the follow-up, the children's health, educational performance, school attendance, self-confidence, social behaviour and emotional and behav-ioural progress in the two types of placement were very similar. However, about half the children in each group where the children had moderate or severe emo-tional and behavioural problems were not receiving help with them.

Placement endings

By follow-up, almost three-quarters (72%) of the children placed with kin remained in placement, compared to only over half (57%) of those with unrelated foster carers. A major reason for this difference is that placements with unrelated foster carers were quite often a prelude to another kind of placement, whilst this was rarely the case with the kin placements which were generally intended to provide long-term care. The placements of a similar proportion of children in each type of care disrupted (18% and 17%).

Chapter 5

Placement Outcomes

Within the study, two measures were used to assess placement outcomes: the first related to the quality of the placement for the children and the second was placement disruption. We wanted to know whether children's experiences before the placement were linked to these placement outcomes, or whether factors relating to the carers, the children's behaviour or the support they received from children's services or elsewhere during the placement were more important. This chapter falls into two parts: the first focuses on pre-placement issues and the second on those that emerged in the placement itself.

Outcome measures
Placement quality

The quality of the placement was a researcher rating, which was based on all the available evidence from children's case files. This rating focused on how far placements met the needs of the children, and where outcomes were satisfactory for the children but not their carers, the placement was rated as being satisfactory for the child.

Placements were rated as being either (a) a satisfactory (good quality) placement for the child overall or (b) a placement where concerns had been expressed about the child or the placement or where there was other evidence that the placement was negative for the child (problematic or poor quality placement). Concerns included anxieties by social workers or others (for example, other family members, teachers or health visitors) about the well-being of the child in the placement; concerns about the carers' parenting skills or their ability to protect the child adequately or other indications that the situation was negative for the child (for example, if they were being bullied by other children in the placement). Where the quality of the placement varied over time, the rating was made in relation to the situation at follow-up.

Ratings of placement quality were not significantly different between the two groups of children, with 66 per cent of the children placed with kin and 73 per cent of those in unrelated foster care being rated as having satisfactory placements, whilst 34 per cent of kin placements and 27 per cent of foster placements were rated as problematic (see Table 5.1).

Table 5.1 Researcher rating of study placement quality

	Kin placement		Unrelated foster care	
	Number	Per cent	Number	Per cent
Satisfactory placement	94	66	93	73
Problematic placement	48	34	35	27
Total	142	100	128	100

DURATION OF THE PLACEMENTS

The average number of months in placement at the two-year follow-up[21] was 57 months (4 years 9 months) for children placed with kin compared to 47 months (almost four years) for children in unrelated foster placements and, although the placements with kin lasted longer, the difference between the two groups of children was not statistically significant.

We did, however, find that placements with kin that broke down or ended for any other reason, including planned endings, had lasted significantly longer before they ended (on average 37 months) than had those with unrelated foster carers (on average 24 months). As a result, children living with kin were significantly more likely, than those placed with unrelated foster carers, still to be in their placement two years after we had selected the sample.[22] At follow-up 72 per cent of children with kin remained in their study placements, compared with 57 per cent of those placed with unrelated foster carers.

As we have seen, a major reason for this difference is that more placements with unrelated foster carers were intended to be a staging post for another kind of placement, whilst this was rarely the case with the kin placements.

Placement disruption

Our second outcome measure was placement disruption. When the children who had had planned moves were excluded, we found that 20 per cent of kin and 22 per cent of unrelated foster placements had disrupted by the end of the follow-up period[23] (see Table 5.2).

Table 5.2 Placement disruption, excluding the placements with planned endings

	Kin placement		Unrelated foster care	
	Number	Per cent	Number	Per cent
Continuing	102	80	69	78
Disrupted	25	20	20	22
Total	127	100	89	100

We found, as expected, a significant relationship between the two outcome ratings: a higher proportion of the poor quality placements in both groups (but a particularly high proportion in non-relative care) had disrupted by follow-up (37% of kin and 64% of unrelated foster placements), whereas only 12 per cent of satisfactory kin and 9 per cent of good quality unrelated care placements broke down.

Factors that related to outcomes

The local authorities

The highest proportion of problematic placements was in LA3 (49%), compared to just 8% in LA4 (see Table 5.3). As we saw earlier, LA3 had the highest level of deprivation, the largest number of drug-using parents and the highest proportion of kin placements (41%) of all our authorities. In addition, most of their children's social workers were employed by an agency rather than by the council. It is possible that the threshold for approval of kin carers was lower there or that monitoring was poorer as a result.

Table 5.3 Quality of kin placements by local authorities

Kin placements	LA1 (Per cent) N = 35	LA2 (Per cent) N = 42	LA3[*] (Per cent) N = 41	LA4[**] (Per cent) N = 24
Satisfactory placements	71	62	51	92
Problematic placements	29	38	49	8
Total	100	100	100	100

[*]Fisher's exact test, $p = 0.001$.
[**]Fisher's exact test, $p = 0.05$.

There were also significant differences between the local authorities in the disruption rates in family and friends placements. As can be seen in Table 5.4, no kin placements disrupted in LA4, compared with between 13 per cent and 33 per cent in the other authorities. This may be a chance finding since the numbers were small. However, it is worth noting that more of the kin carers in LA4 were approved as foster carers (96% as compared to a maximum of 75% in the other authorities) and more showed high levels of commitment (79% did so as compared with 52 to 71% of carers in the other authorities) and these factors were related to lower levels of disruption. In addition, fewer of the children in this authority had serious problems, none were beyond control (as compared with a fifth in the other authorities) and fewer carers in the authority were under strain. As we have seen, LA4 also had the highest proportion of good quality placements.

Table 5.4 Disruption in kin placements in local authorities

Kin placements	LA1 (Per cent) N = 30	LA2 (Per cent) N = 39	LA3 (Per cent) N = 38	LA4[*] (Per cent) N = 20
Placement continued	87	67	79	100
Placement disrupted	13	33	21	0
Total	100	100	100	100

[*]Significance $p < 0.05$ (chi-square = 10.307, df = 3, $p = 0.016$).

Pre-placement factors
Children's age, gender, ethnicity and health

There were no differences in outcome by children's gender or ethnicity for either type of placement. However, whilst children with multiple health problems such as severe physical disabilities and sensory impairment did well with both kin and unrelated carers (see also Berridge and Brodie 1998), those who had more minor health conditions, such as asthma, eczema and other similar long-term conditions had fewer satisfactory kin placements than would be expected and more of their kin placements disrupted. This appeared to be because children with these more minor conditions presented higher levels of behaviour problems and their kin carers were under more strain. This difference was not significant in unrelated foster care.

The child's age at the time the study placement was made was closely related to whether placements disrupted in kin care (see also Altshuler 1998; Terling-Watt 2001; Webster, Barth and Needell 2000). As would be expected, the younger children were when they were placed, the less likely their placements were to break down. The kin placements least likely to disrupt were those for children who were placed under the age of five (only 12% disrupted), closely followed by those where children were placed between the age of five and ten (16% disrupted). In contrast, over a third (37%) of young people placed when they were aged ten or over broke down (see Table 5.5).

Table 5.5 Children's age at the start of the study placement with kin by placement disruption

Kin placements[*]	0–4 years		5–9 years		10+	
	N	Per cent	N	Per cent	N	Per cent
Placement continuing at follow-up	44	88	37	84	20	63
Placement disrupted by follow-up	6	12	7	16	12	37
Total = 141	50	100	44	100	32	100

Significance $p = 0.005$ (chi-square $= 12.677$, df $= 3$, $p = 0.005$).
[*] Missing information on one child.

Non-relative foster placements followed a different pattern. Whilst there were similarly few disruptions for children placed under five (13%), there were considerably more disruptions for children placed aged five to ten (35%) but fewer breakdowns for young people placed aged ten or over (19%).

These differences raise interesting questions. It is possible that the low disruption rate for the five to ten age group in kinship care is because, as we shall see later, many of the kin carers had been closely involved with the children before a permanent placement with them was made: for example, they had often looked after the children for weekends and sometimes for extended periods when the home situation was difficult and in the process developed close relationships with the children. The higher disruption rate for the older children in kin care might relate to difficulties in dealing with adolescent acting out behaviours, something that foster carers who regularly look after young people become more experienced in managing. However, the numbers of children in each age group in this study are too small to rely on and it is possible that with higher numbers the patterns in the two groups would be more similar.

Parental adversities: parental drugs misuse

In both kin and unrelated care, placements were more likely to be satisfactory if the children's parents had not misused drugs. Over half (55%) of the children in kin care whose parents had misused drugs had satisfactory placements, compared with almost three-quarters (74%) of those whose parents had not. Similarly, in unrelated foster care, 55 per cent of children with drug-using parents had satisfactory placements, compared to 81 per cent of their peers who had not had this experience. This was not explained by the age at which the children left their parents, difficulties between carers and parents or contact. Nonetheless, this finding echoes that of previous research (Barth and Brooks 1998), and the complex needs of children in these situations are likely to create vulnerability and require high levels of service and support (Grandparents Plus and Adfam 2006; Hunt 2003; Kroll 2007; Patton 2003).

No other parental adversities, or the total numbers of parental adversities, related to the placement outcomes of the children in either group.

Children's adversities: high numbers of adversities and multiple separations from parents

It was striking that when children had experienced a high number of child-related adversities (see Chapter 3), that is seven or more, their placements were much more likely to disrupt when they were in unrelated foster care. However, this was not true for those with kin. This suggests that kin carers may be more likely than unrelated foster carers to continue to care for children with very troubled backgrounds than unrelated foster carers.

Children who had had many separations from their main caregivers and who were placed with unrelated foster carers had more disruptions than the children who had not had this experience (28% v. 14%) but the difference was not quite significant. There was no corresponding finding for children placed with kin. Information from the case files and interviews shows that children in kin placements had often stayed with relatives on a number of previous occasions before their arrangements became permanent. Staying with grandparents or an aunt at times of need may have had a less negative impact on children's feelings of belonging and continuity of care than if children had experienced moves to different unknown foster carers. In contrast, children with no available kin had more often moved to different unrelated foster carers each time the situation at home broke down.

Children's previous emotional and behavioural difficulties

Children with a history of behavioural difficulties before the study placement had poorer outcomes in both settings, that is their placements more often disrupted and were of poorer quality, no doubt because such behaviours tended to re-emerge in placement. For example, children who had previously shown defiant behaviour at home or school, who had truanted or fought other children, had less satisfactory placements in both settings. Similarly, a history of stealing, damaging property or truanting was related to higher breakdown rates in both settings. Past school exclusion was also closely related to disruption, particularly in kinship care.

Some specific previous emotional difficulties (such as fearfulness and bed wetting) were linked to lower levels of placement quality in each setting but a variety of previous emotional problems such as eating problems, depression, self-harming and being over-suspicious of others, as well as having shown a high number of emotional difficulties, were more often related to placement disruption in unrelated but not in kin care. However, this may principally be because these behaviours were so much more often recorded on file when children were with stranger foster carers.

Behaviours related to hyperactivity, (that is restlessness and lack of concentration), whilst not linked to placement disruption, were significantly linked to poorer quality placements for both groups of children. Again, these behaviours probably continued into the placements and were difficult to manage. In kin care for example, 38 per cent of restless children had satisfactory placements, compared to 71 per cent of those who did not display this behaviour. There were similar figures for unrelated care. Hyperactivity has been shown in previous research to be related to poorer outcomes in children's placements (e.g. Farmer, Moyers and Lipscombe 2004; Quinton et al. 1998).

The numbers of previous difficult behaviours were grouped into 'high' (11–20), 'medium' (6–10) and 'low' (0–5) and the higher the total numbers of previous difficult behaviours, the less likely children were in both groups to have satisfactory placements. However, our analysis showed that in stranger foster care the disruption rate rose significantly as the numbers of previous behavioural and emotional problems increased but that this was not the case for kin placements. This suggests that kin carers are more likely than unrelated carers to continue to care for children with very difficult behaviour than unrelated carers.

Carer characteristics

When we focused only on the placements with kin we found that there was no difference in the quality of placements with different relatives. However, children who were placed with their grandparents were the least likely to experience disruption when compared with other family or friends (see also Harwin *et al.* 2003; Hunt *et al.* 2007). Only 8 per cent of the placements with grandparents disrupted compared with 27 per cent of those with aunts and uncles and 30 per cent of those with other relatives and friends. This compares with 23 per cent of placements with unrelated carers. The lower likelihood of placement disruption with grandparents as compared with aunts and uncles may be because there were less often other children in the family (11% of grandparent and 63% of aunt and uncle placements) and research has shown the link between placed children having a negative impact on other children in the family and placement disruption (see e.g. Farmer *et al.* 2004; Sinclair 2005b). We had thought that this finding might also be because grandparents have a particularly strong sense of kinship obligation, but no differences were found between our ratings of the levels of carer commitment in the different groups of relatives.

In contrast, outcomes were not affected by whether the placements were on the maternal or paternal side of the family, were with single or couple carers or included a step-relative. Twenty-one children lived in households with a step relative and most of these (19) lived with grandparents and their partners. Two children lived solely with a step-parent who had continued to care for the child when their relationships with the child's parents ended. Only one of these placements had ended by follow-up. The placements with step-relatives therefore compared well with other placements in terms of placement disruption and there was no difference in terms of quality.

Placements with siblings and other children
CHILDREN PLACED WITH SIBLINGS

The placements of both groups of children were less likely to disrupt if children shared the placement with their brothers and sisters (see also e.g. Berridge and Cleaver 1987; Sinclair 2005b).

SIBLINGS AT HOME WITH PARENTS

One issue that we wished to explore was that of children in care whose siblings remain at home with parents. This may mean that the child has been singled out as a scapegoat for the ills of the family (see Quinton *et al.* 1998; Rushton and Dance 2003) or that their parents (sometimes, for example, as a result of the child making sexual abuse allegations) have rejected them. The authors' previous study showed that adolescents in this situation were frequently pre-occupied by concerns about their brothers and sisters who remained at home, especially if they had previously played a protective or parental role with them (Farmer *et al.*

2004) and Sinclair and his colleagues (2004) found that children who have siblings at home are more likely to experience a disruption in non-relative foster care than those who have not.

In this study, in both kinds of placement there were more disruptions when children had siblings who continued to live with their parents (although the difference was only significant in unrelated care). However, the quality of their placements if they continued was not affected. This finding may reflect the benefits to placement stability of sibling groups being placed together (see above) or the difficulty when a child has been singled out for rejection.

LONE CHILDREN

Children in kin placements with no other children had more disruptions (29%) than those who lived with other children (15%) (siblings or young relatives) but the difference did not quite reach significance. The relationship between lone children and disruption in unrelated care could not be tested since so few appeared to be placed in families with no other children.

Some lone children living with grandparents told us that they were lonely and bored, especially when they lived in an area where there were few, or no, other children to play with. They sometimes compared their situation unfavourably with former placements with other children in non-related foster care.

Factors during the placement

Once placements were made, a number of factors affected their outcomes. This section includes issues such as the presence of siblings or other children; the children's emotional and behavioural progress in the placement; their educational performance and school attendance; carer commitment and strain, and the support offered to the placement by social workers.

Friendships

The placements of children with few friends were at risk of poor outcomes in both settings, although the numbers for whom there was information on this were small.

Education
SCHOOL ATTENDANCE

Poor school attendance was related to disruption in both settings, but particularly so in kin care, although the numbers again were small. Kin placements were also significantly less likely to disrupt when attendance at school had improved after the placement began, suggesting that children had settled into the placement and were amenable to direction. In general, regular attendance at school was significantly linked with better quality ratings for both types of placement.

EDUCATIONAL PERFORMANCE

When children's educational performance was clearly below their ability level there were more disruptions in both settings. In addition, when children had received statements of special educational needs, there were significantly more placement breakdowns in unrelated foster care but not with family and friends.

Behaviour and self-confidence
EMOTIONAL AND BEHAVIOURAL PROBLEMS

When children had emotional and behavioural problems at a level that required remedial help, both types of placement had an increased risk of disruption and the quality of the placements was poorer. We cannot tell however, whether the children's behaviour resulted in poor quality placements or vice versa. Placement outcomes probably result from an interaction between the child's behaviour and how carers respond to it. Previous research suggests that carers find it difficult to maintain their warmth, sensitivity and determination to work with children when they show persistent difficult behaviour or lack of attachment. The carers may then withdraw or become more aggressive in their parenting, ultimately leading to placement breakdown (Farmer et al. 2004; Quinton et al. 1998).

In addition, when children were reported to be beyond control they had higher levels of disruption in both types of placement.

CHANGES IN EMOTIONAL AND BEHAVIOURAL DIFFICULTIES

In kin and unrelated foster care, placements were more likely to be of satisfactory quality and less likely to disrupt when there had been improvements in children's behavioural and emotional difficulties. Conversely, more placements disrupted when children's behaviour deteriorated. However, it was interesting to find that when children's behaviour deteriorated (or showed a mixed picture of changes for better and worse), considerably more of the kin than the unrelated placements continued (56% as compared to 27%). These findings again may suggest that kin are more likely to persevere with children when there are difficulties.

SOCIAL BEHAVIOUR

Unsurprisingly, the placements of children in both groups, whose social behaviour was acceptable to adults and other children, were less likely to disrupt and more likely to be satisfactory than the placements of children whose social behaviour was not acceptable to others, but the information on this issue was limited.

SELF-CONFIDENCE

The placements of children who were generally confident about their own abilities in both groups were less likely to disrupt and more likely to be of satisfactory quality, but numbers were small and we cannot tell whether good quality placements resulted in children having more self-confidence or whether children with positive feelings about themselves were more likely to have satisfactory placements.

Carer commitment

One of the factors that did make a difference to placement outcomes was whether there was evidence on children's case files that their carers demonstrated particularly high commitment to them. As we have seen, more kin carers (63%) demonstrated very high levels of commitment to the children in their care than unrelated foster carers (31%). In kinship, but not in unrelated care, significantly fewer placements disrupted when carers were highly committed to the children. For example, only 11 per cent of kin placements with highly committed carers disrupted, compared to 35 per cent where there was no evidence of such commitment.

In both types of placement, the commitment of the carers was significantly related to the quality of placements.

Strain on carers

Despite high levels of commitment to the children in their care, some carers in both groups were struggling to cope with the demands made on them by caring for the children and, as mentioned earlier, significantly more kin carers than unrelated foster carers were showing such signs of strain.

Placement quality was less satisfactory when carers showed signs of strain and significantly more placements in both groups also disrupted when this was the case, with particularly high levels of disruption evident in unrelated care (52% of strained unrelated placements disrupted as compared with 29% of strained kin placements). As a result, by follow-up, when kin carers were under strain, approaching three-quarters (71%) of placements were continuing. In contrast, only half (48%) of the placements continued when strain had been evident among unrelated carers.

These findings together indicate that kin carers were not only more likely than unrelated foster carers to show particularly high level of commitment to the children they looked after but also that they persevered beyond the point where unrelated foster carers conceded defeat.

Children's services support
APPROVAL OF KIN AS FOSTER CARERS

As seen earlier, by follow-up two-thirds of the kin carers (67%) had been assessed and approved as foster carers for the children (whilst for 20 there was no information about this). The kin carers who had not been approved as foster carers by follow-up included not only those who had been assessed and not approved because of concerns about their health or ability to care for the children but also those who had been granted residence orders or were supported by means of Section 17 payments.

Placements with kin carers who had been approved as foster carers were significantly less likely to disrupt than those where they had not been approved. Over a third (36%) of the kin placements that had not been approved disrupted, compared to only 14 per cent of those that had been approved (see Table 5.6). This could be because the approval process excluded kin carers with greater difficulties and/or because approved kin foster placements received more support. Issues about approval are discussed in depth later.

Table 5.6 Approval of kin carers and placement disruption

Approval of kin as foster carers by follow-up	Placement continued at follow-up (Per cent) N = 87	Placement disrupted (Per cent) N = 20	(Per cent)
Carer approved as foster carers by children's services	86	14	100
Carer not approved as foster carers by children's services	64	36	100

Significance $p < 0.05$ (Fisher's exact test, $p = 0.029$).

SOCIAL WORK SUPPORT AND SERVICES

When kin placements were of poor quality, visits by social workers were more frequent, with 85 per cent of the children in problematic placements being visited regularly by social workers, compared to 63 per cent of those in satisfactory placements. This echoes other findings, which show that strained kin placements were visited more regularly by social workers, whereas this link was less pronounced in unrelated foster care. On the other hand, when unrelated foster placements were of poorer quality the carers were more likely to be provided with other support such as respite care, nursery provision, family support services, foster carer support groups and training courses.

It appears then that kin placements and unrelated foster placements are treated differently when there are concerns about the placement. Kin placements in difficulty were visited more often by social workers, and, although there were exceptions, were not offered other support services. In contrast, unrelated foster placements in difficulty were more likely to be offered a range of services to assist the placement.

In keeping with this, when children had often been seen alone by the social worker there was a tendency for kin placements to disrupt more often, presumably because social workers saw the children with more serious problems more often. On the other hand, unrelated placements had higher levels of disruption when children were awaiting or had received mental health services (again indicating higher levels of problems).

Supervised contact

When contact was supervised either by social work staff or the carers themselves, there were significantly fewer disruptions in kinship but not in unrelated foster placements. It appears then that supervised contact makes a particular difference in kin care.

Allegations

Formal allegations of maltreatment were made against 12 kin and six unrelated foster carers. However, half of the allegations against kin were unsubstantiated, compared to only one of the six made against unrelated foster carers. The rates of substantiated allegations were the same in the two types of placement (4%). In most cases where allegations were made, the placements had been rated as problematic, that is of poor quality.

Two of the unrelated foster placements were terminated as a result of the allegations and all six of these placements had ended by follow-up. In contrast, one of the kin placements was terminated because of an allegation whilst five of the 12 kin placements continued at follow-up as the allegations were judged to be unfounded.

The duration of unsatisfactory placements

About half of the placements which disrupted did so within the first two years (60% in kin and 50% in unrelated care), with a higher proportion of the kin placements lasting over six years before disrupting.

When placements were unsatisfactory, social workers moved children out of unrelated care much more quickly than out of kin placements. As a result, we found that unsatisfactory kin placements continued for significantly longer than poor unrelated foster placements. Twenty-seven per cent of the children in unsatisfactory kin placements remained in those placements for over six years, compared to only 5 per cent of children in unsatisfactory unrelated foster placements; 40 per cent of the children in unsatisfactory kin placements stayed in their placements for between two and six years, compared to 29 per cent in unsatisfactory unrelated foster placements (see Table 5.7).

There seemed to be two reasons for this. Some kin placements continued when social work monitoring was infrequent and referrals about concerns (often from other family members) were disregarded. In other situations, social workers allowed standards in kinship care to fall considerably below those that would be accepted for other children. We will return to discuss this in more detail later.

Table 5.7 Placement duration and the quality of placements

Placement time	Kin placements		Unrelated foster placements[*]	
	Satisfactory placement (Per cent) N = 93	Problematic placement (Per cent) N = 48	Satisfactory placement (Per cent) N = 93	Problematic placement (Per cent) N = 35
Less than 2 years	17	33	18	66
2–6 years	55	40	58	29
More than 6 years	28	27	24	5
Total	100	100	100	100

[*]Significance $p < 0.001$ (chi-square = 27.100, df = 2, $p < 0.001$).

Poor standards in placement

At the extreme, standards were extremely poor in a small number of the placements with kin (10%) and this will be discussed in detail later. Assessment of carers did not appear to protect children, because eight of these 14 carers had been assessed and approved as kin foster carers for the child. Very poor standards were also in evidence for seven (5%) of the unrelated foster placements. There was no significant difference between the rates of these very poor placements in the two kinds of care. Six of those with kin and one in unrelated care were still continuing at follow-up.

Further analyses: logistic regression

Since a number of variables were significantly related to our two outcome variables, we used logistic regression analyses in order to gain more understanding of the extent of the contribution of individual factors to these outcomes. The variables used included some which were known prior to placement and others which emerged as placements progressed. Some of the variables had to be excluded from the analysis because the numbers were small or there was too much missing data, in particular about some of the children's behaviours from before and during the placements. The factors included in the analyses are shown in the Appendix on page 241.

Predicting disruption in kin care

When we then looked at the factors that best predicted disruption in kin placements, the final logistic regression model included the variables shown in Table 5.8.

Table 5.8 Predicting disruption in kin care

	Odds ratio	P
Child's age	1.137	0.041
High carer commitment	0.14	0.001
Child beyond control	12.738	0.001
Contact was supervised	0.166	0.006

These results show that placements where children were older, beyond control, there was an absence of high kin carer commitment to them and contact was not supervised, were highly likely to disrupt. This model was highly significant ($p < 0.001$).[a] However, a number of variables that may be important were not able to be included in the model, such as whether kin carers were approved as foster carers and whether children were placed with their siblings. The only factor here that would be known about in advance of placement is the child's age; although it may be possible to gain some idea of carer commitment when assessments are conducted. This model highlights the importance of supervising contact when problems emerge that may undermine placements and providing assistance when older children are placed and when young people show challenging behaviour.

---

a   The Cox and Snell R^2 for the model is 0.273. The test of the model coefficients found the model to be highly significant (chi-square = 40.156; df = 4, $p < 0.001$).

Predicting poor quality placements in kin care

The factors that best predicted poor quality or problematic kin placements are shown in the final logistic regression model in Table 5.9.

Table 5.9 Predicting poor quality placements in kin care

	Odds ratio	P
Child truanted prior to placement	3.109	0.038
High carer commitment	0.16	0.001
Carer struggling to cope/strained	5.951	0.001
LA3	3.333	0.01

Table 5.9 shows that placements where the child had truanted prior to the placement, which were in LA3, where there was an absence of high kin carer commitment and the carer was struggling to cope were particularly likely to be problematic. This model was again highly significant ($p < 0.001$).[b] Two of these variables would be known prior to placement-making: placement in LA3 (the most deprived local authority in the study with high levels of drug-using parents) and a history of truanting from school, which is likely to be associated with this and other difficult behaviours arising in placement. When carers were under strain during the placement and lacked commitment to the child, the quality of the placements was compromised.

Predicting disruption in unrelated foster placements

When we looked at disruption in unrelated foster placements, the final logistic regression model included only one variable (Table 5.10).

Table 5.10 Predicting disruption in unrelated foster placements

	Odds ratio	P
Child beyond control	102	0.001

In non-relative placements where the child was beyond control the placement was highly likely to disrupt. Again, the model was highly significant ($p < 0.001$).[c]

---

b   The Cox and Snell R^2 for the model is 0.277. The test of the model coefficients found the model to be highly significant (chi-square = 46.075; df = 4, $p < 0.001$).

c   The Cox and Snell R^2 for the model is 0.337. The test of the model coefficients found the model to be highly significant (chi-square = 36.643; df = 1, $p < 0.001$).

Whilst quite a number of pre-placement behaviours and other predictors were entered into this model, the only variable that proved to be a worthwhile predictor was very difficult behaviour (being beyond control) during the placement, which was powerfully related to placement breakdown with non-relative foster carers.

Predicting poor quality placements in unrelated foster placements

In terms of the best predictors of poor quality in unrelated foster placements, the final logistic regression model included the variables shown in Table 5.11.

Table 5.11 Predicting poor quality placements in unrelated foster placements

	Odds ratio	P
Parental drug misuse prior to placement	6.192	0.002
Total number of difficult child behaviours prior to placement	1.187	0.013
Regular school attendance during placement	0.06	0.001
High carer commitment	0.027	0.001
Carer struggling to cope/strained	6.019	0.014

Interestingly, rather more variables combined to relate to the best fitting model for placement quality with unrelated carers. So in unrelated foster care, placements where there had been parental drugs misuse and a high level of difficult child behaviours before placement – as well as poor school attendance, carer strain and a lack of high carer commitment during the placement – were very likely to be of poor quality. The model was highly significant ($p < 0.001$).[d]

In conclusion, there were many similarities in the factors that were related to placement outcome in the two settings, but also some important differences. The regression analyses suggest that difficult behaviour in placement is the strongest predictor of disruption in non-related care, whilst this is true in kinship care when combined with other variables (that is higher child age, low carer commitment and contact not being supervised).

In addition, it is worth noting that factors relating to school attendance remained in the models predicting placement quality in both settings.

d   The Cox and Snell R^2 for the model is 0.387. The test of the model coefficients found the model to be highly significant (chi-square = 62.64; df = 5, $p < 0.001$).

Summary

Outcome measures

In evaluating the outcomes of placements for children, two kinds of outcomes were considered. One was a rating of placement quality which assessed how well placements met the needs of the children and the other was placement disruption. Overall, there were no differences in the quality or disruption levels of kin and unrelated placements.

However, kin placements lasted longer principally because of the higher number of planned moves in care for children with unrelated foster carers. As a result, kin placements were more likely than unrelated foster placements to be continuing at follow-up.

Factors that were not related to placement outcome

There were no significant differences in outcome in terms of children's gender, ethnicity, previous maltreatment or parental adversities, with the one exception of parental drugs misuse. In addition, there were no significant differences in outcome in relation to whether kin placements were made on the maternal or paternal side of the family, with single or couple carers or included step-relatives.

Local authorities

There were differences between the local authorities on both outcome measures. It was interesting that the authority that had the highest level of deprivation and the highest proportion of kin placements also had the most of poor quality.

Pre-placement

AGE

There were higher levels of placement disruption in kin care when young people were over the age of 10 at placement. In contrast, in non-related care disruption levels were highest for children placed between the ages of 5 and 10.

PARENTAL DRUG MISUSE

In both settings placements were of poorer quality when the children's parents had misused drugs.

PREVIOUS EXPERIENCES OF CHILDREN

As expected, the behaviour of children before the placement was linked to disruption and quality in both types of placement. For example, children who had previously showed defiant behaviour at home or school or who had truanted had less satisfactory placements in both settings. Similarly, a history of stealing/damaging property or truanting was related to higher breakdown rates in both settings. Past school exclusion was also closely related to disruption, particularly in kinship care. In addition, restlessness and lack of concentration were significantly linked to poorer quality placements for both groups of children.

In stranger foster care the disruption rate rose significantly as the numbers of previous behavioural and emotional problems increased but that this was not the case for kin placements. This suggests that kin carers are more likely to continue to care for children with very difficult behaviour than unrelated carers.

CARER CHARACTERISTICS

Grandparent carers had the lowest disruption rates. The disruption rates for other relatives and friends were at fairly similar rates to those for unrelated foster carers. There was no difference in the quality of placements with different relatives.

PLACEMENTS WITH OTHER CHILDREN

The placements of children in both groups were less likely to disrupt when they were cared for with their brothers and sisters, and on the other hand more likely to break down when some of their siblings continued to live with their parents. Children in kin placements with no other children were at greater risk of disruption than those who lived with other children, although the difference did not quite reach significance.

During the placement

CHILDREN'S BEHAVIOUR IN THE PLACEMENT

Both types of placement were more likely to disrupt when children had the kind of problems that clearly required remedial help. Not surprisingly, children with such difficulties had less satisfactory placements in both types of care. It is worth noting again that almost half the children with such problems in both groups were not receiving any remedial help.

Children who were reported on file as being confident and behaving well socially had better outcomes in both types of placement, whilst those with poor peer relationships did worse in both. Restless behaviour and lack of concentration within the placement were linked to poorer quality placements in both groups.

Both types of placement were more likely to disrupt when children were beyond control or when children's behaviour worsened, (or showed a mixed picture of changes for better and worse). However, more of the kin (56%) than the unrelated (27%) placements continued in spite of such difficulties. This suggests that kin are more likely to persevere with children when there are difficulties.

EDUCATION IN THE PLACEMENTS

When children's school progress was poor there were more disruptions in both kinds of placement, whilst children with statements of special educational need had increased levels of placement breakdowns in unrelated but not kinship care. Poor school attendance was related to poorer quality placements in both groups. It was also related to disruption in both settings, but particularly so in kin care.

CARERS

Approval of family and friends as foster carers was linked to higher levels of stability and this could be explained by the approval process excluding carers where there were concerns about their capacity to care for the children or because approved kin carers received better support and financial assistance than those who were not approved, or both.

High levels of carer commitment to the children was positively related to the quality of both types of placement but in addition in kinship care significantly fewer placements disrupted when carers showed these high levels of commitment.

Both types of placement were of poorer quality and more often disrupted when carers showed signs of strain but the disruption levels were higher among strained unrelated carers. As a result, more of the placements where kin were under strain were continuing at follow-up (71% v. 48% in unrelated care). This again suggests that kin persevered after strained unrelated foster carers conceded defeat.

SOCIAL WORK SUPPORT AND SERVICES

Kin and unrelated foster carers were treated differently when there were concerns about the placement. Kin placements in difficulty were visited more often by social workers, and, although there were exceptions, were not offered other support services routinely, whereas unrelated foster placements in difficulty were more likely to be offered a range of support services.

When contact was supervised by social work staff or the carers themselves, there were decreased levels of disruption in kin but not in unrelated foster placements.

FORMAL ALLEGATIONS OF MALTREATMENT AGAINST CARERS

The level of substantiated formal allegations of maltreatment against carers in the two groups was the same (4%), but more unsubstantiated allegations were made against kin carers. Social workers tread a difficult line between treating concerns expressed by relatives seriously, whilst protecting good placements from malicious allegations made by relatives who, for whatever reason, may be trying to undermine placements.

DURATION OF PLACEMENTS

We found, unsurprisingly, that in both types of placement the better quality placements were less likely to disrupt. However, when placements were unsatisfactory, social workers moved children out of unrelated care much more quickly than out of kin placements. As a result, we found that unsatisfactory kin placements continued for significantly longer than poor unrelated foster placements. This was probably because over time social workers became less involved with monitoring kin placements, were less inclined to intervene in poor kin placements or discounted concerns expressed by other relatives.

About half of the placements that disrupted did so within the first two years (60% in kin and 50% in unrelated care), with a higher proportion of the kin placements lasting over six years before disrupting.

Now that we have compared the kin and non-related foster care placements, we turn, in the next section, to look in more depth at the key issues in kinship care that arose from the interviews with kin carers, children, parents and social workers and from an examination of the histories of all the cases in the study.

Part III

Overviews and Kin Carer Perspectives on Kin Placements

Chapter 6

Placing Children
with Kin: Assessment
and Financial Support

After reading each case file during the study, we wrote a one to three page summary of the history and the main issues in each case. We then conducted an in-depth analysis of all the 142 case summaries of the placements with family and friends. In a situation where there is so little information about kinship care we thought it was important to provide a picture of the full range of placements and the issues that arise. This also ensured that in-depth information was available on the placements that caused difficulties as well as those that went well, since the interviews were likely to be biased towards the ongoing successful placements.

In addition, we analysed the interviews with 32 kin carers. Of these, 14 were maternal grandparents (11 couples, two single grandmothers and one single grandfather), seven paternal grandparents (six couples and one single grand-mother), four maternal aunts and uncles (three couples and one lone aunt), three paternal aunts and uncles (two couples and one lone aunt) and four friends (of whom one was the parent of the child's friend, one couple had been friends of the mother, one single step-mother and one single step-father). It is worth noting that 6 of the 17 grandparent couples included a step-grandparent (four step-grandfathers and two step-grandmothers) and that one aunt was the wife of the child's maternal uncle who had left the family. In comparison, with the total file sample, we interviewed more grandparents (66% of the interview sample and 45% of the file sample) and slightly fewer aunts and uncles (22% of the inter-view and 32% of the file sample) and friends (12% of the interview and 18% of the file sample). We did not interview any older siblings or cousins (5% of the file sample).

Of the 32 carers we interviewed, 16 had been approved as foster carers; whilst 14 were caring for children on residence orders (although nine of these carers had originally been approved as foster carers and had only made a residence order application later). In two other cases, grandparents were looking after three grandchildren, two of whom were fostered and the third of whom was on a residence order for which no allowance was paid. In one of the other residence order cases, no allowance was paid, making three in all in the interview sample in this situation. The average age of the female kin carers was 56 (with a range of 35–73 years), whilst for the male carers it was 58 (with a range of 38–82). The average age of all the kin carers in the interview sample was 57. This is similar to Pitcher's small study (2002) where the average age of grandparent carers was 54 but somewhat higher than that of kinship foster carers in Sinclair's study where it was on average 44 for the primary caregiver and 46 for their partner (Sykes *et al.* 2002).

In this and the next two chapters, for each theme the broad situation will be sketched out using data from the 142 case file summaries, supplemented by more detailed information about the experiences of the carers from the 32 interviews. The names and some of the details of the cases have been altered to preserve anonymity.

In this chapter, we look at the children's backgrounds before they began to be looked after, how they came to be placed with relatives or friends, the arrangements for assessing and regulating the placements and the financial support provided.

The children's backgrounds and the start of being looked after

Social workers have the difficult task of deciding whether and when children should be separated from their parents. Nonetheless, it was striking that in a small number of cases children were left for a long time in damaging circumstances before they were removed (see also Ward *et al.* 2006). In our judgement, this occurred in 12 per cent of all the placements with relatives and friends. All too often, by the time children were no longer living with their parents, substantial harm had been done and they showed severe behaviour difficulties in their placements with family or friends. We did not examine how far this was true of the placements with unrelated foster carers, but there is no reason to suppose that they would have been different.

These cases tended to show that there were long-standing concerns about the children and often many referrals to children's services but that it often took one specific incident, generally sexual abuse or a violent assault, for the children to be removed (see also Tanner and Turney 2003). A few examples will illustrate the progress of such cases.

The Green family were known to children's services after the youngest child was severely injured. For the next four years, there were many referrals about the two remaining children who had become withdrawn and isolated, were often left in bed all day, were harshly punished if they misbehaved and were living in neglected, dirty conditions with parents who drank and a step-father who was violent to the children and their mother. It was not until the oldest child was aged 13 and his step-father attacked the child's younger sibling with a knife that both were removed on an emergency protection order and placed with their maternal grandmother.

Steve was a boy with severe learning difficulties, both of whose parents also had learning difficulties. Children's services became involved because there were concerns that Steve was smearing faeces, being locked in a cupboard and subjected to violence by his father. A relative, who had been convicted for offences against children, was a frequent visitor and the sexual boundaries in both the maternal and paternal families were seen as blurred. When Steve reached the age of five it was agreed that he would spend each weekend with his maternal grandparents, as a result of his father's increasingly cruel behaviour towards him and a particularly violent attack on his mother. He was soon living full time with his grandparents and his sister joined him four years later after her father sexually abused her.

Ayesha was one of five siblings whose parents misused drugs. Her father had been charged with assaults on three women including Ayesha's mother, who also suffered from depression and had made a number of suicide attempts. The parents' relationship was violent and volatile. There were many referrals over a period of three years because the children were left alone and neglected, they lost weight and were scratched and bruised. When Ayesha's two-year-old sister was admitted to hospital after an accident at home, care proceedings were started and the three older children were placed with their grandparents. The children's guardian recorded on file that she was concerned that it had taken so long for action to be taken with these children.

Whilst these are extreme examples of children left for particularly long periods in harmful circumstances, most of the children had experienced a range of such adversities and, as we have seen, they formed the background to the difficulties that children brought with them to their placements with family and friends.

Placements made with high risk relatives

The case file analysis showed that, when parents had been in care, their children were more often placed with unrelated foster carers than with family or friends. In addition, we were interested to see how consistently social workers avoided placing grandchildren with grandparents who had ill treated their own children. We found that the fact that a mother had had considerable problems in adolescence or had experienced maltreatment did not preclude placement of her children with her parents, although social workers might have exercised particular caution in making such placements. Certainly, we found that a number of mothers were concerned that their children had been placed with the parents who had maltreated them or whose problems had affected their parenting. For example, a mother who had been physically abused by her father and another mother who had been abused by her own mother were concerned when their children were placed with these grandparents, as was another parent whose mother had not protected her from sexual abuse. Some of these grandparents nonetheless managed to provide adequate care this time round.

There were a small number of more surprising placements where the children of mothers who had been (or were highly likely to have been) sexually abused by their fathers or step-fathers were placed with these men. This occurred in four kin placements in the case file study. In two, the alleged abuse did not appear to have elicited any specific safeguarding measures. In the other two cases, assessments were carried out to try to ascertain how safe the placement would be for the child. One investigation could not confirm the abuse, although the mother showed behaviours often associated with sexual abuse and had been treated for depression and bulimia. In the other, the relative had admitted his long-term sexual abuse of the boy's mother and had received a police warning. Another agency had conducted an assessment and concluded that the relative's partner had developed an understanding of the importance of protecting the child, that the boy himself knew what action he could take if he was approached inappropriately and the abusing relative had received some treatment. However, four years later concerns about the risk posed by the carer were still being expressed.

How the children came to be placed with relatives or friends
Initiating the placements

Generally the relatives or friends who became carers had known the children for some time. As we have seen, in many cases, the relatives had often looked after the children in the past and had had regular contact with them. Some of the grandparents had taken their grandchildren for regular weekends or for long periods to help the parents or provide a home for the children when the parents were unable to care. Aunts and uncles too had sometimes provided this kind of assistance. More rarely a grandmother had moved in with her daughter for a while to help her look after the children. Friends had also often, but not always, had considerable involvement with the children before taking them on a longer term basis. Some such families had been a frequent place of refuge for children from difficult home circumstances.

The move to kin sometimes occurred when a parent left the children with their relatives or a friend during a domestic crisis, which led to them staying there long term; or a regular weekend stay became a more permanent arrangement. In such situations, the relatives, friends or the parents initiated the placement, usually with the assent of children's services. In only a few cases had the relatives who came forward known the children much less well before placement, sometimes because they lived in another part of the country. For example, one grandmother described how she and her husband had told their son, the children's father, that they would be willing to look after his children and how readily this offer of help was then taken up by children's services:

> We hadn't had no relationship with them really. It was just before Christmas. Originally they were going to foster carers and Roy said something to us and I said, 'Well we would always help you Roy if there's a situation.' Social services didn't know we existed and so he phoned his solicitor and they were quite interested because Clive is a scout leader and I used to run playgroups for ten years. The social worker was adamant they were going to another foster carer and they would have gone the next day. And she come up here, seen the house and decided that there was quite a suitable accommodation and that we were suitable if we went through the right channels to do it.

The placements with friends occurred in a number of ways. Sometimes, children went to the parents of a school friend who took them in or parents would ask one of their friends to care for the children. Friends would also offer to take children when they realised that they needed a place to live. Occasionally, a social worker (or, in once case, the school) asked a family friend or neighbour to take a child as an emergency measure and this became a longer term placement.

Some placements started as short-term whilst other carers knew from the start that they would be likely to have the children for a long period. In a few such cases, although carers were told that the placement was temporary, it later appeared that the social worker was hoping that it would become permanent.

Placements made by social workers

More rarely, the placements were made by social workers. When relatives had regularly had children to stay, social workers sometimes knew of this and might approach them to ask if they would take the children, or social workers involved kin at the suggestion of one of the parents, especially if the relatives had let the department know that they wanted to look after the children.

When carers had spent a long time caring for the children because the parents could not do so, they had sometimes felt growing alarm about the poor standards of care by the parents, whom they were often also trying to support. In such circumstances, a number of relatives had first approached the local children's services to report their concerns about the children. When the department took action, the social worker might then seek to place the children with those relatives. It is worth noting that other relatives had not realised quite how bad things were for the children even when they had been actively involved in efforts to help parents cope with their children.

Care proceedings

Another clear pattern was where care proceedings were instigated and the social worker then actively searched out and assessed any suitable relatives. This was sometimes on the initiative of the children's guardian. Occasionally, the courts asked the parents who could take on their children and they suggested a particular relative, or hearing about the court case led a relative to offer to take the children. In these situations, the usual procedure was for the child to be placed with unrelated foster carers while the relatives were assessed and these placements with kin only occurred after the assessment was completed.

Moves from foster placements

Whilst many of the moves were from parents (or other relatives) to a friend or relative, there were also occasions when children moved to a kin carer when a foster placement was ending or breaking down or in a planned move from foster care. In three cases, relatives or friends who had provided regular weekend respite placements for the children's foster carers offered or were asked to care for a child longer term.

Not infrequently, a relative heard on the grapevine that the children were in care and contacted children's services to offer to take the child. A friend carer described her efforts to locate the children and offer to have them:

> A friend it was who phoned us and said he'd heard that the kids were in care. And he knew how close Jack was with the kids, and we basically phoned round all the social services in [the city] and [the surrounding area] until we found which one they were placed with, and then straight away, we went to see the kids. Then we had to go to court.

In one unusual case, an aunt and uncle who had often had the children to stay had to fight for them to come and live with them when they were in foster care, because the mother was against this. A subsequent child psychiatrist's report confirmed the strong bond between the aunt and the children, but it took 18 months before the children were placed with them.

Later moves within the kin network

A few children moved to live with a family member after an older relative, usually a grandparent, had died or become very ill or when a placement with another relative had broken down. One child went to an aunt who was herself the victim of domestic violence for two months, then back to his parents briefly, before going to another aunt for a month and then to a third aunt with whom he stayed. In another case, when a grandparent couple struggled to manage both grandchildren, an aunt offered to take one of them and the arrangement worked well.

Sibling placements

Sometimes, family members would meet together to decide on arrangements for caring for a relative's children. At other times, social workers approached a number of relatives to try to orchestrate arrangements. Often children would then be shared out amongst extended family members. For example in one case, a 6-year-old went to the maternal aunt, the 8-year-old to his paternal grandparents and the 12-year-old sister to the maternal grandparents, whilst the 2-year-old was adopted out of the family. In another case, one sibling went to family friends, another to the paternal aunt and uncle, a third to a maternal aunt and a fourth to another maternal aunt who later adopted her. In a third case, the oldest child went to the maternal grandparents and his sister of four went from there to the maternal aunt and uncle because of the competition between the two when placed together, whilst the 2-year-old sister was with unrelated foster carers and the fourth child, who was born later, stayed with the parents. These arrangements were often between family members who knew each other well and there were usually high levels of contact between the siblings.

When families made such arrangements they were accepted readily, rather than trying to make a placement in which all the siblings could be placed together and they generally worked well. However, occasionally the social worker did not accept offers of help from a family member and this seemed to be where only part of the sibling group was placed and no other family member was offering to help. In one such case, the social worker took a 3-year-old boy to a children's home to be with his siblings, moving him from the grandmother who looked after him for the first three months of his life and for the ten months before he went to the children's home. The reason for this move was not clear but there may have been a plan to place the children together, possibly for adoption. However, in practice this did not eventuate and the boy was returned to his grandmother at the age of 5, whilst his siblings were placed with her a year later. In another somewhat similar case, the paternal grandmother and her husband took their two grandchildren aged 5 and 8, but the placement broke down after a few months because they could not manage both. Although they were willing to keep the 5-year-old, both children were removed with a plan to place them together for adoption. Three years later when no adoptive placement had been found the granddaughter was placed back with the grandparents.

However, it was more common for one relative to take all or most of the whole sibling group. One grandmother who could only take three of her five grandchildren mourned the two youngest who were adopted. Occasionally, a relative was managing some of the children but became overloaded when other siblings were also placed. In one such case a maternal grandmother who was looking after four of her grandchildren was assessed for her ability to care for a fifth sibling. Even though the grandmother became ill and said that she could not cope, this child did join her, leaving her struggling to cope.

There were also a number of examples where social workers put pressure on relatives or friends to keep children, even when it was to the detriment of their own family, as for example when the child was unable to get on with the carers' children.

It was interesting to find that sibling moves within the family could affect children. One girl who was living with friends resented it when her older sister went to live with their grandparents. Another child who lived with her grandparents could not understand why her youngest sister had gone back to live with their parents and she had not.

Making the decision to take relative children

When the idea of children moving to their relatives or friends was mooted, the carers would generally discuss this fully with their children and sometimes with other relatives before making their decision. As one step-grandmother said:

> Yes, we discussed it with our children; in fact we discussed it with all the whole family because we knew that Jason was going to be here until he got to the stage where he was independent enough to leave home. So we obviously had to make sure that the girls were happy with that. Me and Keith discussed it for hours and hours and we went through everything that we could possibly think of that could be an issue at all, and at the end of the day, Keith said, 'I will not push you into anything,' because obviously it's his grandson, but I was going to be the main carer, so the final decision had to be mine because I would be doing a lot of the work for Jason.

The health difficulties of the carers and contingency plans

Almost a third (31%) of all the family and friends carers had severe health difficulties, considerably more than was the case with stranger foster carers. Older grandparents sometimes had a number of health problems and a few needed daily assistance to manage their lives, even before they took on their grandchildren. For example, Mr Leigh was a grandfather who had had four heart attacks, suffered from angina and had breathing difficulties. His wife had rheumatoid arthritis. Mrs Billings was diagnosed with lung cancer whilst looking after her grandchildren. Mrs Clark had a heart condition, hypertension, glaucoma and chronic obstructive pulmonary disease. Her husband, the children's grandfather, had diabetes and hemiplegia. Two grandfathers had had strokes and, in one of these families, his wife was providing 24-hour nursing care. A number of these carers coped only because their adult children lived nearby and gave them daily assistance.

The carers did not dwell on their health difficulties. Indeed, one grandmother was anxious to ensure that the detail of her difficulties would not be passed on to her social worker, in case it was thought to jeopardise her care of the children:

> 'Cos I don't want to think that this is anything the children's going to suffer 'cos I'm not well. I don't tell anyone. They has to know I'm all right. I'm on medication and I'm fine.

It was not uncommon for families to have given considerable thought as to who might care for the children if the current relative carers could no longer continue.

Such contingency plans usually involved another family member, such as an aunt, who was already well known to the children. Sometimes this had been fully discussed and in one case put in writing and signed. At other times it was verbally agreed or understood, or occasionally was a hope harboured by the caring relatives. Friends less often had explicit plans, although at the prompting of children's services, the sister of one friend couple who were unwell, had agreed to take the boy they were looking after, if necessary. One carer thought that the child would go into independent living and another into care if they could no longer look after him, whilst a few thought it likely that the children would return to their parents or that an older sibling would take over. However, where relatives were caring for a severely disabled child it could be that no other family member would feel able to take on the child's care. Such relatives caring for children, whose physical or learning disabilities meant that they would not be able to live independently as adults, faced the worry of wondering what would happen to the children in the future.

Children who moved to live with elderly grandparents when young, often later experienced their grandparents' ill health and occasionally their death. Whilst this might be considered a disadvantage of some kinship care placements, the children usually moved to live with another relative, which no doubt assisted in the continuity of their care and probably also helped them to deal with their loss.

Overcrowding

It was not uncommon for there to be overcrowding in placements with family and friends. Unlike unrelated foster carers who plan when to take children, and are assessed as to how many they are allowed to foster, kin take in children with no such plans and often at short notice. Some go to grandparents who are living in accommodation only just big enough for them alone and others join aunts and uncles with large families where there is little extra space for a group of siblings. It was therefore notable how often the case files did not mention whether the accommodation was suitable or large enough or even how many children there already were in the household. Nonetheless, as we have seen, there was clear overcrowding in 22 per cent of families and there appeared to be problems that were not elaborated in the files in a further 13 per cent, making difficulties in at least a third (35%) of the placements with family and friends.

Sometimes, kin were able to sort out the difficulties themselves, moving to larger rented accommodation or exchanging houses with another family member. Others were left awaiting the allocation of a larger house by the local housing department, with mounting tensions and pressure on relationships as the lack of space caused arguments to erupt.

Dealing with overcrowding

The carers were often imaginative in making enough space for the children. In one case grandparents were looking after four grandchildren and still had the children's father and uncle living with them at home. They were planning to make one of the bedrooms into two rooms. In another, the grandparents had a two bedroom house and looked after their three grandchildren, so they partitioned one bedroom and used one of the living rooms as another bedroom. However, they would have welcomed more help from children's services with their housing:

> Had we been in council accommodation we would have got it, being private no. You fit them in but you would think that you would be able to get some sort of grant where you might have been able to have added on perhaps another bedroom.

It was remarkable how flexible families were prepared to be. In one family, one of the grandsons slept in their caravan in order to have his own bedroom. Similarly, a friend couple acquired a second-hand summerhouse for their son to use as his own space, as there was friction when he was sharing his bedroom with the much younger boy who they were looking after. They were hoping to get a three-bedroom house or to be allowed to convert the loft in their council house, but neither had been approved when we interviewed them. Two sets of carers built a fourth bedroom in their loft when their nephews and nieces came to live with them.

Other families made do with what they had. For example, an uncle and aunt had five children when they took their niece into their three-bedroom house, so the four boys shared a room as did the two girls; whilst a grandmother in a one-bedroom maisonette, who was joined by her two grandchildren, ended up sleeping on the settee.

A number of families made major changes such as moving to a new area in order to have the children or in one case selling the house they lived in because, after the grandmother had reduced her working hours in order to care for her grandson, she and her husband could no longer afford the mortgage.

Complex households

Sometimes, there were complex households with a number of adults as well as children. For example, one set of maternal grandparents took their 14-year-old grandson into their family, which already consisted of the child's mother and another of their adult children and her two children – making four adults and three children. In another case, an aunt and uncle lived with the aunt's father who was chronically ill, her brother who was the children's father and his three children, so that there were four adults and three children in the household. This family did manage later through their own efforts to move from a three- to a four-bedroom rented house.

The pressures of overcrowding

In the family just mentioned, when the children came to live permanently with them, the relationship between the aunt and her partner broke down and he moved out of the house. In three other cases, the carers separated after the relative children joined the family and it seemed likely that the new caring responsibilities, compounded by overcrowding, had put these couples' relationships under strain.

The case files did sometimes note that overcrowding was putting pressure on the placement. In one such situation, a paternal uncle and his partner, who lived in a one-bedroom flat, accommodated their 10-year-old nephew who had been excluded from school and who was aggressive and uncooperative. Not surprisingly, this placement disrupted after only two months.

Local authority responses

Local authority responses to these difficulties were varied. In two cases children's services or the housing department provided financial help to build an extension onto the house to provide enough space, but in another two cases help to build an extension was refused. There were no apparent differences between the families where help for an extension was and was not agreed and they were all placements made by children's services.

Social workers were sometimes active in putting pressure on housing departments to provide more suitable accommodation, and occasionally although not very often, a child's placement with kin was delayed until more suitable accommodation was available.

Arrangements for approving and regulating placements and providing financial support

Most of the children who were looked after by family or friends were eventually placed under fostering regulations, after an assessment of their suitability had been undertaken. As we have seen, initially many were placed under what is now Regulation 38 of the Fostering Services Regulations 2002, awaiting a full assessment and were later approved as foster carers. Fostering allowances paid to relative carers were generally lower than those paid to unrelated foster carers, in spite of the Munby judgement (*R. (ota) L.* v. *Manchester City Council* 2002), which clearly states that local authorities may not discriminate against friends and relatives who are foster carers by paying them at lower rates. A smaller proportion of kin were encouraged from the start to apply to the court for residence orders, and the local authority had discretion to pay a residence order allowance. However, it is worth noting that a Family Rights Group survey found that 40 per cent of authorities limited residence order allowances to children who had been in care prior to placement with family and friends (Morgan 2004).

Local authorities made the lowest financial contribution when the social worker was successful in persuading the carer to apply straight away for a residence order. In one such case the maternal grandmother was paid £25 a week from Section 17 funds and was advised to apply for a residence order, even though the father opposed this step. Another grandmother had been paid a small allowance until the residence order came through, at which point the allowance and all other help ceased.

A small number of placements, especially those with friends, were considered to be private fostering arrangements or remained as private arrangements between the parent and the relative or friend, whether or not the local authority gave any financial assistance. In at least two of the cases, which had been classified as private fostering arrangements, the local authority paid very little, arguing that they had no responsibility for placements made under these arrangements. In another case, friend carers were approved as foster carers after 10 months, during which time they had been paid £25 a week from the Children in Need budget, even though they were struggling financially and the female carer was a student.

As we have seen, placements made under Regulation 38 require that an assessment is made within six weeks. In practice, many files recorded that two to three years passed before the carers were approved as foster parents and in a few cases it appeared that the carers had never been approved. Local authorities often made weekly payments at low rates (typically £25–65) from Section 17 funds until the carers were approved as foster parents. However, they did not always do so.

The basis of decisions for approval as foster carers

It was not clear on what basis it was decided whether to seek to approve family or friends as foster carers or whether to suggest to them that they should apply for a residence order. Some relatives who appeared to be offering quite adequate care were routed via a residence order. However, it was clear that when the carers were considered to be unsuitable to be approved as foster carers, they were often advised to apply for residence orders (see also Hannah and Pitman 2000). The paradox of this policy was that carers who already had difficult backgrounds or problems of ill health were further disadvantaged by having to pursue residence orders that carry no obligation to provide payment, offer lower rates when payments are made and provide no social work support or monitoring. For example, one grandmother was considered to be 'grossly overweight' and had a number of health difficulties and so was advised to apply for a residence order. In another more unusual case, police checks revealed that a male relative had a previous conviction for indecent exposure to a young girl. The first social worker decided not to support their application to be foster carers for the children. After the carers complained, another social worker undertook a further assessment and supported an application for a residence order.

Carers who had been urged to apply for residence orders from the outset were often not aware that fostering was an alternative. Indeed, one grandmother who was looking after six grandchildren on residence orders had understood: 'We're classed like carers. We cannot be foster parents because we're family.'

Foster carer approval

However, decisions to approve relatives or friends as foster carers were not consistent and were sometimes made when kin had backgrounds of offences[24] or other problems. For example, two sets of relatives with convictions for fraud (and in one case assault) were assessed as having good parenting skills and approved. More controversially, relatives were approved to foster two children in spite of an allegation of indecent assault on a schoolgirl a few months earlier. The police thought the relative was guilty, but the social worker disagreed and the approval went through. There were continuing concerns throughout this placement about the carer's relationship with the child and these later proved to be well-founded.

A particular dilemma in a number of these situations was whether to approve as foster carers kin who had severe health difficulties. Some were approved whilst others were not. For example, in one case a grandfather had a heart condition and asthma and the grandmother had a severe back problem and agoraphobia but they were approved as foster carers before the child went to live with them.

Concerns about health could also lead to delays in approval or more rarely a decision not to place. In one such case, approval was delayed after the medical report showed that the carer, who was a neighbour, had epilepsy that was not well-controlled and agoraphobia, as well as having convictions for theft. The doctor was concerned about her ability to care for the children. In another case, approval was again delayed because of concerns about the grandfather's heart condition and his violence to the children's father. The social worker suggested that the grandparents apply for a residence order instead, but the mother opposed this. In a third case, approval was withheld and placements with other relatives made, because both grandparents had serious chronic heart and other medical conditions and were overweight. Certainly, many of the kin carers did have quite serious health conditions but succeeded in caring for children in spite of this and often with minimal support from children's services.

Occasionally, where an assessment revealed concerns about the carer's parenting, additional support was provided. Mrs Hall and her partner were already looking after one granddaughter and were assessed as to their suitability to look after their grandson as well. Two separate assessments revealed some concerns, particularly about the couple's ability to provide adequate behavioural boundaries but a substantial package of support was provided, including a family support worker and regular respite care, and the grandson was placed when he was almost two years old.

There were a few cases where children did well in spite of the unpromising circumstances of the carers. Leonie, as seen in Chapter 4, was placed with relatives who had mental health difficulties and longstanding problems with their own children, but she settled well and was happy. In another case, the mother was vehemently opposed to her children being placed with their maternal grandmother who had ill treated her as a child and had an alcohol problem but again the placement went well.

We picked up only a few cases where children's services not only declined to approve but also ended a placement, although this may have been an artefact of our sampling procedure. These cases are considered in Chapter 8.

The time taken to approve kin as foster carers

The time taken to approve relatives or friends as foster carers was again very variable, although it was not always recorded on the case files. It could take as little as four months or as long as three years. In a few cases, as we have seen, carers had never been approved. The cases that were dealt with most expeditiously were those where there were care proceedings and the social worker had to report to the court on the progress of the assessment. Others appeared to be accorded much lower priority. In just one case in the interview sample, the assessment of the grandparents started when their grandson was still with his mother, because it was thought that he might need to be removed from her.

The carers' experience of assessment

In the interviews, we asked the carers about their experience of being assessed as foster carers for the children they were looking after. Some carers had little to say about this, perhaps partly because it had often occurred quite a considerable time earlier. When the assessments had been conducted within the statutory period of six weeks for Regulation 38 cases, they were fairly brief and involved a few meetings and a series of police and health checks and reports from the school. Even when the assessments had occurred at a later stage, they were often recalled as being completed rapidly. One aunt described the process thus:

> One minute we was…and then the next minute they rushed all through these checks you've got to go through, all the crime and criminal checks and whatever. They'd gone through all those very quickly and we'd been passed like that. One weekend to the next we'd gone from nothing to approved foster carers – well relative foster carers.

A grandmother had found the process painless: 'They could see we was a caring family, so they just come around and saw us and I suppose we was being assessed at the time.'

A few carers knew that these assessments were much less detailed than those for unrelated foster carers, either because they themselves later moved to ordinary fostering or because they had friends who fostered.

In contrast, other carers commented that there had been hours of interviews in which they had had to talk at length about the past, that a lot of questions had been asked or that there had been 'millions of questionnaires'. For example, one grandmother said:

> Yes we had to…hours and hours of interviews, go right back through everybody, right back through the family, everything – yes. And they weighed it up before a foster panel. Arthur and I went…we all went up, and we were in there I think 10 minutes because we were family and they just did it.

Another grandmother said: 'It went on for ever.'

A small number of carers told us with pride that all the reports had shown considerable improvements in the children so that they were confident that the assessment would be positive.

Three of the carers remembered assessments that lasted from 8 to 12 months. One grandmother commented that she and her husband had provided respite care for their grandchildren for a long period previously, but she could understand that the eight-month assessment was a process that had to be completed. Other carers were less sanguine. An aunt and uncle were surprised that the assessment did not take into account the fact that they had already looked after their nieces for six months and found the social workers reluctant to let them take over the care of the children. Indeed, it was 18 months before the children were placed with them:

> We had to justify ourselves in respect of, are you worthy to look after the children? Well the way it was put across, we were total strangers. Although the

social services knew that we'd looked after the girls for six months… And I know they have to ask questions and things like that, but they were unnecessary because social services were OK about us looking after them before – it was as if we'd got to fight for what we thought were ours really.

One grandparent couple had faced a solicitor, other relatives and a children's guardian who had suggested that they were too old to take the children.

In two cases in the interview sample, the exploration of the carer's past had been painful, bringing up as it did difficult issues of abuse in the past. In one of these, a single step-father had had a psychiatric assessment because of the abuse he had endured and he described it as follows:

Oh that was awful; I mean that was absolutely awful. I had this woman come down, this psychiatric assessment. She came for three sessions, five hours a session, and at the end of the first session, I was sat there for three hours crying because she'd gone so deep into my psyche, and I had some abuse at boarding school…and then she wrote up this report saying I was a likely child abuser. And it was absolutely devastating, so then I had to go back to court. I had more psychological assessment to do with the here and now so I could explain to them, 'Yes, I was fully aware of the problems I have but I've learned to deal with them.' But social had a duty to make sure that the placement's going to be safe and I understand all that. Everybody used to say to me, 'We're amazed that you stuck in this because we've really put you through the mill.'

In contrast, the police checks that were an inescapable part of all these assessments so alarmed the long-term boyfriend of one single aunt, that he ended the relationship.

One grandparent couple had found the method of assessment demeaning:

It was vile, the assessment. I mean we'd raised children, we'd never done anything wrong – and then all of a sudden you're sat in a room and your parenting skills are being – and you feel like somebody who's had their children removed…really demeaning. And at one point I said, 'How dare you? I haven't asked to be sat here, I haven't asked for all this to happen, it's just, we've been pushed into a corner.' We hadn't done anything wrong. It was traumatic enough that we were about to have our lives turned upside down again.

This grandmother found the subsequent training 'mind-boggling' since she considered that she was being told how to bring up a child, when she had already successfully brought up her own son.

Family and friends were often reassured during the assessment that their standard of living would not fall but found in practice that these reassurances were hollow. For example, one aunt and uncle who took three children in addition to their own two said:

We were saying 'Well, financially we're not bad, we're OK, we've got two kids, we've got a house – we can go on holiday if we can once a year and we've got a nice car and stuff.' And they said, 'No we don't want to take that away, we want the other kids to come in and obviously enjoy that as well.' So it was a case of, 'No, we will help financially' and that didn't materialise whatsoever.

A step-grandmother had the same experience:

All the promises that were made beforehand, that we wouldn't have to worry about money. This was one of the things we said ourselves…we'd got to be sure we could afford to take him on. Not for us to benefit, but for that child not to want for anything because I always said I would never raise a child on benefits… And they assured us that he wouldn't want for anything…and then I found out it was like, round about £20 a week.

An aunt and uncle said:

We felt very let down from social, from the beginning really, I don't think anybody come in and painted us really a true picture. I don't think we realised the impact on our own kids, because it changed. I mean yes we knew they would have to sacrifice a bit but I don't think we realised just how much that they would have to sacrifice.

Pressure for kin carers to apply for residence orders

Some time after relatives and friends had been approved as foster carers, social workers would often begin to put pressure on them to apply for a residence order. Residence order allowances, as we have seen, were paid at lower rates than fostering allowances. At that time, these allowances also generally stopped when the child reached the age of 16, although at least one of our authorities later decided to pay residence order allowances up to the age of 18,[a] providing that the child was in full-time education. Some carers, who had obtained residence orders, as we have seen, received no allowance at all, whilst a few only received payment after involving others as advocates on their behalf. In addition, social work involvement ceased with the making of a residence order.

Moreover, although children's services often paid the court costs for the residence order hearings, not all did. Some carers had themselves paid the full costs of applying for a residence order and one couple whose income was so low that they received Family Credit represented themselves in court to save costs. When relatives paid a solicitor to represent them in these court cases, they were often left with a substantial debt, which took a long time to clear (see also Richards 2001).

a   The Adoption and Children Act 2002 amended the Children Act 1989 to allow residence order to be extended to the age of 18 at the request of the applicant for the residence order.

Of the 32 carers interviewed, six had paid for a solicitor either for the court hearing for a residence order or for earlier care proceedings. This placed them under considerable financial pressure. One grandparent couple had paid £3000 for court costs and another grandmother had incurred a significant debt paying for a solicitor. She commented:

> It ruined me. When we moved into this house I couldn't even afford to buy any carpet. It was really, really hard for me. And buying Ailsa's clothes as well, because she'd got nothing when she came. I didn't have a cooker for three weeks because I couldn't afford to have it connected. I got in a lot of debt. I really got in a lot of debt.

Another grandparent couple were already looking after their oldest granddaughter on a residence order with no allowance and then paid for a solicitor when the two younger children came to live with them. They used up £6000 of their savings in the first year and the grandmother had by then given up her part-time job, so reducing their income. Eventually, the social worker arranged for the grandparents to be approved as foster carers for the two younger children:

> And we made arrangements to see the social worker who was Jenny and we explained to her the situation, and she said, 'Well I can't understand why you're not getting anything, because you're fostering more or less.' So anyway she made enquiries and it went before a panel, but they wouldn't class us as foster carers, we were just caring relatives. So they openly admit what they pay, what they're paying us now is a joke.

The files carried many accounts of the efforts social workers made to get carers to take out residence orders, with one social worker frequently complaining to the carers how much money the family was costing children's services, even though the grandparents in question were clearly under strain caring for their grandson. These efforts were sometimes initiated at reviews and were in some cases linked to a desire on the part of children's services to apply to discharge care orders and to reduce the numbers of children in care. In the interviews too, carers often described the way in which social workers tried on a number of occasions to persuade them to apply for a residence order and some felt under a great deal of pressure to do so. They felt that the arguments deployed by social workers were not always fair:

> Social services want you to take a residency order. I said, 'What does that mean?' He said, 'It means that the boys would be permanently with you then and there's no chance that they'll be moved,' and I said, 'Financially what will that mean?' He said, 'Well you may get an allowance.' I said, 'Well does that mean 12 quid a week or something?' I said, 'No. They're quite all right as they are.' And then I

got all this, 'Oh you're refusing to take a residency order.' I'm not showing much commitment to the boys.

Social workers sometimes introduced the subject by suggesting that if the relatives did not apply for residence orders, the children might be placed for adoption, even though there was no apparent intention of doing this:

> Because the reason we did it is because, because we fostered, they could take them off us at any time for adoption. And to safeguard that, they recommended we went for the residence order – so that's what we did.

It was surprising to find that some social workers would apply pressure on carers to go down the residence order route even when continuing children's services involvement was clearly needed. For example, a year after an aunt was approved as a foster carer her social worker tried to persuade her to apply for a residence order, even though the mother and step-father still threatened to remove the child from placement and the department had earlier started care proceedings to avert this, only stopping because the child became upset. The withdrawal of social work support would clearly have been inappropriate. In another case, the carers, who had been the mother's employers, were left to fend for themselves after a residence order was made. They had originally offered to keep the two boys for a few days when the mother disappeared. They struggled to care for the boys who were soiling, disobedient and aggressive. They felt that children's services had pushed them into keeping the children and then pulled out. After this placement ended, Mrs Grant made an official complaint to her local children's services department saying that she had needed assistance with the children's behaviour and with the father's aggression during contact. These difficulties had had a negative effect on her personal, family and business life – so much so that her relationship with her husband had been jeopardised and her business was threatened with closure.

In contrast, in three other cases in the case file sample, children's services had agreed not to try to persuade carers to apply for a residence order because the children clearly needed the protection afforded by care orders and social work involvement.

Disadvantages of residence orders

Many carers agreed to apply for a residence order, sometimes on the incorrect understanding that there would be no financial disadvantage and we found in the interviews that they often felt tricked when they discovered the true situation. One carer who found that she was now getting £34 less a week said:

> I said, 'Will my money drop?' 'No, no,' she said, 'money won't be no different at all.' And when I had, I was flabbergasted because I opened it and it was only 13 pound had gone in the bank. I thought this is not right.

Another aunt was advised more realistically that she would lose birthday and Christmas payments, but that otherwise there would be little difference. However, a week before the court hearing the picture changed when the social worker asked her to sign a paper agreeing that the arrangement to make payments would be reviewed every two years. This relative was later approved as a foster carer for an unrelated child and so became aware, too late, that the residence order allowance and other help for her nephew would (at that time) at best have continued until he reached the age of 16, unlike the situation in unrelated foster care:

> But what I didn't realise at the time and I've only learnt the last couple of months is now Carl has lost all his college education and he will get no help later on whatsoever. And because of his learning difficulties, he is the child that is going to need further education. [Fostered] children now at 17 or when they leave school they get a plan made out for them – he's going to lose all that – they can go on to do driving lessons and things like that. We don't mind our financial bits that we lose on but I feel that Carl has lost out on an awful lot, it wasn't explained when we went for the residency order. I think it was really unfair that they didn't explain to us exactly what Carl would lose out on, otherwise I think I would have definitely thought twice.

It is encouraging that the White Paper 'Care Matters: Time for Change' (DfES 2007) has revealed plans to legislate to raise the age at which a residence order ends from 16 to 18. There are, however, other advantages when kin remain as foster carers because looked after children become the responsibility of leaving care teams, which can provide a range of practical and financial services denied to those on residence orders. Indeed, those young people in our interview sample who were the responsibility of leaving care teams were receiving excellent advice and help, including generous financial assistance – for example, payments for driving lessons and college trips.

The advantages of residence orders

Some carers, however, were willing to apply for residence orders and did so some time after they had been approved as foster carers. These carers looked forward to leading a 'more normal' life, no longer having social work visits and reviews and to the end of asking for permission for the children to stay away overnight with their friends (as was then generally required), having to have babysitters police checked or being unable to apply on their own for a passport for the child.

> Interviewer: But having the residence order has that worked out better for you?
>
> Aunt: Yes it's worked a lot better. At least you haven't got those [social workers] coming every month. I used to detest that. 'Cos they only used to come in and

just sit. Just to see how you were really. You can tell them that on the phone, you know. To me it was wasted time.

One family saw it as giving them the chance to move away from the area. In addition, some families saw residence orders as an opportunity to prevent a parent trying to take the child back, give the child more security or provide a situation in which they felt they were 'adopting the child as [their] own'.[25] In line with this, one grandmother saw it as having psychological advantages for her grandson:

> But psychologically for the boy, it's going to make a great deal of difference to him. As soon as I mentioned this is what social services wanted us to do, how did he feel about it because if he didn't want it then we wouldn't have gone ahead with it. And he just jumped and he said 'Oh yes, it'll be better won't it? Because I will be yours and I won't have to go back to Mum.'

Resistance to applying for residence orders

Although it is often assumed that relatives prefer to keep children's services at a distance, relatively few of the carers we interviewed (only four) clearly very much disliked social work involvement, found it very intrusive and therefore benefited from this aspect of residence orders. In contrast, many carers resisted the suggestion of a residence order precisely in order to keep social workers involved, often because of difficulties with the child's parents or other family members and sometimes to ensure adequate continuing financial support. Five of the carers we interviewed refused to agree to apply for residence orders, three because of the costs and two because they wanted to maintain children's services involvement. In one of these, the grandmother agreed to a residence order for the older granddaughter who wanted to minimise social work visits, but refused for her younger sister who had a lot of problems.

In a sixth case, where the department was pressurising the grandparents to apply for a residence order, they rightly pointed out that this would only be acceptable if concerns about contact were dealt with:

> They have recommended it for a while, two or three years. They want Gerry off their books – they don't need him to be there any more. We will. It's just a question of getting this contact, lots of contact. That is the big stumbling block because social services can't get them sorted out, the contact, so how Jim and I would I don't know.

Indeed, children's guardians were often so concerned at the prospect that children's services would withdraw from cases once a residence order was made, that in the case file sample they insisted in four cases that a supervision order or a family assistance order was made in conjunction with the residence order, in order to oblige children's services to provide continuing support. However, these orders are of limited duration.

In two other cases, the move to apply for a residence order was opposed by the children's guardian when the case came to court, on the grounds that it would place the carers under financial pressure and that the safeguards of the pre-existing care order should be maintained. In one of these cases a residence order was made nonetheless and children's services paid only a small weekly allowance, in spite of their reassurance to the court that the family would incur no financial penalty by continuing with their application.

Case closure and residence orders

When carers agreed to give up the relatively advantaged situation of being approved foster carers to take out a residence order, children's services closed their cases. This occurred even in situations when carers were clearly struggling to deal with children's behaviour. In one such case, the maternal grandparents were finding caring for their two young grandchildren extremely difficult. The children were showing very disturbed behaviour and their GP stated that the grandparents needed more assistance and respite. However, the community support worker who had helped in the holidays was withdrawn when the residence order was granted and the case was closed.

Carers were sometimes surprised by the complete withdrawal of support after a residence order was made. One grandmother had been paid a small allowance until the residence order came through, at which point the allowance and all other help ceased altogether. She experienced this as very abrupt and as being 'shut out':

> Pauline (my social worker) asked me to go for the residence order – they were helping me financially with Sharon's keep. Once I'd got that residence order it was stopped. I had to pay for my own solicitor. The solicitor had £250 off me before he'd even write a letter. I told her Sharon needed counselling. She had one session and that was it. No help with having a night – we haven't been out together on our own now since, oh god, four, five years? Once I'd signed that in court that was it. And I phoned her up once after and I was told by social services I was nothing to do with them now. They would have nothing at all to do with me. They just shut me off, didn't they?

Even carers, who had been glad at the prospect of no longer having social work visits, could feel left alone with any subsequent difficulties:

> And relief when they get off your back when you've got that residence order, but then reality hits you and you think, 'God, I'm on my own with it.' And it does really, really come hard.

Consideration of adoption by kin

In a small number of cases, plans for adoption by family or friends were considered. In one case, the carers who were friends of the child's former foster carers planned to adopt but the plan was changed to long-term foster care for financial reasons and because of opposition from their own children. In another case, the maternal aunt and uncle were willing to adopt and were approved as foster carers but did not proceed with adoption because they thought that the children's mother would oppose it. In a similar case, an aunt and uncle chose not to apply for an adoption order because they felt that it would cause difficulties in family relationships, but were re-considering this decision when the child was five because by then it was thought that the mother was much less likely to remove the child. In practice, they continued as foster carers. In just one case in the sample, an aunt and uncle adopted their disabled niece after she had been with them for 12 years.

Placements made without children's services involvement

Those carers who were approved as foster carers did at least in theory have the option of refusing to pursue a residence order. The carers who were at the greatest financial disadvantage were those who had in the first place agreed to take on the child of a relative or friend without children's services involvement. In these cases in our sample, children's services generally took the view that the children were not their responsibility and refused payment if the carers later requested help. In one such case, a grandmother was caring for her three granddaughters because of their mother's drug dependency and prison sentence and approached children's services when she could no longer cope financially. The grandmother was approved as a foster carer for the children and paid the fostering allowance initially, with a panel recommendation that the grandmother pursue a residence order. The grandmother who worked full-time and supported her ageing parents could not afford the legal costs of an application. Nonetheless, children's services declined to pay the legal costs of the application and were not prepared to continue to pay the fostering allowance.

Another carer, who was the mother of the child's best friend, looked after her for four years before being approved as a foster carer. This occurred only after she made a complaint. The department claimed that the carer had instigated taking the child:

> I think what they're trying to say is, from what I read in the letters, they're trying to say that I went down to her house, took her out of her house, brought her home and said, 'I'm going to look after this child'.

In similar cases, it was not clear if any payment was made or only very small amounts were given. In one case, friends who had been bringing up a child without any help, turned to children's services after a fire destroyed many of their belongings. Since this was considered to be a private fostering arrangement, even though the child was accommodated, a monthly £15 clothing allowance was all that was agreed.

Financial issues

Particular financial hardship

Given the low incomes of kin, many of whom were on income support or pensions and the low levels of foster care and residence order allowances paid to them, it was not surprising that there were frequent reports on file that carers were suffering financial hardship. It was particularly difficult when there were periods during which carers were not paid or they were paid at rates well below the fostering allowance, as for example during the first months or even years of placement. One grandparent couple received no financial help with their six grandchildren for the first 12 months of placement. There was hardship too when the placements were considered to be private fostering arrangements since any Section 17 payments tended to be unreliable and relatives made many telephone calls to social workers to try to get payments made.

Under-payment and over-payment

On a number of occasions, there was confusion about whether or not the carers should be receiving child benefit. Generally, carers do not receive child benefit when they are paid a foster care allowance but do when the children are subject to residence orders. This could lead to under- or over-payment. In at least three cases the carers were underpaid. In two instances this was because the authority assumed the carers were receiving child benefit when they were not and reduced their allowance by this amount. In one of these cases, it was calculated that the carers had been underpaid by about £8000 by the time it came to light.

There was one case of overpayment when it was found that the grandparents had been receiving the fostering allowance and child benefit:

> I don't know who it was said, 'Oh, you're breaking the law, that's theft. You can't have family allowance and money from us.' And I said, 'Well I didn't know.' And he said, 'Well you should have done.' And luckily the social worker said, 'Oh yes, I knew,' and I think because it was a genuine mistake I didn't have to pay it back. But it was quite a lot of money – well to me.

In another case an overpayment on one child was dealt with by deducting what was owed from the allowance for the sibling.

Payment of additional allowances

In a few cases children's services agreed either to pay higher allowances or to fund extra services for carers. In two cases, children's services contributed financially to enable grandparents to employ a nanny to help out with the children when their business made it difficult to care for the children without assistance and, in another, fees for a private nursery were paid as there was no local authority provision locally. In four cases, where the carers had particular difficulties such as dealing with the father's violence or acute health problems, the higher rate enhanced boarding out allowance was paid. However these seven cases are only 5 per cent of all the kin placements and, whilst probably an underestimate (as not all such help would be recorded on file) they do not suggest that many exceptions were made.

Parental contributions to the placements

There was little information on the files about parental contributions to these placements with kin. In just one case, the father paid £13 a week to the parents of his daughter's boyfriend with whom she was living, this being the amount he had previously paid in maintenance. In a second case the father paid towards a new school uniform. In a third, the parents were reported to be unreliable about paying for the child's keep or expenses. Certainly, the interviews did not reveal that parents contributed financially to these placements or that they were generally in a position to do so.

Caring for financial gain

On four occasions, the files reflected a concern that the relative carers might be caring for the children principally for financial gain. In two such cases an aunt and uncle said that they would not continue to care if they did not get an allowance and this was refused because children's services already entertained doubts about the quality of the placements and were content to move the children. In another case, members of the extended family suggested that the aunt and uncle might be motivated by money and in a fourth case, relatives who had provided poor care were upset when the two children returned to their father, as they were said to have become reliant on the allowances they received.

Of course, in practice a much more usual situation was for the carers to forego money in order to look after the children, sometimes giving up their jobs to take on the children or spending their savings to finance their care.

Involving advocates in order to gain financial assistance

A few carers had to involve others as advocates before they were paid their full allowance. This friend carer, who was looking after two children, involved a solicitor and a voluntary organisation:

> After I put my official complaint in and they received letters from my solicitor, I suddenly got this letter saying that changes have been made to the caring relatives allowances and it's been reviewed and it's been put up, and it's been put now to, from £194 I was getting, to £554 a fortnight.

One grandmother went to her local councillor and headmaster to put pressure on children's services to pay her an allowance after she got a residence order, whilst a friend carer was paid a small weekly allowance, until after three years she complained, was approved as a foster carer and paid the fostering allowance.

One grandmother told us in interview that she resorted to threatening to give up her grandson to apply leverage to receive payments:

> Well I was disgusted because the little bit of savings we had we'd spent. And in the end I said, 'Well either you give me money or you get him and you put him into care, which is ridiculous, because he is happy and he is settled here, and his school reports were good. So, you want to disrupt this child, and if you do I shall make sure the local press hear about it and everybody else.' Because I thought it was disgusting. So eventually the money arrived.

The carers' views about the adequacy of financial help

Kin carers varied in their views of the adequacy of the financial help they received. Many of those who received an allowance felt that they had been able to maintain their previous standard of living overall, although they were stretched to manage holidays or activities for the children, especially when they were looking after more than one child. For example, some kin carers found it hard to afford day trips for the children, activities to keep them occupied in the school holidays or school trips, so that occasional one-off payments to help with these items would have made a difference. However, other carers made it clear that they were suffering financial hardship and some were barely managing financially and had had to take out loans for essential items.

Those who knew a little about the allowances for unrelated foster carers were aware that kin were paid at lower rates:

> The family is different. If the next door neighbour had them then they get all the other allowances with it like birthday money and holiday money and things like that.

> Relative carers fostering allowance or something, you didn't get the full, because they says oh you're relatives – you only get a third of it or something. You don't

get the whole foster allowance, which meant that you didn't get the uniform help, you didn't get the clothes, you didn't get the holidays.

And all I've ever been told is, caring relatives aren't entitled to this, caring relatives aren't entitled to that, they don't get no holiday grants, you don't get no clothing grants, you don't get pocket money, they don't get extra money at Christmas or on their birthday, you don't get any support whatsoever of any kind. You don't even get a social worker of your own.

As I say foster carers, they told us how much money they were getting, it was practically double what we were getting, and then on top of that…they pay for not only the holiday of the child but they help out the holidays for the whole family.

Just one set of grandparents in the interview sample said that they received an additional £100 at Christmas, birthdays and for holidays.

In addition, a number of carers, when talking about finance, said that they had not been out in the evening for many years. For example, one carer said:

They've been with me just over a thousand days, I've had fifteen nights off, fifteen trips out and actual nights when they haven't been here has been about six.

This was partly because of the difficulty of paying for approved child sitters who were expensive, plus the additional costs of going out. It was an even greater problem for carers who received no allowance or where the special needs of the child or carer made caregiving very expensive.

One disabled male carer was able to get some financial help towards babysitting only after the children's guardian discovered how little help he was receiving. He was very isolated and starting to withdraw:

It was only a couple of weeks ago when the children's guardian…came to see us all…and was absolutely amazed that I had no proper support. I'm supposed to get special fostering support, I'm supposed to get someone to come and see me to talk purely about how I'm coping and mentally, am I getting enough other stimulation in my life? And I'm a bit cross about that. I need a bit more support really – it's only been in the last few months that I've actually convinced them to give me some extra money. Had a cheque last week for £162 towards babysitting costs, which is great.

Two sets of carers in the interview sample had asked the social worker if respite care could be provided for a few hours during the holidays but were told that the cost would be deducted from their allowance. The cost of a few hours care would have exceeded the low allowance the carers were receiving. Neither was able to afford it.

Some carers, particularly when they first took on children, asked their local children's services if they could provide help to fund the newly arrived children to go on holiday with them, but this was either refused or given on just this first occasion:

> Because it was three children, which made five people…the holidays are really expensive…because our one stipulation was we were giving up everything else but we didn't want to give up our two weeks holiday in the summer, because we'd just started where we could go abroad. So I asked them if they could possibly help by £400 and we would put the rest because we had to have two rooms. We got quite a snotty letter didn't we off of Ben Turnscrew – said they would do it this year but not again.

A couple of families who took a large number of children could not transport them without buying a bigger car, which also involved higher insurance costs. However, no help was given towards this, even though neighbouring unrelated foster carers occasionally had such assistance. Taking on a group of children could be very costly at first, especially as was often the case, when they all required new clothes and carers often used their savings to finance this.

Social workers were generally more willing to provide help with bedding, bunk beds or clothing when children first arrived to get the kin family up and running (see also Farmer and Parker 1991). If relatives started to care for a baby they might receive a pram, car seat or cot. However, requests for help with moving house, even when necessitated by the arrival of the children and when carers were disabled, met with little success. As one elderly grandmother put it:

> I asked them for help for moving the furniture and they couldn't help me. I asked them if they'd give me more time to move from the flat to here and they gave me a week. And I had to decorate all the house right through.

Help with school uniforms was also given sparingly:

> I says to him, basic outline of what he needs is going to be about £150 and that is as cheap as I can get it. 'Oh um, caring relatives don't get clothing grants,' and I said, 'He needs that for secondary school, I've got other children, I cannot afford that. I'm doing you a favour by the children living with me, you need to start helping me out a bit.' The social worker went off anyway and discussed it with the manager and they moaned and moaned about it. So they come back to me with: 'We're going to give you £75,' but 2½ years on I'm still waiting for it.

Another relative couple said that in six years they were only once given £11 for a school uniform even though their financial situation was dire. A particular difficulty arose in relation to replacement of items that the children destroyed, such as replacing a carpet ruined when a disturbed child wet and soiled it on a regular basis.

One of the most concerning situations we encountered was that of grandparents who took on the care of their five-year-old granddaughter, who was already so disturbed that no foster carers could manage her. The grandfather had just had major surgery and his health deteriorated to the point where at interview his wife was giving him 24-hour care. Even though the grandparents were approved as foster carers for this girl, they were paid only £50 a week and received no child benefit. As a result, they were living in straitened circumstances with very high expenses caused by their granddaughter's special needs and destructive behaviour:

> She'd got into David's room and she'd pushed his computer monitor off the desk, the processor she'd pushed off and she'd picked up and she'd thrown it at the wall. She'd totally smashed his computer system, she smashed all his work, his disks, everything. In that time she totally smashed up in my older son's bedroom – and he came back and it was all his work, his exams, and he had to spend the time going round all the class members going back to the school and trying to get the stuff he'd stored – it'd gone. We had to cancel our house insurance when Tanya came, we couldn't afford to pay because we were so skint. So in the end we took out a loan and replaced the system, not the same grade but we replaced our system for David. It ended up that we, instead of borrowing about £900 we'd got to pay back over £2000. And this was because Tanya had a tantrum.

This grandmother added:

> If you're a foster carer you get a certain amount of money a week to look after that child. They also get money when it's a child's birthday to pay for the presents, they get money at Christmas, they get money for a holiday every year, if they need uniforms it's paid for, if they damage anything in their home it's paid for. If they've got a special diet it's paid for – everything. Then why are somebody like in our situation where they give you a pittance and don't help you with anything [else], I can't get my head round. Surely that should be the other way round, if you haven't got the income surely they should help you with clothing? Why give it to the people who've already got? I think as a family we've been let down and I think Tanya's been let down.

These carers could not afford to give their granddaughter a birthday party at a pizza restaurant as all her friends had done. When they cooked food for a birthday celebration at home, the girl was so disappointed that she smashed the plates and threw the food on the floor.

A number of kin carers gave up their jobs to look after the children or changed from day to night time shifts, leading to a loss of income. However, they did not complain about this, seeing it as a necessary sacrifice to look after the children. They did, however, talk about how tired it made them, when a full day with the children was followed by a night shift. One such grandparent who had lost money by giving up her good full-time job was most concerned that, as a kin carer, her three grandchildren were not receiving the help they needed with their disturbed behaviour:

> I've told them – I'm a cheap option, I am. I don't care what anybody says. It's not the fact they get, you know, what the foster carers get, it's what the kids don't get. Because if they'd been with an ordinary foster carer I believe they would have got the treatment they needed.

The carers' attitudes to payment

Several carers were at pains to explain that they used all the money on the children and that they did not expect any element of reward in their allowance. They commented: 'It's not done for the money,' 'We didn't make any money out of it,' 'I don't want to benefit financially through having the children.' They emphasised that they had always worked for the money they got and did not want to ask for help. Some social workers had told them they should ask for what they needed, but they disliked asking as it made them feel as if they were begging. One carer who had no allowance said the social worker knew her financial situation and so she should not have to tell him about her needs.

In spite of this attitude of pride and self-reliance, they were well aware that they were saving the local authorities money and were critical of departmental penny-pinching or reluctance to make regular payments. As one grandmother put it:

> We do get our works pension but all in all, that's what you work for, for yourself. I know if it's our own children you don't get paid for looking after them – but it wasn't our fault.

One grandfather said that the financial side was poor in view of their extensive responsibilities for their severely disabled grandchild but added: 'Like we're grandparents so we view it a bit differently I think.'

Summary

The files and interviews showed that kin were active in offering to care for these children and had very varying experiences of assessment, with some feeling demeaned by prolonged assessments that did not take account of their previous experience of looking after the children. However, most of them came under pressure from local authority social workers to pursue residence orders even when there were unresolved issues requiring social work intervention. The financial payments made were at lower rates than those for unrelated foster carers, were often much delayed and some carers had no financial help at all. As a result, some kin carers and the children they looked after experienced considerable financial hardship. Family and friends care seemed to be an area in which local authorities tried hard to limit spending, so that the conditions for kin carers compare unfavourably with those for unrelated foster carers.

In the next chapter we consider the behaviour of the children in the placements and the services provided to help them.

Chapter 7

Placement Progress: The Children's Behaviour and Service Provision in Kin Care

In this chapter, we look at how the relationships between the new and resident children were negotiated, the behaviours of the placed children and the services that were provided to the carers and children.

Relationships between the children

Difficult relationships with other children

It was clear that carers' own children had to readjust when new children joined the family. Generally, this was made easier as the newly arrived children already knew them quite well. Nonetheless, some children were jealous when their relatives came to live with them, feeling that they lost out on their parents' attention. This was particularly a problem when the new children were attention-seeking or if bedrooms had to be shared with others who needled the resident child or did not respect their property. One resident child, Stuart, became very distressed when the two children placed with his parents stopped their weekend visits to another relative, so depriving Stuart of the exclusive attention of his parents at weekends. Another boy, whose cousin of the same age had joined his family, was very jealous and became aggressive and unhappy.

The children of the family sometimes complained that the looked after children were favoured or treated more leniently than they were by their parents or that other relatives showed more interest in these children, who had joined their family, than in them. A few resident children openly resented the children placed in their families and rejected them, such as siblings who resented the

131

arrival of their two cousins because their pocket money stopped as their parents could no longer afford it. There were also a few cases where the newly arrived children were themselves intensely jealous of the children of the family and destroyed a resident child's precious belongings or stole things from them. Children with serious behaviour difficulties, in particular could have a negative impact on resident children.

Often these initial problems were resolved, but in some cases they were not. In one such case the placed child caused so many arguments that the cousin her age left her own family to live with another relative. Children who went to live with their own friends' families generally got on well with their school friends. However, occasionally these friendships too came under strain and the placements foundered.

Sometimes, the carers had to look out for their own younger children who experienced aggression and violence from the newly arrived child and who in turn would sometimes imitate their aggressive or destructive behaviour. Occasionally, a placed adolescent involved a younger relative in activities that placed them at risk. For example, Susie at 15 was sleeping with an 18-year-old boy, was truanting and verbally aggressive and her 12-year-old cousin was copying her behaviour. In addition, at least 11 children (8%) in kin care showed sexually abusing or very sexualised behaviour to their cousins or other relatives and such behaviour was sometimes minimised by social workers who were anxious to maintain the placement (see also Farmer and Pollock 1998).

Good relationships with other children

However, relationships between children were often good. Sometimes, older related young people were very fond of the placed children and mothered or spoiled them. In one such case this went too far and the placed child was having difficulty with peers because of this overindulgence. There were a number of reports of particularly good relationships between the placed child and either other children in the family or the adult children of the carers who lived nearby. Older resident children could act as good role models or a 'steadying influence' for placed children. They could help them settle into the family or school or would make sure they were not being bullied. Even when the children of the family had felt a little pushed out at first, they often became protective of their relatives. Cousins sometimes made firm friendships with each other and one child living with her maternal aunt and uncle was said to 'fit like a glove' in the family, whilst another young person who went to her friend's parents was reported to be 'good fun' and 'good company'. Placed adolescents sometimes found satisfaction in looking after a baby or toddler born to the carers with whom they were living.

Sibling relationships

Occasionally, sibling relationships were poor. In sibling groups, especially large ones, siblings sometimes competed for the attention of the carers. In one such case, two siblings competed so much for the attention of their grandparents that they were split up. When one sibling moved to a relative some time after another, as quite often occurred, there was an increased likelihood of sibling rivalry and a need for the 'pecking order' to be re-established. In a few cases, the carers favoured one placed child over another, either because one was a blood relative and the other was not, or because the characteristics of one child evoked dislike or special liking. Occasionally, a less favoured or less well-settled sibling moved out.

Explaining the situation to other children outside the family

Whilst many children welcomed living with a relative as more normal and less stigmatising than being looked after, a few were taunted by other children about their birth family or experienced bullying because they lived with relatives or friends rather than with their parents. Whilst some children were confident at school about being able to explain that they were living with kin, other children were afraid of being teased for not being with their parents:

> I said, 'Well, where did you get that idea from?' 'Oh, that's what my friend said – I live with old fogeys.' So yes, he had a bit of a struggle, going to school and not having normal parents. (Grandmother)

Advice to carers and children about how best to deal with such situations would be useful.

What children called their carers

Some children called their relative 'Auntie Jan', 'Nan' or in one case 'Mummy Nanny' but others, especially those who were younger and where the carer had young children of their own in the house, called them 'Mum' or 'Dad'. It was especially hard for young children to understand why they could not call their carers 'Mum' and 'Dad':

> I mean we were always Nanny and Grandad; we've always been Nanny and Grandad to him. Within days of him coming here to stay, I would say if Pete was in the kitchen, 'If you go and ask Grandad he'll get you a drink, he's in the kitchen.' He would walk straight out into the kitchen and say, 'Daddy can I have a drink?' And I think because him and Shannon were so close in age, he just wanted what the girls had; he wanted the Mum and Dad.

In this case, the social worker objected until it became clear that the child felt singled out as different by not being allowed to call his long term carers 'Mum' and 'Dad'.

The children's behaviour in placement

As we have seen, overall the children living with kin showed similar levels of behaviour difficulty to those placed with unrelated foster carers. From analysing all the 142 case file summaries of kin placements we found that one in five children placed with family or friends had no particular difficulties and at the same time did well in placement. In contrast, some had very severe behavioural and emotional difficulties. These relatives and friends often described the children who joined their families as angry children who took out their feelings on the people looking after them or destroyed property, whilst some had not been taught to use a knife and fork or to clean their teeth. There were descriptions of children who swore and bit at school, urinated on the furniture or banged on the door if their carer left them for a moment to go to the toilet.

Some more detailed examples will help to show the severity of the problems that these children brought to their placements with kin.

A court order was made on Mandy after a long history of poor care. Her mother had severe health problems, her step-father had mental health difficulties and both had alcohol problems and frequent hospital admissions, leaving Mandy neglected and out of control. At the age of 7 she was placed with her uncle and aunt. Mandy was diagnosed as having ADHD and excluded from school on a number of occasions. Her behaviour was described as being 'anti-social and aggressive, swearing, kicking, defiant and self-harming by cutting her wrists'. She had shown sexually abusing behaviour in the past and again in her placement with her young male cousin. The placement was under great strain, especially when the aunt felt that her daughter was emulating Mandy's behaviour.

Scott was physically abused by his step-father, who was a violent man, and he experienced many moves in his early years. After a spell with his grandfather he was placed at the age of 8 with a friend of his mother's and her husband. Scott had moderate learning difficulties, a limited attention span and elements of an autistic disorder with difficulty relating to people. At the beginning of the placement Scott was destructive: he cut his clothes and bedding and broke

> toys. He was soiling every day, showing sexualised behaviour and stealing from the carers. There were reports of increasingly difficult behaviour which included Scott burning a carpet, running away, talking to strangers and cuddling up to people he hardly knew. There was also friction between Scott and the carer's younger son.

A grandmother told us about her 5-year-old grandson, Owen, when he joined the family:

> He was wet, messing himself, eight, nine times a day. I mean I was always washing and that… Breaking things, ripping all the wallpaper, I mean I'd just done all the bedroom right out and he stripped the wall right off…made great big holes in the tiles in the ceiling. Take light bulbs out, put his finger in the socket with the switch still on…put a toilet roll down the toilet, block the toilet up. You had to watch him 24–7. It's eased up a bit but you cannot trust him anywhere like in the toilet on his own, because he put loads of toilet paper down the thing… He'll go out in the kitchen, you've just given him a great big dinner, he'll go out there, start nicking food out the cupboard, after having a great big dinner.

Owen had shown some improvements but was still very difficult for his grandmother to manage.

Several children like Owen were reported to eat voraciously and to take food from the house, as if they could not trust that their hunger would ever be assuaged. Given their backgrounds, it is not surprising that children often joined kin families with a legacy of disturbed and challenging behaviour that put their placements under considerable pressure.

The progress made in placement

Good progress

After reading each case summary the researchers rated whether the children had or had not made progress overall in terms of their behavioural and emotional adjustment whilst in their kin placements. (Educational progress was also noted when there was sufficient information about it). We also considered some of the apparent reasons for lack of improvement.

In spite of their experiences, many children made remarkable progress once they were placed with kin. The case summaries showed clear evidence of such progress in 44 per cent of the 142 kin placements. Some examples will help to illustrate this.

An emergency protection order was made on Meera when she was 18 months old because she was failing to thrive with her mother. She could not walk or talk and was much neglected. She was placed with an aunt and uncle. Within three months she had changed from 'a very sad dejected baby to a bright, happy and much loved little girl'. By the age of 8 she was very close to her aunt, occasionally soiled, had panic attacks in shops and had learning and speech problems. However, she later took 12 GCSEs and went on to the 6th form at school where she worked hard with excellent attendance and was achieving 'A' grades in her subjects.

Ricky had grown up in a chaotic home; physically abused by both his parents and affected by his mother's mental health difficulties and periodic overdoses. At the age of 12 the parents of a friend were asked to care for him for a few days and he remained with them thereafter:

'When we had Ricky he was a pretty sick child really – he slept in the cupboard; wouldn't sleep in a bed – he was sick all the time, anorexic – wanted to kill himself. It was terrible. But I was the right one for him. I would stay up at night with him and we would talk. And it was very, very hard, because the first three years the parents were fighting a lot between themselves and then the father remarried. His new wife had got two children, and I think Ricky found it all very hard to deal with. And it was a mess. But you know I worked through it gradually. Because I would stay up and talk to Ricky, or I would go in when he was crying, and I used to say to him, "Look Ricky, the only one that's getting hurt here is you. You've got your whole life ahead of you".'

Ricky had been in the placement for two years when an assessment was completed and he was described as a 'happy, cheerful boy who laughs a lot. His attendance at school is 100 per cent now and he wants to go on to college after school. He is also much more confident in his general demeanour.'

A number of the children in the study were born with drug withdrawal at birth and needed time in a special care baby unit after birth. Most of these children (5) were placed with relatives when still very young and as a result they generally did well even though some developed severe health or developmental problems:

Chris was born with opiate withdrawal and at the age of four months went to live with his great aunt and family. It emerged that he had global developmental delay. He also had a physical disability, speech, language and health problems. In spite of considerable overcrowding the family cared very well for Chris. He attended nursery three times a week, had speech therapy and Portage (an incremental learning system individually designed for each child). By the time he was nearly four he was said to be mixing well with his peers at school and to be confident at nursery with improved speech but poor concentration.

Little progress

Some children made little progress in the placement on which we focused because the carers were overwhelmed and could not cope with the child's behaviour.

Satya had been neglected and scapegoated by her parents and had no toys or books. After three brief episodes in foster care, a placement with her aunt, which began when Satya was nine, ended after three months because the aunt could not cope. Satya moved to live with an uncle and his partner in a one-bedroom flat, but this placement disrupted after two months because of Satya's behaviour. Her subsequent placement with her grandmother lasted nine months but ended because she too could not manage her behaviour.

Lack of progress in some placements appeared to be partly because children had continuing needs for which they received little or no help.

Graham was aged eight when he went to live with his aunt and uncle after long-term neglect, parental substance misuse, domestic violence and maternal mental health problems. Before this placement Graham showed a variety of difficult behaviours: temper outbursts, lack of social skills and stealing. Bedtimes were a problem – he was frightened of the dark and always wet the bed. He was also soiling and damaging his clothes. Although Graham and his brother appeared more settled with their aunt and uncle, their behaviour continued to be difficult to manage and they did not make progress at school.

There were also a few children who appeared to be progressing initially but whose behaviour later deteriorated, either as they moved into adolescence or as the result of a setback, such as in one case sexual abuse by a teacher at school.

> Roxanne had lived with her disabled grandparents since the age of three. Her grandmother had chronic arthritis, limited mobility and a visual impairment. After her grandfather died when she was ten, Roxanne began to abscond regularly and often went off with men she had only just met. Her school attendance fell dramatically and she was bullied and teased at school. Her grandmother felt unable to cope.

In another such case where a teenage girl was truanting from school with a friend and demanding designer clothes, her grandmother's uncertainty about how to cope was magnified because she was afraid she 'would go the same way as her mother'. Whilst difficulties in dealing with children as they reached adolescence occasionally posed particular problems for older family and friends carers, on the whole this was not the case. Indeed, as shown in Chapter 5, placement disruption rates were lower for grandparents than for other kin or non-relative foster carers. In contrast, as we have seen, when young people were placed with kin carers as teenagers, there were more disruptions than when they were placed under the age of ten.

There was a small group of children who failed to make progress because, as will be seen in Chapter 8, their kin carers provided a very poor standard of care and some of these children showed great improvement when they left the kin placement by moving to respite care, another placement or their parents.

The carers' experiences of dealing with the children's behaviours

In addition to describing the children's behaviour, the kin carers were asked at interview to complete the Strengths and Difficulties questionnaire (SDQ) (Goodman 1994) about the children's emotional and behavioural difficulties. The carers of 20 children aged 5–16 completed the SDQ. The Strengths and Difficulties Questionnaire is scored on five categories and the level of strengths or difficulties indicated by the score is divided into normal (total difficulties score 0–13), borderline (total difficulties score 14–16), and abnormal groups (total difficulties score 17–40).

More than a third (35%) of these children were in the abnormal range on the total behaviour score (the proportion in the general child population is 10%).

Although only 20 SDQs were completed, this finding is supported by evidence from another recent study following up 40 children three to nine years from being placed with kin after care proceedings (Hunt *et al.* 2007) where exactly the same proportion of children showed behaviour in the abnormal range. These findings suggest the persistence of behavioural and emotional difficulties given that the children in both studies had been with kin for a number of years (see Table 7.1).

Table 7.1 Kin carers' SDQ scores at the interviews

Category	Normal		Borderline		Abnormal	
	Number	Per cent	Number	Per cent	Number	Per cent
Prosocial score	16	80	2	10	2	10
Hyperactivity score	11	55	2	10	7	35
Emotional symptoms score	12	60	5	25	3	15
Peer relationships score	10	50	3	15	7	35
Conduct difficulties score	10	50	3	15	7	35
Total score	10	50	3	15	7	35

In the interviews, kin carers described how they had attempted to deal with the children's behaviours. An aunt was one of a number of carers who described giving a child space to confide her worries. Her niece had been abused in care:

> She'd read the statements, she couldn't understand why she and her brother had been taken into care, why they wouldn't allow me and Uncle John to take them away…the first day we saw them. She said, 'I wanted to come with you and you wouldn't take me,' and I said, 'I couldn't sweetheart,' and we explained the reason why. And she was OK with that but there were occasions when she was troubled and we used to say to her, 'What's the matter bab, what's the matter?,' and she's saying, 'Nothing,' we'd say 'OK then, you tell me when you're ready.' And then it might be, as I'm tucking her in, and then Becky would say, 'Aunt Susan,' and I'd say 'What sweetheart?' 'You know when we were at Heather's? [the foster carer's] 'Yes,' 'Well Heather did this, Heather did that,' and then Becky would upset herself and I'd say, 'But you're out of there now darling,' [and she would say] 'Yes but I feel sorry for the other children.'

Some kin carers, who had received no outside help, tried everything they could think of to help the children they were looking after. One grandmother said:

I must admit it is tough because I do fight a lot thinking, am I doing it right? Where can I get the help that I need to try and change their food, to try and give them the concentration they need? And it feels like it's all – my brain is constantly working.

When children stole from other children in the family or destroyed their property, the advice given by social workers in such situations was sometimes seen as difficult to use. An aunt described how a social worker cautioned her against punishing her nephew for this behaviour, saying that it was part of an emotional problem. This was seen as unfair by the other children in the family who decided to take their revenge. It had also allowed the boy to feel that he could do whatever he wanted:

> We'd got five kids. He was taking things from the other kids; he was going to the girls' bedroom and pinching their things. He was going into the other lads' [rooms] and he's taking their stuff, and he was wrecking the things, taking the CDs and scratching on them. He was deliberately violent… Social services saying well you must ignore it, you can't chastise him for it… We can't be seen to condone what he's doing if it's wrong because we've got another four sitting there and [the social worker] saying 'Oh yes, but there's more social, deeper social aspects of this and there's reasons behind it.' Then he developed this 'couldn't care less attitude' then, because it's a case of we couldn't touch him, we couldn't do anything – so he was just doing whatever he wanted. And of course we couldn't condone that because then the violence started because the other kids were starting to hit him.

A similar point was made by a grandmother who felt that her management of her behaviourally challenging grandson was compromised by the expectations on her as an approved foster carer. Her grandson was aged four when he first went to live with his grandparents:

> They give you all these rules that you've got to abide by, what we do in foster care, and about how you punish the children, they've got to be treated really special. So you're in a situation where you're losing before you start – you get a social worker come in and they will tell that child [what] adults and parents can't do. He still says it: 'You can't shout at me, you can't do this to me, you can't do that to me' and he's ten. Well that authority was taken away. They undermined me. When you've got a member of your family come to stay with you and you love that child so much, and then all of a sudden you've got to treat that child like a foster kid in care, it's so hard.

A few carers had been forthright with social workers when they disagreed with their advice:

We had the children and if they didn't agree with the way I was disciplining them 'cos I know I am a disciplinarian and mother did report me for smacking. Social services was, 'You do not smack Mrs Burton' and I said, 'I'm sorry, it's now or never and if you don't like the way I am – just take them away.' Couldn't do that.

Some carers were trying to support one of the children's parents as well as managing the children's behaviour. One grandmother who was rung up two or three times a day by the children's mother explained how she had had to learn to deal with this:

When she [the mother] was really bad she would be ringing up here two or three times a day and I really cracked to the doctor one day and he said, 'She's always going to be there, you've got to get over this.'

Difficulties in coping with the children

As we have seen, nearly half (45%) of the kin carers struggled to cope with the children in their care. There were many reports on file of relatives who were on their last legs, where the situation was out of their control or the placement close to breaking point and of carers who were worn down by the child's behaviour. Sometimes, additional difficulties were caused by one of the children's parents living in the home with the carers and children or by behaviours such as sexualised behaviour directed at the carers' children. In some of these situations, the children were progressing very well even though the carers were finding it hard to manage. In others, the children displayed quite serious continuing difficulties.

Twenty-five of the carers whom we interviewed completed the General Health Questionnaire (Goldberg and Hiller 1979). As can be seen in Table 7.2, just under a quarter of the carers had total scores in the clinical or sub-clinical range, suggesting that they were under a great deal of strain.

The number of carers completing the GHQ was small, so little can be made of these scores. However, other research has shown that kin carers, especially grand-parents, tend to be in poorer physical and mental health than non-related foster carers (e.g. Hegar and Scannapieco 1999; Minkler et al. 2000) and experience considerable stress (Fuller-Thompson, Minkler and Driver 1997).

Table 7.2 General Health Questionnaire of the kin carers at interview

	Normal range (scores 0–4)		Sub-clinical and clinical range (scores 5–21)	
	Number	Per cent	Number	Per cent
Somatic symptoms	12	48	13	52
Anxiety symptoms	15	60	10	40
Social functioning	2	8	23	92
Depression symptoms	21	84	4	16
Total scores	19	76	6	24

Service provision

Social work contact

The case files often lacked details about social work visits to the children and their families. Some files showed that social workers were actively involved in supporting placements. Others recorded visits at lengthy intervals, a succession of social workers and cases that were unallocated or where review meetings did not meet the statutory requirements. Quite a number of cases had had a succession of social workers with long periods without a worker allocated. In one case, where the placement with a relative carried some known risks, there were six different social workers and infrequent visits. Sporadic social work contact also led to referrals for services that did not eventuate and were not then followed up, so that some kin carers were left to search for help on their own.

This variable social work contact may have been one reason for the lack of services provided. However, many of the service gaps were in cases that did have social work involvement and may in part reflect an attitude that kin should be able to look after children without assistance. It is possible that a view that kin could manage without help is fuelled by ideas about the strengths of family and friends carers. In one such case the social worker made the assumption that close family ties trumped other difficulties. The child had many problems, was suspended from school and was cared for by his aunt who was unwell and struggling to cope. The social work report read:

> As the child is 'in family' [the placement] meets all of his physical, emotional and cultural needs. He presents no problems in the home except when the police are called.

Such views may also be related to attempts to contain the costs of these place-ments, since, as already shown, there were many attempts to minimise payments to support kin placements.

However, the low levels of social work contact also led to lack of oversight or monitoring of cases, and this was one reason why some of the situations, in which children lived for many years with carers who provided poor care or who abused them, were able to survive for so long. One exception to this lack of service was when it was thought that a kin placement would be lost if services were not provided.

Out of authority placements

In five cases, the children went to live outside the placing local authority and in four of these there were tensions between the two authorities. In one, the author-ity had to make a number of requests before the child received help and in two others the receiving authority provided no assistance.

Proactive social work help

In a small number of cases the children's social worker had been highly proactive in setting up or supporting a kin placement. It was not clear what led to such active intervention, but it seems likely that it was related to the individual prac-titioner's view of the importance of these placements in securing permanence for the children. In one, the children moved a great deal between the mother and their maternal grandmother. For over a year the social worker worked hard to organise a permanent placement with the grandmother with the mother's co-operation. After a great deal of work, the children were placed with their grandmother and remained there. However, when the social worker left, the case became unallocated.

Another social worker provided a high quality service to an aunt and the children she looked after. She visited fortnightly and talked to the children and their aunt separately. When she was off sick this placement broke down. As soon as the social worker returned to work she managed to get the placement rein-stated. She also arranged for an independent agency respite carer to take the children for some weekends and applied for additional financial help when it was needed. The social worker realised that the aunt's perseverance was a great help to these children and had protected them from having unstable care careers.

A third social worker tried hard to support grandparents who had the task of looking after four demanding small children. She felt that the carers needed support, encouragement and frequent visits to assist them. She tried to arrange respite care with the mother taking two of the girls for some weekends, although this was not successful. When this social worker left she too was not replaced. A fourth example of particularly good social work was provided by a freelance social worker employed because the children had moved with their aunt and uncle to a distant county. He visited the placement regularly and conducted Life Story work with both children.

The carers' experiences of relationships with social workers

Experiences at the start of the placement

Some relatives had been afraid that they would not be able to keep the children at the beginning:

> When you first have the children, you're frightened that you might not be doing the right thing because then you're frightened they're going to come and take them away again, because you don't know the system and things like that.

A few kin carers had found that court hearings, assessments and investigations at the start of the placement had necessitated a great deal of contact with children's services and felt that, 'Our lives were taken over for a certain length of time.' One grandmother said that she felt it was: 'Just overpowering, all the meetings and that, because when we first went to a meeting there were so many people there, school teachers, doctors.'

A grandparent who had been involved in a plan to assess a schizophrenic mother's capacity to parent her children, necessitating a lot of trips to the psychiatric hospital for contact, had found this period of children's services involvement intrusive. In contrast, others who had attended regular child protection or other meetings had managed this without difficulty.

Turnover of social workers

Carers often had the experience of a high turnover of social workers, sometimes with gaps where no worker was allocated. This could cause difficulties when problems arose:

> As soon as they got used to it and then got to know us and realised…that we weren't the ogres that she [the mother] was making us out to be, there would be a few months with no social worker for the two of them, then we'd have another one so you'd have to go through this getting to know people again and so on. This one we've got, she's brilliant isn't she, she's brilliant.

For some carers, having no social worker was hard:

> She left the other year and we found it quite hard – there was quite a long period when we had nobody. Tom had no social worker and that was hard because we had no one to turn to.

Positive relationships with social workers

Relationships with social workers varied widely. Some relatives praised the children's social workers highly. For example, one grandmother said: 'We know they're on the phone if we ever need them.' A grandfather said: 'Steve never came often did he, but he was always there if you needed him.' A grandmother commented about her social worker: 'She's wonderful, she's always on the end of a phone but we mainly cope with the problems ourselves, it's just if we have a query or anything.' An aunt said of children's services: 'They've been brilliant all the way along. Yes they worked with us and we worked with them and there weren't major problems.' A friend carer was delighted by the praise she had been given by her new social worker:

> She's really nice too. She's been to the house three times and we've just had a meeting now. And I was so chuffed because she said she had lots of children, and that Sharon was the most focused and the most confident and the most happy, and I thought that was lovely.

Some carers who had had bad experiences with some social workers were fulsome in their praise for a social worker who broke the mould:

> Our regard for her is massive, it's absolutely huge. If you wanted a social worker, Caroline King would be the person I'd recommend to anybody. She was so honest.

A number of carers praised social workers for their help over educational issues. Others felt that the workers had helped to place boundaries around parental contact.

Poor relationships with social workers

Others had less happy experiences:

> I had this social worker for probably about a year and I said, 'Do not send that man to my house again because he will not be stepping over the doorstep,' and they said, 'Oh have you got a problem then?' I said, 'He's the rudest man I've ever met. Do not ever send him to my house again.'

> If there's any problems I don't contact social services any more. It's only be if something really bad happened. I don't bother with them any more. They've ignored everything I've ever said to them; they have treated me like rubbish. They've insulted me enough times and they insulted my partner and it's not on is it?

> I mean the times I've tried to phone. [They] said, 'Ooh we'll get them to give you a call back' and you'd still be waiting for the call back three days later – we were

sort of at the bottom end of the priority list – it made you feel like you weren't very important.

One grandmother, who explained that children's services had been unwilling to backdate payments, identified an attitude from social workers that grandparents should undertake caring without requesting assistance:

> But because I was his grandmother and because we were retired and because we seemed to have a comfortable home and a car, and he was well clothed and well fed, and well shod, and seemed happy and content, [we'd] done no more than grandparents should.

Negative experiences of social work involvement

Even when family and friends were managing the children well and were providing a much needed service, some felt that, at times, social workers and their managers treated them in a high handed way:

> I got angry because of the letter we'd had off that woman at social services, and I think how dare you, you know, because at the end of the day I don't care who it is, whether it's social services, whether it's the Queen of England, you should have your say and they shouldn't think that they can say what they like and you can't say anything.

> It was how he was on the phone. He was very, as though he didn't want to talk to me. I threatened I would go to [a voluntary agency]. And the minute I told them that I'd phoned them up [the voluntary agency], they was OK.

> I hadn't let them know where we were going [on holiday], it's true. Because he [the worker] didn't get told personally, he was quite stroppy.

> [The social worker] was a nasty piece of work, real nasty piece of work, and every time we went to see Greg or we had a meeting with Greg, you always felt that he was trying to threaten you all the time. He would have no hesitation in telling you that, 'Well if you don't have the children you know they'll finish up in care.' You felt that he was trying to save social services as much as he could save.

Even though some kin carers stood up to social workers with whom they disagreed, many recognised the importance of working with, not against, children's services: 'It's better to have them on your side.'

Some carers had rather more difficult experiences. One had asked for help with a girl with a very difficult background and found that the social worker was, instead, recommending a long-term foster placement:

> They tried to move June. I had a social worker came on the scene and she was here for about five minutes and she was making all these decisions, 'Oh this isn't right and that's not good and we need to take her and move her somewhere.' And

> then I'm saying, 'I need help with this, I need someone to advise me, I need some training.' And I was on the phone every five minutes just saying 'Please, please, it's just all falling apart,' and that. And their answer to that was, 'That's all right we'll just take her.' No, that's not what I asked for. That's not good for that child.

When a worker from a children's rights group got involved and discovered that June did not want to move, the decision was changed. The carer then made an official complaint through her solicitor, with the side benefit that her money was significantly raised:

> As soon as I had the letter come through saying that an official complaint has been logged and it's under investigation, then suddenly I got this letter saying, 'Oh yes, things have been changed, and you're going to be getting this much money from now on.' I went, 'Whoa, that's like more than double what I was getting before.'

One grandmother told her daughter, the children's mother, that she would not be getting the children back, but felt that this should really have come from the social worker. Another grandmother who rang to ask why the children had not had a review for two years was subsequently criticised for trying to involve the children's mother in their care.

How being a kin carer differed from being a parent or an unrelated carer

A number of kin carers commented that it was harder to bring up these children than it had been to bring up their own:

> It's hard work, it's a lot harder bringing this one up than it was bringing the other three up.

> I think it's more difficult, I think as well the kids are different, because I think to myself what am I doing different now to what I done with Karen, Jill and Dave [her own children]. I'm not, I'm doing exactly the same thing, but the kids I think are more challenging.

This was partly because they themselves were older but was more often because the children often had behavioural and emotional difficulties by the time that they came to live with kin. As we have seen, a few relatives, especially grandparents, were fearful that as the children grew older they might get into the same kind of trouble as their parents, such as misusing drugs, whilst one grandmother said that she spoiled her granddaughter to make up for her past experiences. In addition, as already noted, a few carers said that being an approved foster carer could interfere with ordinary family life because they could not discipline the children as they wished.

Several carers also explained that being a kin carer was harder than being an ordinary unrelated foster carer because of hostility from the child's parents and lack of action to assist with this:

> [With] family care and that child comes to you, you haven't got the protection from social services and everybody else, like you've got if you're a foster carer. Because the foster family deal with that child, they don't have to deal with that child's family. They don't have to have the abuse and the contacts. And everything's arranged by social services. When you're a family carer then we had his mother threatening us.

Those kin carers who knew foster carers were well aware of the differences in the support provided for them. For example, one severely disabled grandmother pointed out the routine services available to the foster carer of another of her grandchildren:

> She's got her own support worker, plus she's got this woman that comes and takes Frank places after school – and it's two things I don't have. Frank breaks anything, she gets in touch with the support worker and she gets refunded for it.

There was a general feeling that kin got a poor deal, especially when compared to unrelated foster carers:

> You're not going to get any help, is basically what I was told, you're not entitled to support or any type of help whatsoever, only foster carers get that. Sorry there's nothing we can do about that. That's the rules, deal with it or we can put him somewhere else.

> I sometimes do feel out of my depth, really, and it's strange because they said to me if I become a foster carer I'd have a back-up from the foster system, but because I'm his grandmother I don't.

Some carers also recognised that they did not know what they could ask for and yet would not be told:

> I do feel that there are other families that are in this situation and they don't know what their rights are and they're not going to be openly given their rights.

> No one's said, 'This is what we can offer.' It's almost been like left to you to say 'Well is there this or is there that?'

A number of carers also told us that when they asked for services they were told that as relatives or friends they were not entitled to help, something that effectively disarmed most carers:

> [They said] I'm not entitled to it.

> They seem to have a rule for foster carers that are foster carers, but not foster carers that are grandparents or aunts and uncles. They do less for you, they give you less help.

Review meetings

A few carers mentioned that they could not be open about difficulties in review meetings when the children's parents, to whom they were related, were attending:

> And so his mum chose not to go. Neither of them went to the meeting. So I thought, it's a lot easier for me, 'cos I could be quite open and express myself. And that's the other thing I find very difficult, because she's family, she's my sister-in-law. I'm actually saying stuff that she doesn't particularly want to hear about her son, 'cos she thinks there's nothing wrong with him and he's a good boy.

> Once I've started talking they back me up, but I've initially wanted them to actually start that conversation and me actually butt in if you like, the other way around. Because then [mother] looks at me, I'm just really classed as a bad person, but really she can't see that all I'm trying to do is actually help her son. You see I didn't have all this when I fostered Jules [an unrelated child].

Many of the carers said that they only saw the social workers when a review meeting was due. The reviewing officer at one review for a very disturbed boy took the social worker to task for offering so little support when the alternative would have been an expensive out-of-county placement. Sadly, in spite of this, little change took place.

The difficulties posed by some kin carers

However, there were specific difficulties in helping some kin carers. In a few situations, the family dynamics served to keep the social worker on the periphery of events (see also O'Brien 1999). For example, a few social workers felt that a mother was playing off the carer against children's services so that both parent and carer became hostile to the social worker. At other times, extended family members colluded with the parents against the caring relatives. When the extended family was locked in conflict it was also hard for the worker to make a significant impact.

Other kin carers resented the restrictions imposed by children's services and tried to keep social workers at a distance. They responded variably, as we have seen, to the demand to get permission for holidays abroad and overnight stays with friends (which was a common expectation at the time); and to the requirements for police checks on the adults with whom the children stayed. Some complied; others got the child's friends to stay in their house instead, whilst others ignored the restrictions:

> Oh I don't tell them about it. Oh God, they'd have everybody in the village filling out police check forms, he'd never have a friend left would he? I mean most of the kids at school don't know he's fostered either. So I just said, 'Well in that case I shan't ask for your permission if you think you'll refuse it,' because I'm not asking to do anything silly. I've taken him to America twice because I have relations over there.

A few kin carers took the view that such restrictions represented 'interference' in their lives. Others considered that these demands restricted the children's social life and felt that they showed a lack of trust in their judgement:

> Yes, I mean it's like it with Tracey's sister. They haven't got any children, they spoil him to death but I'm not supposed to leave him out there. Have done a couple of times but I'm not supposed to. And I do feel a bit embarrassed and it's almost as if social services don't trust your judgement – that you're not going to leave him [with someone unsuitable]. You just wouldn't, after what he's been through, you wouldn't. If anything you are a bit ultra-careful with him.

One family was described by the social worker as a 'very enclosed family who do not cooperate with the social services department' and one where the sexual boundaries were unclear. When an investigation was conducted into a sexual assault by the non-resident father, the grandparents became openly hostile and the relationship with children's services deteriorated further.

One single carer, whose disciplinary methods were harsh, was aggressive with her social workers and with the school when there were concerns about the child being hit or being taken out of school during the school term:

> Well he sat there, he said, 'I've got it wrote down here that you hit her.' I said, 'What? And I'm a childminder and you think I'm going to hit Fay, you must be, got a screw loose or something.' As though I hit Fay I'm going to hit the little ... You can see for a fact she's happy enough – couldn't see the floor, toys is every-where.

There were also a few carers who were openly hostile to the parents and who restricted their contact with the children, actions that social workers again found it hard to influence. In a few instances, carers actively blocked help for the children. Occasionally, this appeared to be partly to cover up the poor care they were giving them. Overall, when we looked at the cases where carers were extremely uncooperative or resentful of children's services, these were often families that later emerged as having provided particularly poor care.

Specialist services for the children

Carers were generally positive about help from medical services including paediatric consultant appointments and the services of a bedwetting clinic, although one child had waited two years for a speech therapy appointment.

Given the considerable behavioural and emotional difficulties of the children placed with kin, we examined which specialist services were provided for them. As we have seen, mental health services were arranged for 28 per cent of the children placed with family or friends and 29 per cent of those with unrelated foster carers. Of course, it is possible that more children in both groups received services, but that these were not recorded on the files.

Of the children in kin care in the case file review, six saw child and adolescent psychiatrists, of whom three were only for assessments. Child psychiatrists provided direct work to three children, one of whom had been sexually abused and two of whom had witnessed a parent being killed. A paediatrician was involved with another child who was thought to have attention deficit disorder (ADD).

Child psychologists provided direct work for another six children and in two of these cases they also supported the carers in the difficult task of looking after the children. This included an aunt who had no children of her own, who was ably supported to cope with her disturbed nephew. Educational psychologists undertook direct work with four children.

Another 18 children were involved in therapeutic help from a variety of other sources, including by a specialist therapy team, by Child and Adolescent Mental Health Services (CAMHS), Family Centre workers and the NSPCC. One child whose placement was fragile had attended therapy three times a week for four years. Intensive work was also provided to help two children who were confused about why they were living with their relatives, whilst counselling was provided for four other children who had been maltreated or were suicidal. One child saw a school counsellor about identity issues and another was receiving bereavement counselling. In a few cases, engagement was brief or consisted of only one session, whilst the kin carers blocked one referral for therapeutic help to a specialist unit.

In addition, five children engaged in Life Story work, two with local authority social workers; one each with a nursery worker, a family support worker and a freelance social worker. In spite of this assistance, one of these young people blamed children's services for breaking up her family. Plans were in train to do Life Story work with one other boy to help him come to terms with his past, on the recommendation of his therapist. In addition, two sets of grandparents had attempted such work themselves:

We'd got a folder and we sat down and we did a life story folder and we put in photographs and all the times and everything, right up to date for him to read, have a look at – and photos with all the different names in his family. It took a long time, it was a big folder but easy reading for him to look at. They didn't even do that, we did it off our own back. For him to remember because at such a young age, he couldn't even remember who we were.

Work with the children and carers

A family aide or support worker was involved in working with either the child or the carers in eight cases. In one, the worker visited regularly for three months to help a grandmother with a small baby. In another, a support worker had taken two children out for an hour a week to give their grandmother a break at the beginning of the placement. In a third, a support worker was involved after a second child was placed with the grandmother and there were uncertainties as to whether she could manage. Two others worked directly with the carers on parenting skills, whilst another provided activities for a boy who was excluded from his special residential school.

Although, as we will see, there were often quite acute conflicts between the kinship carers and the parents and other family members, work with the families as a whole appeared to be rare, although some commentators advocate this approach (see e.g. O'Brien 1999, 2000; Doolan *et al.* 2004). Family therapy was provided in one case. In another, counselling for the family was arranged to deal with tensions between the grandmother who was the carer and the mother. In a third case, the child had been used as a go-between in arguments between the mother and the relative carer and the social worker had arranged a meeting to try to negotiate better relationships.

Assistance for the carers

Direct work with the carers

In only eight cases (6%) had kin carers themselves been involved in counselling. One carer recognised that some of her own issues were interfering with her ability to provide optimum care for the child and others received help in dealing with children's disclosures of maltreatment or advice about child management.

Foster carer groups

Kin carers appeared very rarely to be involved in the foster carer groups that unrelated foster carers attend, although some knew about them. One aunt, who did attend, found the meetings very useful:

I thought, 'This is stressing me out, this is stressing me out,' but when I go to the fostering meetings, they'd say, 'Let it become his problem and not yours,' the best advice they could give me. So I'd make it his problem, not mine.

One carer was very enthusiastic about attending a group but was told there was no group locally. In the one authority where a dedicated kin carer group existed, one set of carers attended and two others tried unsuccessfully to locate the group.

We asked the family and friends carers if they would have joined a special group for kin carers, and there was considerable enthusiasm for the idea, although a number were still not sure if they would actually attend. Certainly, carers generally felt that the groups for unrelated foster carers would not have been suitable for them. One grandparent couple, who had attended training with ordinary carers, thought a special group for relatives would be useful because they considered the issues to be rather different to those for other foster carers, whilst another grandmother thought such a group:

Would have been ideal because there was times when you wondered if you'd been doing it right, or is anybody else going through this, you know.

Similarly, the grandmother of a severely disabled young person commented: 'You can feel totally out on a limb and on your own if you don't talk to somebody like that.'

One carer could see the potential of a group to enable carers to meet each other and provide mutual support. Certainly, unrelated foster carers gain considerable support from individual contact with other carers who they meet through foster carer groups (see for example Farmer *et al.* 2004; Sinclair 2005b).

Parenting skills groups

We found reference to a small number of kinship carers (7) who attended a parenting skills group to assist them with behaviour management skills, either because the children they were looking after were particularly difficult or showed sexualised behaviour or more often because their own parenting skills were considered to be deficient.

Training

Few carers were encouraged to attend or had attended training, although four of those whom we interviewed said that they had received information about the training courses provided for non-related foster carers. In contrast to the situation for unrelated foster carers who routinely attend such courses, the carers who did attend training were usually those where children's services had concerns about the carers' poor parenting skills, lack of parenting experience or that they were looking after children with particularly severe difficulties. One grandparent couple who did some training said that the other unrelated foster carers felt sorry for them and were helpful. An aunt who had completed two training courses run by the local health visitors had found them 'an eye opener'.

An exception was an enterprising grandmother who had attended several training courses and found them useful:

> Because I had the fostering payment they used to send through all the courses that they used to do. So I don't think I was actually supposed to do them because I wasn't actually a general foster carer, but I did actually go on a lot of the courses – a lot of them were absolutely brilliant. I learned a lot on the courses, especially with the education system because I've never heard of ed psychs, or the SENCO, and it did explain all his [her grandson's] issues. And it was nice getting views from foster carers and I learned a lot from them, but they were also just as curious about me being a kinship carer, and picked things up from me.

Formal and informal respite care

Given the ages of some of the carers, their poor state of health and the large numbers of children placed, we examined how often respite or short break care was provided (see Aldgate and Bradley 1999; Greenfields and Statham 2004). The case files showed that regular respite care was arranged for eleven sets of kin carers (8%), most of whom were grandparents. This usually involved weekend care, which varied from fortnightly to six-weekly. Those carers whose children received such regular respite care found it very helpful:

> And he loves, he absolutely loves going up there. It's freedom. We can go out, yes that's about the only time you can get drunk. (Grandmother)

> And now I do get respite every weekend with Neil and I've got to be honest, that is so valuable, so so valuable. And he'll leave at five o'clock teatime and he'll go to another foster family who live on a farm and they will keep him then until say five o'clock on Sunday and bring him back here. And I've got to honestly say, without that I think the place would now break down because I really need to recharge my batteries, and to give some quality to [my own daughter] – more like a break from each other, and we call it our little holiday for the weekend. (Aunt)

Another three carers were provided with occasional respite care either to enable them to take a holiday or during times of illness or stress. As previously noted, two other sets of carers who ran their own businesses employed a nanny to look after the children when the call of their work left them unable to care themselves. In one of these, children's services provided financial support. One other child was cared for by a formal shared care arrangement where one set of friends provided care during the week and another set at weekends. Others had requested respite without success, either as we have seen, because they could not afford it or because their request was refused.

Interestingly, when kin carers requested respite care, social workers sometimes tried to arrange it with the children's parents or other relatives. In two such cases, another relative was approved as a respite carer and this was successful. In another two, the arrangements had been made with the mothers and were not sustained either because of disagreements between the mother and kin carers or because the mother's circumstances changed, leaving her unable to continue. Other efforts to arrange respite with children's parents had not got off the ground, either because the children returned with worsened behaviour or because the parents could not be relied on.

Eighteen other carers (13%) received regular help from family members. This ranged from three arrangements where the grandparents provided daily or holiday care to enable the caring aunt and uncle to maintain their jobs; to situations where other relatives took the children for regular weekends or provided regular babysitting; to adult children and other extended family members who visited frequently and helped out. In one, the mother helped the grandmother every day and this led to the children's return to her.

Thus while about one in five of the kin carers had access to help from either extended family members or from respite carers, the remainder did not. There were a good number of situations where regular respite care might have provided a much needed break for the carers and lessened some of the stress of caring.

Whilst a number of kin carers had originally provided respite care for the children to relieve either the parents or more rarely foster carers, many were not given this service when they became full-time carers:

> We did laugh one day and say, 'Well, we need respite care now and we used to do it ourselves for them and we need it now.'

Gaps in the help provided

As we have seen, very few (6%) of the kin carers had a family placement worker, although the one friend couple with particularly high needs who did, found that this worker kept changing and so they relied more on the children's social worker. In another two cases, the children's social worker requested that a family placement worker become involved to provide more support for the carers. A number of carers commented that non-relative foster carers always had family support workers whilst kin carers did not.

Practical and other help for the carers

On the evidence in the case files the researchers judged that in 30 per cent of cases either no services were provided for kin carers, or those offered fell far short of what was needed. Practical help for carers in looking after children in particularly difficult circumstances was often lacking. For example, one grandmother who took on five children under the age of eight received an offer of help with housing and an arrangement that the great aunt would provide respite care, but no other assistance.

In the interviews, some of the carers identified specific services that they felt they needed but that had not been available. A few wanted counselling for themselves, some wanted money to cover child sitting to allow them to go out occasionally and a number wanted respite care, especially at the beginning of the placement. A few had wanted a support worker to take the children out for an hour or two to give them a break, particularly during school holidays, or financial help to pay for an After School Club. Carers had difficulty too when schools sent children home frequently for misbehaviour. One file recorded the problems of grandparents who wanted help to move house because of the frequent interruptions by the parents who lived in the same street. Another carer said that 'a bit of recognition would be nice, someone to come and say thank you, because Linda isn't my daughter.'

Others said that they had needed help to deal with contact issues and to place boundaries around how often parents saw the child or telephoned them, especially when for example daily telephone calls from a parent were having a negative impact on the child and undermining the placement. A few carers made it clear that they would have welcomed help to understand the behaviours of the children they were looking after.

When carers had needs of their own, over and above those related to managing the children, these received little attention. One grandmother was struggling to cope with three grandchildren and having difficulty in coming to terms with the fact that her daughter was in prison for a very serious offence. Another grandmother who was looking after her two grandchildren because their mother, her daughter, had died was still grieving eight years later but did not know how to get help for herself.

Carers with health difficulties

Carers who had chronic health conditions often did little better. Most carers, who had little mobility, were housebound or had a major disability, received no additional services for the children or for themselves. It was notable that their difficulties did not seem to be taken into account in the services that were offered and some, as already noted, relied on family members to assist them. Indeed, while ill health was sometimes considered to disqualify carers from being approved as foster carers for a specific child, it remarkably rarely elicited additional help.

Services for children

There were considerable gaps too in the services provided for children. Those with serious emotional and behavioural difficulties often received no direct work. Max was an 8-year-old boy who, with his siblings, lived with his disabled aunt. He was so difficult to control in school that a residential school was recommended. It was a year before the aunt was offered any assistance in managing him. In another case, a psychological assessment recommended counselling for a 14-year-old girl who was placed with her grandmother but none was provided, although the children's guardian had been so concerned about service needs that she had successfully opposed the authority's application to discharge the care order.

Some carers had tried hard to get help for the children they were looking after without success:

> We've been trying for three years to get him to have some sort of, somebody to talk to.

> I told her Megan needed counselling. She had one session and that was it.

> I mean I've asked four times now, for a support worker, and they said no. They said you weren't allowed it because you were a relative not a foster carer.

Another issue, already noted, that emerged in the interviews was that kin carers who were looking after disabled children or those with disorders such as autism worried about what would happen as the young people reached the age of 18. Whereas unrelated foster carers might reasonably assume that children's services would make some arrangements for the young people, there was no such reassurance for kin carers.

The lack of information given to the children about the reasons for the placements and plans for the future

Although we gained little insight from the files into the children's feelings about their placements, a small number clearly did not understand why they were living with a relative or friend and not with their parents. This has also been shown to be true of some children in foster care (Cleaver 2000) and in other studies of kinship care (Aldgate and McIntosh 2006; Doolan et al. 2004; Hunt et al. 2007; Messing 2005). In one case, this was revealed when a care leaver wrote on an exit questionnaire that no one had talked to her about why she was living with her grandparents. Junior too was confused about why he was living with his grandparents and with whom he would live in the future. He said he had been told he was living with relatives because his mother was re-decorating the house. Julia who showed distressed behaviour after contact with her mother, who was putting pressure on her to return, was confused about the reasons why she was living with her aunt and uncle. Simon who lived with an aunt and uncle did not know who his parents were, although he saw them at family gatherings. In a few cases it was clear that the children blamed either the kin carer or children's services for not being able to live with their parents.

It is likely to be considerably more difficult for kin carers to explain to children why they are not living with their parents than it is for unrelated foster carers, since kin sometimes have strong feelings about the reasons for care, may feel responsible for these difficulties (Crumbley and Little 1997) and may themselves have reported the concerns that led to the children being separated from their parents (Spence 2004). Explaining to children why they cannot live with their parents is clearly an important task for social workers or other professionals to undertake, especially as without training or advice, kin carers are not in a strong position to know how best to approach this topic with children and, in many cases, seemed to have avoided it. It was interesting that when we asked the kin carers what the children understood about why they were living with them, they often said that they did not know and had clearly either not felt able to broach this topic or not seen the need to do so.

One enterprising 12-year-old girl, dissatisfied with her aunt and social worker's explanations about why she was not living with her mother, asked to see her case records. She was shown her parents' and the social workers' statements from the file, which satisfied her need to understand. In addition, one grandmother was pleased that the children had attended family therapy sessions with their mother, so that they could hear their mother describing and taking responsibility for the events that had led them to need the placement with their grandparents.

Plans for the children's future also need to be discussed with them. In one case a boy living with family friends was anxious that it would 'all go wrong' and he would not be able to stay with them. These are areas of routine practice that might benefit from more attention in work with kin carers.

Summary

The files and interviews showed that the children placed with family and friends had high levels of emotional and behavioural difficulty, as would be expected in a population of children with similar experiences to children in care. Kin carers often struggled to manage these difficulties, especially when they received few or inadequate services. They welcomed and sometimes relied on those social workers who supported them in this task but many wanted more social work assistance and in particular wished for services for the children in their care. However good their parenting skills, most kin carers were not prepared for the severe difficulties these children brought with them to their placements. Nonetheless, a few kin carers resented the restrictions associated with social work involvement and saw it as interference. A number of specific issues for kin carers have been highlighted, such as the conduct of review meetings when parents are present and the need for information to be given to children about the reasons for their placements and about plans for the future.

Now that the children's behaviours and the services provided have been described, we turn to consider in the next chapter children's contact with their parents and other family members and the impact on the kin carers of looking after the children.

Chapter 8

Caring for Children:
Contact, Standards of Care
and the Impact of the Children
on the Kin Carers

This chapter examines children's contact with family members, how well carers were able to protect children from their parents when necessary and the few placements where standards of care were unacceptably low. Finally, the impact on the carers of looking after the children will be considered.

The involvement of the extended family
Positive involvement
One of the characteristics of family and friends care is that the children looked after by relatives, in particular, are usually included as full family members by the extended family:

> But you see all my brothers and sisters have always given to Kylie, Christmases, birthdays, Easter, so she didn't lose out at all. So they just added one more.

> I think your family take a bit longer than if it's your own child to accept it but over the years they've gradually accepted that he is part of the family and if ever they've treated Luke a little less – like a little bit less money than they've given to Geoff, I've said, 'Look, I want them to be treated the same. I don't want Luke to be given less.' So they've realised now that he's part of the family and always will be.

Often, as previously mentioned, there is an explicit or implicit contingency plan about which relative would take the children if the current carer could not continue:

> Oh yes, if something happened now, Fiona [older daughter] would have her, because she's married and got her own family now, so she can just take her on.

As we have seen, members of the extended family not infrequently assisted the carers by having the child to stay on a regular basis, by babysitting or helping in other ways. Quite often, the adult children of the carers lived nearby and gave their parents regular assistance (see also Farmer *et al.* 2004) whilst, as we have seen, the carers with severe health conditions were often dependent on their adult children who visited daily and assisted with maintaining the home.

Occasionally, one of the parents lived with the grandparents who were caring for the child. More often, grandparent carers had other relatives in the house, such as their other children, who might also provide support. In one such situation, when the grandmother died, one of the resident uncles took over the children's care. A few grandparents were also looking after a grandchild by one of their other adult children or had another adult child and his or her children in the house. In a small number of families there was a pattern of grandparent care, where the grandmother currently looking after her grandchildren had herself been brought up by her grandparents.

Grandparents sometimes provided support when aunts and uncles (or friends) were the carers or vice versa. In one family the grandparents had their grandson every weekend to give the aunt and uncle's children time on their own with their parents.

A few children had moved a number of times between members of the extended family, either when an older relative became too ill to continue, or in the aftermath of a kin carer placement breakdown. Most of these moves were clearly necessary. It was rare for children to have a large number of unplanned moves between relatives, although this had occasionally occurred.

Lack of support and opposition from the extended family

Whilst a number of carers had very good levels of support from the extended family or from friends and sometimes from work colleagues or the church, others had little or no such support. Indeed, a few from the interview sample had actually met opposition from the wider family. This was often because family members thought that the carers should not have agreed to take the child in the first place, and were concerned either about the burden it placed on the carers or about the loss of the carers' time for themselves and their children. For example, one great-grandmother resented the fact that her daughter was giving her time to her granddaughter and not to her. The grandmother said:

> Because none of my family have been supportive with me having Helen. They weren't against it but they never once said, 'Well we'll have Helen for a night. Go and go out for an hour.' Not one of them. And that, it do hurt. They say, 'You should be just starting to go out and start enjoying your own life, and now you're tied down again.'

Occasionally, an older child of the family was angry with their adult brother or sister for being unable to care for their children, such that the relative had had to take over their care. One grandmother said:

> My son was totally against it. He understood with Nicky – he was totally against us having the other two. He felt that our daughter was not playing her part and it caused a lot of rows, a lot of friction.

One maternal grandparent couple who were looking after their severely disabled grandson got occasional financial help from the paternal grandparents if they needed a specific item to help with the boy's disability. However, they did regret that their own adult children did not provide them with practical or emotional support:

> That's the sadness of it all. That's where sometimes we feel we're out on a limb, but I think on the other hand, when you've got social services and all the other bits and pieces, we feel we've got a lot of backup. [What would have helped is] just the emotional backup, if not physically. The fact that you can feel the family are behind what you're doing. There have been times when we've felt that we've been kicked in the backside for looking after him.

In addition, as we will see in relation to contact, some carers had very difficult relationships not only with the child's parents but also with other members of the extended family who criticised and undermined them, and this behaviour sometimes extended to violence and threats to the carers.

Contact

As we saw in Chapter 4, contact levels for children living with kin carers were similar to those for children with unrelated foster carers, except that those with kin carers saw their fathers, aunts and uncles more.

Contact patterns

A number of typical contact patterns emerged. In a small number of cases in the file sample (4%) the mother helped the carers daily with the care of the child in what amounted to shared care. Five of these six carers were maternal grandparents and one was an aunt and uncle. In a few other situations, as we have seen, one relative helped another daily in caring for the children so that the main carer could work. In all these situations, the children had very frequent contact with these other relatives. We have also noted that occasionally a relative provided respite care for the main kin carer, thus also providing regular contact.

Another typical pattern of contact was that the child saw one or both parents at agreed intervals, if the parent remained in contact, and also regularly saw the relatives from the side of the family with whom they were living, as they dropped in and visited. Thus, children living with paternal grandparents often saw not only their father but paternal aunts and uncles and their children, who were their cousins, who were in regular touch with the grandparents. In addition, some relatives would facilitate contact with other family members who lived further away: for example, aunts with the grandmother on the same side of the family. Contact with the other side of the family required more formal arrangements and depended mainly on the interest of these other relatives. In most cases, the carers were happy to enable such contact and a few made efforts to ensure that the relatives on the other side retained contact. In a very small number of cases, conflict between the maternal and paternal sides of the family made this difficult. In a few instances, a kin carer worked particularly hard to maintain contact with a parent who was unreliable, who had disappeared from the scene or was in prison.

When sibling groups had been shared out among a number of relatives, usually between the grandparents, aunts and uncles, as we have seen, they generally saw a great deal of their brothers and sisters, during the many contacts between these parts of the family. On the other hand, when a child's brothers or sisters were in care, the amount of contact with siblings depended on how active the kin carers were in arranging it. Not infrequently, children had younger siblings who had been placed for adoption and with whom contact had either ended or was maintained through letterbox contact or more rarely occasional visits.

In a small number of cases (6) the kin carers had made good relationships with the previous non-relative foster carers often because of their frequent contact with the children during these previous placements, and they maintained the child's contact with these foster carers through regular visits.

Lack of contact

Whilst on the whole the children with kin carers had high levels of contact with family members, a number of children had little contact with relatives. As we have seen, 30 per cent of the children in kin care had no contact with their mothers whilst another 7 per cent of the mothers were no longer alive, and 51 per cent had no contact with their fathers, with another 6 per cent of fathers no longer alive.

A small number of children (6) had little contact with either parent. In one such case, the social worker actively considered involving an Independent Visitor, as a boy living with his grandmother was upset by his parents' lack of interest in him. However, the worker decided that this was not appropriate as the child was living with a family member. In addition, a few children were reported to want to see siblings but were unable to do so.

Termination of contact and contact restrictions

As already noted, there was a court order or a local authority ruling preventing contact in 20 per cent of kin cases. In a few of these, contact had been prevented because the relative had sexually or physically abused the children or had committed offences against other children. In two others, the mother's behaviour upset the children and undermined their confidence so much that it led to termination of contact. In one such case the child was tearing up photographs of herself and saying she wanted to die; in another, the mother was telling the children that she was going to commit suicide. In a case where the father had tried to abduct his daughter from the placement, an injunction was taken out to prevent contact; whilst a parent who had assaulted the kin carer in front of the children was banned from the home.

Contact supervised by relatives

One in five of all the family and friends carers officially supervised contact and in many others, kin maintained a watchful eye to see that contact was appropriate. Occasionally, when there were tensions between a parent and the supervising relative, another family member would step in to undertake the supervised contact. For example, when children were living with an aunt and uncle the contact might be supervised by the grandparents on that side of the family in their home. In a more difficult case, after an unsubstantiated allegation of abuse against the children's father, he moved back to live with the relatives who were caring for his son, Brad, and the kin carer was then charged with monitoring all his contact with Brad. On the other hand, occasionally when supervised contact went well, the parent negotiated with the carer for unsupervised contact and a small number of carers encouraged increasing levels of contact with parents, once they were able to manage it constructively, sometimes needing to convince social workers that this was possible.

All in all, most relatives showed great skill in supervising difficult contact situations with parents and other relatives. They were usually very clear about their responsibility to protect the children they looked after and balanced this with compassion for the parents' situations and awareness that their own ability to care for the children, when the parents could not, could evoke considerable jealousy.

Carers described how mothers would sometimes cry in front of the children and tell them how much they missed them, lavish attention on one child to the detriment of the others or teach the children bad habits, which they later reproduced at home. One aunt told us that the mother would ignore the children while she talked on her mobile phone and then refuse to hear them read, when they wanted to show her how much they had learned:

> He'd pooed himself and he was about five... And I says, 'Well, why did you do that?' and he said, 'Because, I thought if I pooed myself I'd be able to go home.' And he'd literally been with her for about 25 minutes. And he just did not want to be around her, he did not want to be anywhere near her.

Occasionally, supervising contact was more fraught, as for a grandparent who had to prevent the mother bundling the children into the car on a contact visit. In such situations carers had to intervene to protect the children, usually by providing close supervision or, more rarely, by reducing the frequency of contact.

They also had to help children deal with unreliable contact or parents who stopped coming to see them for long periods. One grandparent explained how she dealt with the unreliability of the child's mother:

> What we do now is we don't tell Gus Mummy's coming. So what I do is, if they phone half past nine quarter to ten, I say, 'Oh Gus, Mummy and Daddy are coming, what a lovely surprise,' because over the last year there was a lot of big let-downs. They just didn't turn up.

However, grandparents in this situation felt that they could not make alternative plans when children's parents were due to visit (see also Farmer *et al.* 2004; Sinclair 2005b). Another grandmother described how during supervised contact she would let the children go out with their mother and follow behind at a little distance, in order to let the children feel they had their mother to themselves.

Only a few carers had been able to determine how and when contact would take place, since this only worked if the parent was amenable. For example, one aunt said of the child's mother who had learning difficulties:

> She's never lived far away. And we did make it clear to her that it would become very difficult if she kept coming in and out of here. We knew that would be a problem with all her problems. It can be very disruptive, but she didn't seem to have a problem with that.

Occasionally, carers set the terms in ways that may not have been in the child's interests, including one relative who limited the mother's contact with her children, even after the mother's lifestyle had improved and the children wanted to see her more. However, on the whole, kin carers were not able to set the terms of the contact when it was working poorly, including of course when parents were unreliable or disappeared for months at a time. Contact was particularly difficult when the parents lived very close or even on the same street and came and went as they pleased.

Contact supervised by social workers

As previously noted, social workers or family centre workers supervised contact for children living with kin carers much less often than was the case for children looked after by unrelated foster carers. There appeared to be an expectation that relatives would generally supervise contact and they were charged with supervising some quite difficult situations. Children's services, however, became involved in supervision of contact in a number of circumstances. One was when the parents had very poor relationships with the kin carers and were sufficiently hostile for social workers to step in. Others involved serious difficulties that required professional supervision, such as when the parent or a sibling had sexually abused a child in the family or the parent was patently inappropriate in contact with their children and undermined the placement.

When contact was supervised by social workers, occasionally a relative had reservations about the way in which it was done. One aunt said:

> And the children used to say, 'Why do we have to have social workers there Aunt Jane? They keep making notes.' They make notes, feed it all back to Kevin Brown [the social worker] and that was more ammunition. If Paula [the mother] said anything…that they didn't think was right, they'd turn round and say, 'There's emotional abuse,' and she'd say, 'Well what have I said?' 'You know what you've said,' and she'd end up in tears, the girls would end up in tears, and then she'd say, 'OK well if that's the case I'm not going to see them again.'

Even social work supervised contact could not always keep children safe. Two children were groomed by sexually abusing father figures during such contact and one was pinched and bruised by her mother and half-sisters on several occasions until the contact was stopped.

Other helpful interventions in relation to contact included a social worker who vetted all letters for inappropriate content from an imprisoned father to his daughter and another who had managed to use her influence to insist that telephone contact from the mother stop because of its impact on the children.

Contact difficulties

One way in which contact was very different for family and friends carers as compared with stranger foster carers was in the extent of conflict between the kin carers (usually relatives) and the parents or other members of the extended family, as a result of their shared history. Given these conflicts it was surprising that children's services did not offer more assistance with contact to kinship carers (see also Laws 2001; Richards 2001; Russell 1995). As we have seen, such conflict occurred for well over half (54%) of the kin carers but for only 16 per cent of unrelated foster carers. The difficulties took a number of forms.

Inappropriate parental behaviour and parents with high dependency needs

Sometimes, the parent was drunk or high on drugs when they appeared for contact and the relative had to protect the children, even occasionally by calling the police. One grandmother discontinued the mother's contact because of her partner's heavy drug use and violence and because the mother's behaviour was increasingly out of control.

On the other hand, some grandmothers were divided between trying to meet the needs of their grandchildren and of their needy adult children, who were the children's parents. This was especially true of grandmothers (and a few aunts and friends) who provided a great deal of help to the mothers but at the same time had to be clear about putting the children's needs first. The parents who were helped in this way were sometimes ambivalent and intermittently hostile to the children's carers.

Parental hostility to the placement

Some parents objected to the placement with their relatives and criticised or tried to undermine it. In one example the mother actively worked against the aunt who was the carer, making her task more difficult. The aunt said:

> Mum doesn't always like that I perhaps kept him in, grounded him, you know, maybe possibly taken his TV out of his bedroom. She says, 'It's your TV, you should be keeping it,' so she's undermining me all the time. She does the total opposite to me. His mum would like to keep him very baby, but I'm trying to do the reverse. She's actually doing a lot of damage I think. If she wasn't on the scene, I think I would have got further with Carl.

Parental hostility sometimes occurred because the mother had had a difficult, deprived or sometimes abusive childhood and was reluctant to see her child go to live with the parents who had subjected her to this. Some parents would frequently contact the kin carers to complain about the way they were managing the child or make abusive telephone calls, and the children themselves could exploit these differences. For example, an aunt and uncle described their situation as follows:

> She will only give her mum half the story and then I've got her mum on the phone saying, 'You've done this to her, you shouldn't have kept her in.' I don't know if I actually recommend having a child to live with you in the family, unless, if the parents have died, and you've got the full support of the rest of the family – that's a different situation.

Similarly, a father verbally abused his parents who had taken on his disabled son when neither he nor the mother could cope, probably fuelled by feelings of guilt. One mother, who had asked friends to take her son, later became jealous and aggressive to the carers, accusing them of having stolen her son and also took it out on him:

> Well when it started getting difficult because she was getting very jealous about him calling me Mum and she'd tell him off. But I heard his mother give him a long telling off about it – I wasn't his mum and she was the only mum he'd got and they had to stick together and stuff. So in front of her he'd always remember to call her Mum.

When parents were resentful that a relative was caring for their children, they would often try to assert some control by, for example, punishing the children a second time for any misdemeanours, suggesting that they abscond or refusing permission for them to go abroad on holiday with their carers. In one dispute between the cousin carers and the mother, the child was used as a go-between between the warring factions and became very unhappy. Mothers were sometimes jealous, seeing their children receiving the attention from their grandmother that had been denied to them as children. On just a few occasions, as we have seen, the social worker intervened, by calling a family meeting to try to resolve such difficulties.

When, as often happened, parents promised children that they would return to them or threatened the carers that they would get the children back, kin carers found the experience of contact very difficult. One practical difficulty was that with mobile telephones, carers could not limit or monitor the telephone contact that parents had with their children, even when it might be harmful to them.

A few children were torn between the kin carers and a parent. One child who was living with her aunt would, after contact with her mother, say that she would run away if she was not returned home. In private, she told her social worker that she wanted to stay with her aunt but was afraid of hurting her mother. Another child, who was living with her grandmother who had a difficult relationship with her mother, chose not to see her mother, probably as a consequence of this conflict.

Parental allegations against the carers

In addition, as we will see later in this chapter, parents' efforts to destabilise placements could lead to false allegations against the carers. For example, a mother who had had her children removed, alleged that the children's grandfather, who was caring for the children, had sexually abused her as a child. One child was bribed by her mother to say that her caring grandfather had bruised her, and two other mothers reported to the police or children's services that the grandparent carers were abusing or neglecting their children.

The difficulty for social workers was to decide which allegations were justified and which were not. There appeared to be a tendency to ignore criticisms by parents or other relatives about a kin placement, but in this study whilst half of the allegations were attempts to undermine the placement, the other half appeared to be well founded; although this had generally only been confirmed after the children had moved out and revealed how adverse the placement had been. It may therefore be especially important to give children the opportunity to talk alone to a social worker or other professional at regular intervals, especially when there have been any referrals expressing concern about the placement.

Carer resentment of parents

For their part, a few relatives had strong feelings that the parents had tried to obstruct the children's placement with them or about the parents' original abuse or neglect of the child: 'I can't forgive her sometimes for what she's done.'

Occasionally, the carers made frequent criticisms of the parents within the children's hearing. A few relatives blocked contact with a parent with whom they were angry. In one such case, the uncle would not allow contact in his house, but the aunt liaised with the mother to maintain contact elsewhere. One set of maternal grandparents would only allow the father one hour a week contact and this was not challenged, as it was thought that insisting on more contact would jeopardise the placement.

Open conflict between the carers and parents

In many cases, there were high levels of conflict between the carers and the parents, with some kin carers anxious about the parents' hostile and unpredictable behaviour. Sometimes, arguments between the kin carers and parents erupted during contact. In others, friction arose because a parent was trying to regain custody of the children or frequently dropped in without warning.

Sometimes, poor relationships between the kin carers and parents led parents to stay away. One mother thought that the grandmother had criticised her to the social worker and as a consequence did not visit the children for three years. In another case, the parents were abusive to the grandparent carers when they came for contact, and as a result the social worker supervised contact in the carers' home. However, in a similar case, when the mother threatened the grandparents when she visited, no social work assistance was forthcoming. This grandmother rightly commented that non-relative foster cares would certainly have had help in this situation. Yet, this mother's impact on her son was so adverse that when he started therapy, the therapist arranged for contact to be stopped altogether.

Violence and threats by the parents to the carers

The most serious situations were those where family conflicts were so severe that relatives were violent or threatening to the carers. One father was violent and abusive to the aunt who was looking after her nephew against the father's wishes. When the aunt telephoned children's services for help, none was provided. In contrast, when another mother made abusive telephone calls and threatened to remove her children from their aunt, the local children's services stepped in to support the placement with a plan for an emergency order if she tried to do so.

Another aunt and uncle ended a placement after the aunt suffered continual harassment by the step-father and two assaults by local women instigated by him. The aunt was greatly affected and the family moved from the area, choosing a house that was not big enough to include their niece. In one particularly severe case, care orders were made on Adam and his brother Jim and they were placed with relatives because of disclosures of maltreatment by their father. When he found out where they were living, he sent threatening letters to the kin carers. The police took these threats very seriously and the carers and children had to move twice to avoid him finding them.

Conflict between different parts of the family

In a few cases, there were tensions between the two sides of the family, with one side feeling blamed by the other for the family problems. In one such situation, the mother and maternal grandparents felt that the paternal aunt and uncle carers isolated the child from their side of the family and there was constant conflict over this involving the courts.

In another similar case, the grandparents on one side of the family did not allow contact with the grandparents and aunt on the other. It emerged after the children left this placement that the grandparent carers had been abusing the children, so they may have blocked contact to ensure that the children did not talk about their situation.

Occasionally, the kin carers who were looking after a child reported that relatives on the other side of the family were undermining them or were critical of them. One grandparent couple in this situation were planning to move to escape this pressure. There were also a handful of cases where a grandparent singled out for special treatment the child who had moved in with an aunt and uncle, arriving laden with gifts, whilst ignoring the other grandchildren in the family.

In two cases, one set of relations waged war on the relatives who were looking after the child because of their feelings about the placement. In one, Selena was removed from her parents on a care order at the age of seven and placed with her grandparents. She did well in this placement but children's services recommended that they did not take on long-term care of Selena because of the grandparents' state of health. Instead, an uncle and his wife on the same side of the family were approved as carers and Selena moved to them 12 months later. The grandparents became very hostile to this uncle and aunt and wrote hurtful letters to them. Children's services were so concerned at the threat to the placement that they prevented all contact with the grandparents until relationships had improved. The grandparents fought this ruling seeking help from their solicitor and their MP. Attempts by children's services to broker an agreement were not successful and in the end the uncle got a job offer in another part of the country and the family, including Selena, prepared to move away.

In the other case, three children were placed with relatives on the suggestion of grandparents who felt that they could not offer them a permanent home. However, the grandparents became jealous of the arrangement and resented it when the children referred to the carers as Mum and Dad. When the kin carers decided to move to another town, the grandparents, fearing loss of contact, became extremely hostile and threatened them with violence. The social worker, not surprisingly, had difficulty in managing this complex situation and the carers concluded that children's services 'could not protect them from future conflict' so the placement disrupted.

The impact of contact on children

These conflicts could make the experience of contact fraught for children. Whilst there were more problems when children were living with relatives, some parents came to resent friends looking after their children, even when the parents had instigated the placement with them in the first place.

The case files held quite frequent reports of children who showed distress as a result of contact. Some became more defiant, disruptive or childish after contact with a parent, whilst others became withdrawn and quiet or had nightmares and disturbed sleep. Some children felt rejected by parents who failed to keep in touch or were unreliable or they decided that no contact was preferable to seeing a parent who ignored them when they met. Other children were spoiled during contact, leading to poor behaviour on their return. Children sometimes returned from contact confused after a mother had told them that they would soon be returning to her. One child was noticeably distressed after supervised contact with a brother who had sexually abused her and others were clearly afraid of aggressive father figures. Some children were embarrassed by parents who came to contact visits the worse for wear after drinking or behaved inappropriately, such as a mother who checked her daughter's hair for nits during a birthday party.

A number of kin carers described how children's behaviour worsened after contact and made their task of looking after the children considerably more difficult. A grandparent described the impact of contact with her mother on her eight-year-old grandson:

> We were getting somewhere but when he saw his mum he used to go to pieces sometimes. He gets very angry, very cross.

Another carer said:

> We were still concerned about what she would say to him – it seemed to be that every contact, whatever happened, his behaviour was dreadful before and after – it felt also that she was undermining what we were doing. She was saying things like we were taking him away from her and telling him things like we were the baddies and 'They are keeping us apart my darling and we should be together.'

A grandmother said:

> But when they come back, you've got all the pieces to pick up because she gets worse then, their behaviour is terrible.

An aunt spoke of the impact of contact:

> She'd just literally be naughty. She'd destroy things in her bedroom. She's cut her quilt covers with scissors, slam doors.

In most cases, kin were left to deal with these problems alone, although in some cases social workers took action to reduce contact or arranged for it to be supervised, once early experience showed that the children had been disturbed by unsupervised contact.

In three cases, contact was stopped altogether, on the advice of a specialist. In one of these, a friend carer described how contact with his mother had been affecting the boy she was bringing up:

> Well, [after contact] it would be just no emotion, and then he'd gradually loosen up over a day or so and start laughing – because you never saw him smile when he was with Mum.

In another case, as already mentioned, a boy's behaviour became so bad after visits that contact was stopped completely on the advice of a psychiatrist. This led to a great improvement in his behaviour:

> It was when he was having contact his behaviour got really bad, it deteriorated. Eventually at the review, he'd started seeing psychiatrists and they decided to stop contact altogether. After a few months his behaviour, it got fantastic, [it has] been really good.

Abuse during contact

A few children, as we have noted, were physically or sexually abused during supervised contact or, as we will see in the next section, when relatives had left children with a parent against the instructions of children's services.

The carers' ability to protect children from their parents

Social workers have to assess whether relatives can protect children from their parents when they might put them at risk and it is often assumed that this is a considerable challenge for kin. In extreme cases, children have died when a kin carer allowed them access to a violent parent or one whose lifestyle placed the child at risk, such as in the cases of Tyra Henry and Toni-Ann Byfield (London Borough of Lambeth 1987; Birmingham ACPC 2004). We therefore noted how often this was, in practice, a problem. We found some cause for concern about this in just nine cases (6%). (This compares with 10% of cases made in care proceedings in the study by Hunt et al. 2007.) In most cases, relatives managed the tricky business of putting the children's needs first very well.

In four of these nine cases, social workers ended the placement because relatives allowed unsupervised contact with a parent, leading to two children being injured. In one other case a girl had been sexually abused by her father and the grandparents did not believe this had occurred and allowed her to see the father against her wishes. In two other cases, fathers who assaulted their children were banned from the carers' house and the carers were seen as acting appropriately to protect the children. Two young people were sexually abused or at risk from abuse during visits to the extended family with their kin carers, so the visits were stopped. In the great majority of cases, then, kin carers were able to keep the children safe from parents who might have placed them at risk.

The standard of care in the placements with kin

In most cases family and friends provided excellent care for the children. As we have seen, the files contained many accounts of children with difficult backgrounds thriving once they had moved to these placements. It was noticeable that a number of the young people looked after by relatives achieved GCSEs and went on to undertake further study, but exam results were not routinely recorded on files at that time. We also noted from the interviews that although financial constraints limited the activities of some children, a good number of others placed with kin were involved in a wide variety of leisure activities including sports, Beavers, gymnastics, weight training, dance and karate.

There were, however, 14 cases (10%) in the case file sample where the children's care was judged on our researcher ratings to be of a very poor standard. As already noted, these very unsatisfactory placements continued for significantly longer when they were with kin than with unrelated foster carers. It may be that these placements were allowed to continue precisely because they were with relatives, in which case the standards expected were allowed to fall considerably below those that would be accepted for other children. It may also be that the continuation of the placement occurred partly because of the lower levels of social work oversight afforded to these placements. Some examples will help to draw out these issues.

Two siblings were placed with their relatives because their mother was in prison. One of them did not return to the family after revealing, during respite care, his unhappiness and fear of his kin carers. Frank, who remained, was bullied and beaten by the carers. These concerns were reported to children's services by an aunt and their mother. After seven years in this family Frank returned to his mother where he blossomed and his school performance improved dramatically. The social worker commented on file that if the carers had not been relatives they would have been investigated long before.

Max did well with his kinship carers, getting GCSEs and going to college but his sister was profoundly unhappy and withdrawn and later disclosed inappropriate sexual behaviour from the relatives. Their father had reported his concerns on many occasions. This placement broke down after six years.

Eight-year-old Shane went to live with friends of his parents. He was unhappy and showed destructive and disturbed behaviour. All the family members were negative about him. When he was placed with respite carers, he changed considerably, his soiling stopped and he was happy at school. The social worker frequently questioned whether this was the right placement for Shane and called a meeting to discuss these concerns at which family work and training were planned. However, Shane's behaviour continued to be of concern and the placement was still continuing seven years later.

In the other cases, concerns included poor parenting, harsh discipline, unsafe housing, poor hygiene and inappropriate visitors to the house and, in some of these, when the children left the placement their behaviour and health improved noticeably. In one of these situations, the problems came to light only after a new social worker was allocated who took action to deal with the problems.

When we looked back, we found that eight of the carers in these 14 very unsatisfactory placements had been approved as foster carers, four had not because of concerns about standards of care (although in two, residence orders had been made instead) and in two cases we could not ascertain this from the case files. Foster carer approval, therefore, did not distinguish between these very unsatisfactory cases and others.

In addition to these 14 cases, there were two others where the kin carers (both approved as foster carers) had difficulty in maintaining appropriate boundaries with the children. One placement ended with an allegation that the uncle had physically abused his niece and, in the other, a series of supports were provided to assist the grandparents to manage their grandchildren. In a further four cases there were deficiencies in the placement although the overall standards of care were considered by the researchers to be acceptable.

Allegations of abuse or neglect

There were 12 allegations against kin carers, of which, as previously noted, six incidents were later substantiated and six were not. Only one allegation ended a kin placement although it was later found to be unsubstantiated. This was an allegation by a grandmother that the aunt and uncle carers had physically abused her grandson. He was then successfully placed with another aunt.

Of the six allegations that appeared to be well founded, one was of physical abuse by the kin carers to another child, one child alleged that her friend's mother had kicked her in an argument and one child was bullied by her carer. An aunt had bruised her niece on more than one occasion and a boy, after the placement ended, disclosed inappropriate sexual behaviour by his relatives. Similarly, a grandfather was found guilty of physically abusing his grandsons, when they too had disclosed the abuse after moving out of the placement.

Five other allegations against kin carers were judged at the time to be unfounded. They involved allegations of physical abuse and neglect by kin carers.

Six allegations were made against unrelated foster carers of which five were substantiated and one was not. One substantiated allegation of physical abuse, force-feeding and locking the children in the attic ended a placement. In one of the other founded allegations, the prospective adopters found marks that had been made when the child was tied to a chair and in the other the foster carers had beaten the younger child and treated him differently from their own son. The other allegations were of physical restraint and of emotional abuse and neglect. The unsubstantiated allegation was a mother alleging neglect by the foster carers.

It was interesting to find that substantiated allegations were made in similar proportions in the two types of placement (4% against both kin and unrelated foster carers) but not surprising, in the light of the interfamilial conflicts, that there were more unsubstantiated allegations made against kin (4%) as compared to unrelated foster carers (1%).

The placements that were ended by children's' services

As we have seen, in a few cases kin placements were assessed by children's services as unsuitable and placements not made or rapidly curtailed. Only a handful of ongoing placements with family or friends (5) were ended by social workers because of the inadequacy of the placement. In one, no action was taken until there was a change of social worker. She was concerned that the baby was under-stimulated, the house was dirty and unsafe and the kin carer was leaving the baby with her teenage daughter who was herself out of control.

Return to a parent

Children returned more often to a parent from unrelated foster carers (13% of cases in the case file sample) than from kin (6% of these cases). This was partly because, as we have seen, the placements with family and friends in our study were more often intended to provide a long-term home than an interim placement from which return could be effected. It may be that relatives do provide interim care more often than appears here, but that these arrangements are often informal and so would not appear in our sample (Brandon *et al.* 1999; Packman and Hall 1998). It is therefore interesting to consider the situations (9) in which return did occur.

In three cases, the kin placement was relatively short-term and the children returned to a parent after between six and seventeen months with kin carers. In two others, young people returned to a parent when a care order expired or they became pregnant.

In two cases, a form of shared care led to return. In one, when family pressures emerged in the placement, the grandmother left her husband and moved with her grandson to live with the mother. The child remained with his mother when the grandmother later returned to live with her husband. In the other, the mother shared the care of her children with their grandmother for six months while the mother came off drugs and the children then reverted to the mother's full-time care.

Occasionally, difficulties in the kin placement led to the children returning to a parent. In one such case a plan to return children to their father was brought forward after the uncle left the home and the aunt suffered a series of strokes.

Now that some of the pressures on placements, such as conflict during contact and allegations against the carers have been examined, we look next at the overall impact of the placements on the kin carers themselves.

The impact of looking after the children on the carers

Many of the carers had the satisfaction of seeing children flourish and thrive in their care. They also felt secure in the knowledge that they were providing an essential service to their family or friends and that they had obviated the need for the children to go into care and face an uncertain future (see also Broad *et al.* 2001). One couple were able to stop fertility treatment and focus on their niece.

However, the positives in caring for these children were bought at a high cost for many carers. Some were living in very overcrowded conditions where carers or their children had to give up or share their bedrooms. A few carers had moved house to accommodate the children, sometimes leaving behind places where they had been happy. Most struggled on low incomes to care for the new arrivals. Almost a third of the carers had health conditions, which made caring for children more difficult. Whilst unrelated foster carers plan to foster and this suits their life stage, for family and friends the idea of looking after someone else's children is neither planned nor expected. As a result, they made sacrifices and incurred losses to take the children. Several relatives gave up their jobs to look after the children and this reduced their income and their contact with colleagues who had become friends. This would also have an effect on their pension entitlement later on.

Many kin carers spoke to us about giving up their freedom. Grandparents had often just begun their retirement and had been enjoying going out with their friends and taking holidays. Taking on the children often meant foregoing holidays and postponing retirement indefinitely, so that the leisurely life they might have planned for their old age was never likely to be realised:

> We did have a life of our own, now he's retired. If we'd wanted we can go off to Tenerife – couldn't do that now, because the children are with us. You give up your freedom again don't you – time that you would normally have for yourself after your children are grown up. So yes, you lose that, and I do think you're giving up things but obviously you weigh that up. If you didn't want to do that then you'd say no, I won't have them.

> So we always said whatever happened we'd never have any children after we were 40, so by the time we got to 50-ish [it would] be our time. And we were working towards that – we'd done our duty, you know, we'd brought the children up. My asthma's a lot better down by the seaside, we lived at Seacliffe for a while, it was a lot better. So we were going to buy a little bungalow by the seaside.

> I was just getting used to the fact that I had nobody in the house – that's why we were going to downgrade because we didn't need it, it was only me and John. A nice little bungalow with a garage, and then I end up with three kids on my doorstep!

> This has been five years now almost exactly, last month, 20th of March [my son's] life crashed around us. Lost – yes the dreams that you had. And we realised that our freedom was then finished, but what do you do?

> I had the kids early, great, and then I can just get on with my life and have some fun. And I didn't expect to have my grandchildren. But that's just the way it goes, isn't it? I am resentful sometimes. I don't think any grandparent wouldn't say they were resentful.

A few grandparents admitted to feeling angry about having to take the children and some were guilty about these feelings.

Moreover, older kin carers, especially grandparents, could feel socially dislocated as they did not fit with other parents of the child's age who were younger, or with their own friends of the same age who no longer looked after dependent children.

> We don't fit in with other parents of children the same age or with friends the same age as us.

> Our friends haven't got young children now, they've got grandchildren but with grandchildren, you send them home at the end of the day, so if you want to go out for a meal then, you can. But we've got Steve. And our friends are older, they've got their grandchildren, they don't want our grandchild as well. Mind you they've been good – but sometimes it's nice to go out without children, it's

> nice to be able to go out and be who you'd like to be. And I just think, 'God is it ever going to end?'
>
> Now we've got to the stage, we've lost a lot of friends through it; we really have lost some good friends through it. Because Lawrence and Pam, our good friends, their sons were [our son's] age – well they're off their hands so they're doing what they want. We couldn't. Every time they phoned I've said I've got nobody to have Wendy.

This was particularly a problem if the child had severe behaviour problems and so could not be taken out readily to friends:

> You lose your friends because obviously you haven't got friends at our age with young children. You stop going out, you stop being asked to go out, you can't socialise with people. You become an outcast because you take this child along that they see as a monster and he absolutely wrecks every party, every barbeque, everything.

Some carers found that the time they were giving to the placed children diminished the time they could now spend with their adult children or with other grandchildren. They also lost out on the pleasures of being grandparents as they had to take on the parenting role with its requirement to be the disciplinarian:

> So I suppose you're more like a mum and dad than a grandma – it's like they say, the old saying is, well grandparents they can spoil them, it don't matter, because they hand them back. But if you're in the other situation, you can't hand them back can you. So you've got to be both really. But I suppose no, you go more like parents.
>
> I like being her nan. And I like it when I was a nan she used to come and lay on the top of the bed by me and we'd have a talk, and we'd laugh. But all that went out when I'd got her full-time. Because I've got to get her up, bath her, dress her. And it was a nightmare.

Another big loss was the ability to go out in the evenings. As we have seen, carers often went out very little once they were looking after the children:

> So now, my life, I don't get any social life… Your life alters, it definitely alters. I mean I've seen my sister in law, people going on coach trips and go away on holiday for five days you know, but I can't do none of that.
>
> Things drastically, dramatically changed. You couldn't afford to do things like we did before, because we just didn't have the money for it – you're going out, two adults, and five kids, to get them to the pictures you're talking about a month's wages to get into the pictures.

This was even more of an issue for single carers who could not rely on a partner to give them the occasional night off and could feel very lonely. A few relatives who very much enjoyed looking after children commented that they had never been without children, first their own, then their grandchildren and this seemed to suit them as long as they had support from their family or friends. On the other hand, some of the carers, especially the grandparents, found adjusting to looking after young children difficult and this was exacerbated when they took on a large sibling group.

Many found looking after children tiring when they were older, had less energy and more limited financial resources and commented on the constant demands of young children and of being:

> [a] mother all the time, 24 hours of the day. It's harder this time round, than when I was younger. It's harder.

Some carers were clearly under strain as a result of the difficult behaviour of the children they were looking after.

> He goes on and on and on and he wears me out. 'Cos he wears you out, he mentally wears you out. I do find it very frustrating, it's bloody hard work and I can honestly say the only time I really switch off from Ed is when he's, not even so much when he's gone away the weekend, more when he's asleep in his bed.

> I'm so stressed out – I can't relax. My mind is just so full of so much I need to do and find out, and it's getting to the point where I'm thinking, I'm going to bust soon. Sometimes I haven't coped very well because things do get on top of you and you just don't know what to do. So you just have to dig your way out of a pit. I can't bring them up for the next ten years or so knowing that I'm still going to have to fight to get their schooling sorted, fight to get them help with things, to fight every inch of the way to get them what they deserve.

In addition, three sets of kin in the interview sample were looking after children with profound disabilities, which affected their mobility and speech, one of whom also showed features of autistic behaviour. It made a difference if they attended foster carer meetings or had good friends with whom they could discuss these difficulties, but most did not.

It was clear that kin carers would carry on well beyond the point at which many foster carers would end the placement, and this combination of coping with extremely difficult behaviour and, in many cases, their own disabilities and ill health was a recipe for strain:

> How many grandparents in my condition would put up with a child as bad as what Sally is, and believe you me, when she was here first, she was really bad. Many a times I wanted to send her back, but I put it she's my grand-daughter, how would I feel by putting her back in?

> Vince'd been here a few years, and at one point, every day I was crying and my hair was dropping out on my head, my nerves were shot, they really were.

> We were too old, we had not got the energy to run round with him and do all these things with him and it was really difficult. And my sister came and my mum, but they saw him with us one day and they said 'You have done your best, you have tried your best' and they wanted to contact social services there and then and get them to come down and remove Vince. Because they feared for my health, well they feared for my life.

One grandmother described the extraordinary price she had paid for looking after her violent and destructive grandson:

> It's left us very bitter people. I mean I nearly lost my son, I nearly lost my husband, I nearly lost our home. I've lost a tooth, slipped two discs in my neck; I've now got problems with my neck for life. He slipped a disc in my back through kicking. I've got scars. Financially we're lower than low. And we will always be broke.

When we asked the kin carers about the stresses involved in family and friends care, some talked about the earlier difficulties of knowing that children were at risk when they were still with their parents and worrying about the children until action was taken to remove them. Waiting to hear whether residence orders would be granted had also been stressful.

Sometimes, the task of caring for the children was made more challenging because, as we have seen, a female relative had been charged with protecting the children from the male carer. Over the course of the placements, carers had to cope with additional events, such as a fire set by a child which devastated their home or broken windows when furious neighbours targeted the young person. Some struggled to pay off debts incurred either by young people or by the children's parents or tried to extricate a young person from the clutches of a drug dealer.

Things were made considerably more difficult when conflicts arose with members of the extended family, some of which turned into harassment, threats and violence. This in turn could jeopardise the carers' health and a number had moved house to escape such conflicts. Difficulties during contact were common and, as previously noted, supervising the contact of related parents could be a tricky task, requiring considerable diplomatic skills. Tensions with the children's parents frequently occurred and had a much more malicious and personal flavour than those that arose with unrelated foster carers.

Carers often had loyalties to the child's parent as well as to the child and sometimes felt torn between the needs of each. Some carers, as noted, also provided a lot of support to one or the other parent. However, ultimately they had to put the child's needs first, even if it meant turning their own adult child out of the home. One mother would pour out her troubles to the friends who were bringing up her son, and ignore her son on contact visits. Yet she was also jealous of the carers. As the friend carer said:

> He was sitting on the mat and he fell over and obviously started crying because he'd suddenly plopped over and I automatically went out to grab him but, because his mum was sitting right next to me, I was trying to hold back wondering if she was going. And then realised she wasn't. So I went to grab him and to stop me grabbing him she flung her arms around me and started crying to tell me all her troubles, because she wanted the attention and did not want him to have it.

An aunt described the support she gave to the child's mother:

> I personally think that it's more difficult to foster a child within the family because you've not only got the child's problems and needs and wants...but the child actually sees the parent more, which makes your job more difficult. And in the case of the child I've got now, his mum's got learning difficulties so it's almost like I'm her carer as well because she will phone me three or four times a day.

They were also aware that the children's growing attachment to them was painful for the parents to see:

> Even last year when we were playing down the park he fell off his bike and [his mother] was there and I know it hurt her but I couldn't do anything because he came to me and he wanted me and he didn't want her. And I know that sort of thing really must hurt, and I do feel sorry for her, but she has made her decision.

Grandparent carers were sometimes struggling with feelings of shame, loss, confusion or guilt about the difficulties of their adult children that had necessitated the children being removed from them. When these difficulties included prostitution, heavy drug use and even murder, their feelings could interfere with their capacity to care effectively. One grandmother said she could only manage by compartmentalising her feelings about her drug-taking daughter. Others were still grieving for the death of the children's parents, and had found it hard to move on. Two carers spoke of becoming depressed some time after the children moved in, and it seemed that their grandchildren's demands had interrupted their opportunity to grieve for the death of their own child, the children's parent:

> But yes it was all very traumatic in the beginning. Took us a long time to come out of it but we managed didn't we? We managed, because I think, we wanted to do it and the anger, it makes you go on and on you know. It was only afterwards that I collapsed, I had depression. I'm just feeling better now, five years on.

Some carers found that their marriage came under strain as a result of these abrupt changes in their circumstances, the difficulties presented by full-time child care and the complications of an 'interrupted life cycle' (Crumbley and Little 1997), such as when retirement was postponed and the task of child rearing taken up again. Such strains might not be recorded on case files but nonetheless the files reported as many as 10 per cent of the couple relationships as being under severe strain, with all but two of these breaking down, so this is likely to be an underestimate:

> It's put a strain on our marriage because you get tireder as you get older, and we're having to do things that we don't really want to do. We're having to go places we don't really want to. [Grandmother]

> Oh it was, clearly [putting strain on our relationship] because it's like, you should be free to do your own thing at fifty. Not that I begrudge our Sharon, I don't. But it was like we never had a night out, we never went for a meal together, anniversaries and things like that. We'd always got to take Sharon with us. We never had a private life. [Grandmother]

> So we would be getting into bed and it was like oh, you know, totally, totally exhausted weren't we? And our sexual relationship went out of the window, didn't it really? [Aunt]

A number of grandparent couples, as we have seen, included a step-grandparent who had no blood tie to the grandchildren and no experience of shared parenting with this partner. This could lead to disagreements about child care. A few grandmothers made quite elaborate arrangements to safeguard these second marriages, including living apart so that their partner was sheltered from the everyday care of the children.

A few kin carers felt upset or angry when a young person suddenly moved out to go to other friends or relatives without explanation, or the children they had been caring for were returned to their parents and they did not see this as appropriate.

Unfortunately, contact with children's services, whilst greatly appreciated by most carers, could also involve added pressure when social workers withheld needed services or pressed for carers to take out residence orders at a time when family conflicts were unresolved or the carers' support needs were unmet.

Advice to others

We asked the kin carers at the end of the interviews what advice they would give to others who might be considering looking after the children of relatives or friends. Several said that keeping the children in the family was better than letting them go into care, that they had been able to keep siblings together and that coming to a family member helped to keep the children's lives normal:

It's hard work but you get a lot of pleasure out of it and I think it would be better for a family member to look after them than to go somewhere else. [Grandmother]

I didn't want them going to homes, I didn't want them all split up. [Aunt]

I just think that if a child's taken away and they've experienced something traumatic, the first thing they're looking for is comfort and friendly faces, people that they know, people that they can turn to. [Aunt]

Quite a number of carers emphasised the pleasure of seeing the children grow up and do well and one friend carer said: 'I'd do it all over again'. A few said that it would have been easier if they had had training to help them manage the children and assist them to recover from their past experiences.

However, several carers also emphasised that looking after the children of a relative or friend was hard, could wear you out, was not something to be undertaken lightly and was something that you often did not want to do at that stage:

I would tell them it was a lot of hard work, 'cos you've got to be honest about it. [Grandmother]

I said I'll be honest with you, I didn't want my three. Sheila, I accepted Sheila. I said I didn't want the others, but I got a wife that said 'Yep, I'll take them on,' so I just felt it was my job to support her as much as I could. [Widowed grandfather]

It isn't something we wanted, I mean if you tell the truth it isn't what you wanted because your family's grown up and you think 'Oh I've got time back.' [Grandmother]

They emphasised that potential carers needed to take account of being older than when they had their own children and consider how they would ensure that an only child had plenty of contact with other children:

Think about it very carefully. I must admit I have, especially when times are bad because you do question if you're doing the right thing bringing the child up on your own. I know you can give the child a lot of attention. You also have to realise that you're a lot older than the child, you haven't got the energy, would it be better mixing with more children? I always take him out, we go to clubs, go to swimming clubs, we go all sorts, just to get him mixing because maybe it's not good that he's with an older person all the time. He needs to be with children of his own age. [Grandmother]

They also highlighted the importance of thinking about the effect on their own children:

I would tell them to look very carefully, and I would tell them to think first of their own house and just say well look, if you've got kids of your own, think what you're doing to your own kids. [Aunt]

> And if you can still maintain your relationship with your own children whilst you're dealing with other children that may have severe problems, and how your children feel about it as well. Because a lot of it was, even though the kids really liked the boys and stuff, there has been times when they've gone 'Oh I wish they wasn't here.' [Grandmother]

Many of the carers placed particular emphasis on the importance of sorting things out with children's services before taking the children, not being hood-winked into applying for a residence order and ensuring that enough support was in place for both the carers and children:

> Social services-wise, then if I'd have known what was going to be going on, defi-nitely would have sorted it out before the boys came, I wouldn't have let the wool be pulled over my eyes like I have. I've asked for guidelines on how someone becomes a caring relative as opposed to a foster carer and how they determine that, and how especially they determine it for somebody who's clearly not related to either of the children. [Step-mother]

> Make sure that there is a support package in place before you did it. The rewards are absolutely fantastic but don't try doing it on your own, especially if it is a dif-ficult child. Make sure that you've got some support there. If you need any finan-cial support, make sure that is all done beforehand and I would say to anybody is to get everything that they are told in writing. [Step-grandmother]

> [I'd advise them] to ask a lot of questions. What help would you give them if they wanted a bit of a break? Because taking on somebody else's child full-time is hard. And like, financially if you're on a low wage and what backup you could give, psychological help, like if the child needs counselling through being taken away from its mum. Not just sit and talk to them but give them professional help that helps them explain it all to them. Because Neerosh blamed me for every-thing: I was the wicked nan when she first came. I took her away from her mum. [Grandmother]

> There'd have to be a stipulation that these children would be treated if they need treatment, and if I say that there's a problem that they have to get it sorted straight away. Like I say, I do believe that because I'm a grandparent the children are sort of put on the shelf and they don't get the full extent. [Grandmother]

A couple of carers were not sure that they would recommend anyone to become a kin carer because of the difficulties presented by the child's mother or the lack of support from children's services:

> I wouldn't always recommend that a child is placed within a family unit, because you've got the other pressures, which makes your job doubly difficult. If [the mother] backed me up, that could have more of an impact for Hugh growing up than [instead the mother says] 'Well that's it, I'm going to speak to Janice. How

dare she?' See the difference? That is not backing me up, that's just tearing me apart. [Janice, friend carer]

Summary

Many children with family and friends enjoyed regular contact with members of their extended family, particularly those on the same side (maternal or paternal) of the family as the relative with whom they lived. Contact with parents, however, was often less harmonious, especially if the parents resented seeing their children brought up by those particular relatives or friends. When parents were hostile, they sometimes made active efforts to undermine the kin placements, for example making abusive telephone calls or more rarely false allegations or threats of violence. Whilst on the whole kin carers managed such contact difficulties extremely well, there were a number of cases where more social work intervention was needed either to supervise contact or to place boundaries around parents' contact with their children. However, the level of social work involvement with contact issues was not very high and kin carers bore the brunt of these difficulties. Some children too were distressed by contact with their parents, and in three cases contact with a parent was terminated on the advice of a specialist.

The great majority of kin carers were able to protect children from their parents and only 6 per cent failed to do so. However, the researchers judged that 10 per cent of the kin placements were of a very poor standard and, as previously noted, such very unsatisfactory placements continued for significantly longer when they were with kin, than when children were with unrelated foster carers.

Whilst unrelated foster carers plan to foster and this suits their life stage, for kin the idea of looking after someone else's children is neither planned nor expected. As a result, they make sacrifices and incur losses to take the children. Several relatives gave up their jobs to look after the children, reducing their income and their pension entitlement. Ten per cent of the couple carers found that their marriages came under severe strain as a result of these abrupt changes in their circumstances, with all but two of these breaking down.

Moreover, older kin carers could feel socially dislocated as they did not fit with parents of the child's age or with their own friends who no longer looked after dependent children. They also lost out on the pleasures of being grandparents as they had to take on the parenting role with its requirement to be the disciplinarian and they lost out on friends, holidays and social activities. Many found looking after children tiring when they were older, had less energy and had limited financial resources. Some too had other caring responsibilities for their own elderly parents or a sick partner. As a result, some kin carers came under severe strain.

Grandparent carers were sometimes struggling with feelings of loss and guilt about the difficulties of their adult children which had necessitated the children being removed from them or because they had been unable to take on a full sibling group. Others were still grieving for the death of the children's parents. Tensions with the children's parents and members of the extended family made caring for the children considerably more difficult. Thus, the satisfaction of seeing children do well or at least not go into care were bought at a high personal cost for some kin carers.

Many of these issues have implications for policy and practice, which we address in the concluding chapter.

Now that the placements have been examined from the perspective of the kin carers, we will consider in the next chapter how the placements were viewed by the social workers, children and their parents.

Chapter 9

The Perspectives of the Social Workers, Children and Parents on Kinship Care

The social workers

Interviews were conducted with the social workers responsible for 16 of the children whose carers we had interviewed. Thirteen were women and three were men. One of the male workers was African-Caribbean and was responsible for a young person of mixed ethnicity and another was Asian and was the worker for two white children. The other two children of mixed ethnicity in the group had white social workers. Over a third of the social workers (6) were aged 21 to 39, half (8) were 40 to 51 with two aged 60 or over. Five of the workers were in Leaving Care teams. The children and young people for whom they were responsible ranged in age from 2 to 19. Some were placed alone and others lived with siblings, including one sibling group of four children and another of six. The interviews elicited the social workers' experiences of the kin placements for which they were responsible and also their general views on kinship care.

The social workers' general views about placements with family and friends
THE ADVANTAGES AND DISADVANTAGES OF KINSHIP CARE

In the interviews we asked the social workers for their general views of placements with family and friends. All of them saw a range of advantages in these placements including maintaining a child's sense of identity, culture and belonging; the normality of the situation as compared with the stigma of being looked after; having a shared history with family members who know the child's back-

ground and can answer questions about it later on and children's positive attitudes to being with relatives and knowing that a family member cares about
them. Several of the workers mentioned the high levels of commitment of the
carers to the children and that kin carers persevere where ordinary foster carers do
not. Just one worker mentioned using kinship care to work towards returning
children to their parents.

A number of potential disadvantages were also noted. These included
passing on negative family traditions or dysfunction; the possibility of collusion
and of alliances forming between relatives and parents against the social worker;
the lack of social work control over contact, especially where a parent has un-
limited access to the children in the carer's home and conflicts between the carer
and other family members which are then difficult to mediate. One example of
such conflict occurs when a parent blames the grandparents for their own poor
upbringing:

> Because we do tend to get quite a lot of grandparents looking after children who
> haven't parented that well themselves. Partly the reason why their children can't
> parent is because of the way they were parented themselves. And then we turn
> round and put the children with the grandparents, who the adult children blame
> for why they are the way they are! That's really tricky, and puts a lot of conflict
> between people. And understandably birth parents find that very difficult to
> cope with.

Other disadvantages were carers' poor financial circumstances, kin carers feeling
under pressure to take children (especially during care proceedings) or taking on
more children than they could manage. The social workers also mentioned the
difficulties of working with carers who did not like to be told what to do or, more
specifically, did not seek social work permissions for overnight stays.

ASSESSMENTS

Several social workers considered that it would be better if family placement
workers (or specialist kinship workers) conducted the assessments of kin carers,
partly because they were independent of the family, whereas the children's
social workers sometimes had pre-existing relationships with the carers. This
arrangement was also thought to be preferable because the assessments were
time-consuming and there could be several relatives to assess, some of whom
could be geographically distant, and because of the greater experience and exper-
tise of family placement workers who nonetheless rarely gave field workers any
help or advice with this task:

> It's not always appropriate for the child's social worker to be doing that assess-
> ment. And yet our fostering team won't do it…but certainly my experience on

district is you get no help, advice or work from the fostering team. It's the social worker who holds the case has got to do it. And so in a way that might be a reason why sometimes it doesn't happen, because it is a big piece of work and it's an important piece of work.

This social worker admitted that work pressures could militate against making kin placements when children's social workers are left to do the assessments (see Waterhouse and Brocklesby 1999).

It was generally considered that it was appropriate to be a little more flexible about the standards expected of kin carers than would be the case with unrelated foster carers, in relation for example to bedroom sharing, carers' past offences or difficulties with the carers' own children. An example of such discretion was one assessment where it had emerged that the grandfather's sister had alleged inappropriate touching by her brother when they were children, which she later explained as experimentation. This was fully examined by the worker and at the Fostering Panel and the carers were approved notwithstanding. On the other hand, it was thought that age or the fact that relatives could not stand up to the parents or put the child's needs first would mean that carers were not approved. It could, however, be problematic when relatives were already caring for a child or had assumed that they would be approved, if approval was then withheld. Whilst it was thought that a few relatives found the assessment intrusive, only one worker considered that the six week assessments that were usually undertaken with Regulation 38 carers were insufficiently rigorous.

WHETHER KIN PLACEMENTS WERE THE FIRST OPTION

The social workers said that they always looked first to place a child with their relatives, but some added that they did not always know of possible relatives at that point:

Well in theory, yes [it's the first option in placing a child], but it doesn't quite always work like that. Because sometimes it takes time for other family members to realise the situation, because it's not always obvious to them. And it takes time for them perhaps to come forward.

The general picture seemed to be responding to relatives who presented themselves rather than actively searching out possible kin carers:

If a relative comes forward and that relative has the ability to care for a child, or you feel strongly that that person has the ability to care for a child then you would go through the avenues of looking and checking through. So yes, we would consider – but not necessarily give priority to in the first instance. You have to be absolutely certain that it is right for the child. It might not be right because of family dynamics that could be quite damaging.

THE ADEQUACY OF SUPPORT AND FINANCIAL HELP

Interestingly, over half of the social workers (9) thought that enough support and financial help was provided for kin carers and asserted that the same services were offered as to unrelated foster carers.

The remainder (7) considered that insufficient support and financial assistance were provided. They gave examples of the lower levels of allowances and support and the difficulty in getting services for children with kin:

> Because you do the assessment, you go to Panel. Then if it's approved the fostering admin set up the payments. That's it! Nothing else whatsoever. There's no support.

> I've made several referrals [for community mental health support] and things like that for this particular girl that is placed with her grandparents – and I think their priority has actually been decreased because she is actually not in local authority care – and it's only since grandfather's made a complaint about the department that she's actually been seen as a priority. She was referred [six years ago] and she's only just had an appointment come through, so it's been quite a long struggle.

> Caring relatives don't get a link worker, as like local authority foster carers get to support them. And sometimes I think I find myself taking on that role as well, because if they've got a problem or something like that then they pour their heart out to me. But I do think that they need someone.

> There's no specific [foster carer] group for them, like the fostering service get, and they don't get the support services from the fostering team. The only support they get is from the district social worker…they don't access any of the training.

> It is a massive contentious issue that caring relatives aren't entitled to holiday grant, birthday grants and things like that, what normal foster carers get…and this frustrates not only social workers but caring relatives as well. I really don't know [why it is], because [the carer] is probably doing a better job than most foster carers with the way she's turned Dan around.

> I would like to see them treated more as actual foster carers, because they are doing the same job. Sometimes perhaps made more difficult because of the links with the family. They've got that extra stress haven't they?

Some social workers made it clear that they thought that their local authority regarded kin carers as a 'cheap option':

> I think one of the reasons why we looked at family as a first port of call is because it's financially less costly.

They also felt that kin carers were undervalued:

> I think they are very under-valued, caring relatives. They don't get the accolade that the foster carers get, and yet they do a better job.

A number of workers commented that, unlike non-related foster carers, not only did kin carers not know what resources might be available but nor did many of the children's social workers themselves, since they were not experienced in family placement work. One worker said candidly that social workers did expect kin carers to manage without much support:

> So long as they can access resources, I guess there may be an expectation from some social workers that you kind of let them get on with it. The thing with foster carers is they're in a stronger position and they can say, well actually, I'm entitled to x, y, z. Whereas birth family people don't necessarily know that and may not be told that. If they already know the child I think that social workers do kind of assume a little bit that they're going to be able to cope a bit better than a foster carer that doesn't know the child at all.

Another worker explained frankly that her team manager had told her that her role with kin carers was a strictly limited one:

> I remember the team manager saying that as far as families go, we don't really have an awful lot to do with them – except if there is a crisis or something goes wrong and then we sort of go down.

The social workers' views about the study placements
FINANCES

When we asked how well the carers in the study were managing financially we found that:

> six of the 16 workers had no idea how much they were paid or whether it was enough: 'I don't know how much it is, I don't get involved in the budget.'

> I wouldn't have a clue how much that is …I don't really know [how adequate it was] because I don't know what it was. [The carer] never complained to me that it wasn't.

> I don't know really [if the carers are managing financially]. They're a pretty poor family, they haven't got much money between them, but they're a typical lower working class family. If they're struggling they can come to us for financial support.

The other workers knew more and, of these, over half considered that the carers were managing financially (6) whilst the remainder said they were not (4).

Where social workers were aware of the carers' financial difficulties, they often commented on the inherent inequity of providing lower allowances for kin carers:

I think financially as well we let caring relatives down. I do think that our caring relatives are quite hard done by actually.

I think they struggle yeah, because she has to save up to buy him a winter coat, so yeah definitely they do struggle day to day.

Social workers described how they had had to plead with their managers for small amounts of financial assistance for carers. One very disturbed boy was always asking his grandparents for things that they could not afford and it led to many arguments, so that their financial difficulties were having a direct effect on their already compromised ability to care for their grandson.

THE SUPPORTS AND SERVICES PROVIDED

The social workers described a range of services that they had organised. These included referrals to CAMHS, counsellors and psychologists, an enuresis clinic, a Young Carers' group, a Play Scheme and respite care. Five workers had also provided financial help with items such as beds, school uniforms and glasses, although this had not been easy. As one said: 'It was just like trying to jump through hoops just to get that couple of quid to help.' The Leaving Care workers provided help with job seeking, activities and accommodation as needed.

A few workers had become actively engaged in finding out what the carers and children needed but others responded only to specific requests for help, even though the carers rarely knew what services might be available: 'I can only go on what they've requested really.'

Moreover, many of the kin carers did not like to ask for help. Two workers were particularly sensitive about how difficult this was for them:

They have had to ask for it which I think is quite a shame really, because they don't like asking, you know. They feel quite terrible asking, which is why they are grateful with anything.

They generally don't ask for things. You have to suggest them.

Those carers who had successfully applied for residence orders on the children did not have any social work involvement, except one grandparent couple who were caring for a very large sibling group. It was expected that they would access any services that the children needed through their GPs, as would anyone else in the community.

Few of the workers had been involved at the start of the placement. The two who had, said that the kin carers had needed a lot of support at the beginning of the placement as there were so many adjustments to make and so much new information to absorb.

It was noticeable that, with a few exceptions, the workers described their involvement with the kin carers as not very demanding, not a priority, cases that 'ticked over quite nicely.' Three of them commented on how pleasant it was to visit the family:

He's been a joy to work with and his carers too. I went to visit them a few weeks back and it was lovely, it was just a proper slice of family life…you know, just a typical family life, very promising to see really.

THE SOCIAL WORKERS' INVOLVEMENT WITH THE CARERS AND CHILDREN

Most of the social workers said that they visited every six to eight weeks and focused their attention on the children, speaking to the carers only briefly at the start and end of these visits. The Leaving Care team workers in particular saw themselves as there for the young people rather than the carers. The workers had made efforts to make relationships with the children and often took them out in order to spend time alone with them. Nonetheless, very few thought that the children would have contacted them if they had any worries.

Five of the 16 workers were also providing support for the carers. One of them commented that she tried to take on the family placement worker role with the carers but that her priorities were sometimes then divided between the child and the carers:

Sometimes if there are difficulties…you're the child's social worker…it's very difficult to do that bit [helping the carer] as well.

However, even amongst these five, two provided a rather limited service to the carers. One worker was visiting children who were subject to residence orders and duly defined her role very narrowly:

I'm not really actively involved with the case – my role is just there purely as a sounding board for the grandparents.

The other social worker was dealing with an extremely strained kin carer but kept her involvement to a minimum when things were difficult, saying:

I mean things are pretty stressed at the moment but I mean I tend not to visit at times like this because she is just so all over the place. When things settle down again she gives me a call and then I arrange to go out, discuss things – if things aren't going very well then I do sort of tend to stand back.

This attitude seemed to be in part because there were major concerns about the male carer's failing health but appeared not to take full account of the extent of the desperation this carer felt about managing a child with major emotional and behavioural problems.

CONTACT

Most of the social workers were well aware of the contact issues for these children and their carers but, on the whole, they were no longer live issues and none were involved in supervising contact. Those contact issues that were recent or current were of a somewhat different character to those common in unrelated foster care. They included one young person who was visiting her mother daily in secret to get round her grandmother's limits on her contact, an issue the social worker hoped to tackle; and a father who had refused to maintain contact as long as his children lived with these relatives. Although the social workers were aware of conflicts between the carers and parents, they rarely intervened.

REVIEWS

When children had six-monthly reviews they were described as broadly useful and as similar to those for any looked after child. However, it emerged that the birth parents very rarely attended so the issues that had been raised in the carers' interviews about how difficult it could be to talk frankly when parents were present, did not arise. One social worker had found reviews difficult in the grandmother's house, as there were frequent visitors. It was at the reviews, when consideration was given to plans for permanence, that recommendations were often made to encourage carers to apply for residence orders. One worker commented that the encouragement for kin carers to apply for residence orders was in order to reduce their dependence on children's services.

THE SOCIAL WORKERS' VIEWS OF THE PLACEMENTS

The great majority of the social workers were very positive about the placements and the kin carers and described them in glowing terms:

> They're just exemplary really. The children have done extraordinarily well.

> The love and devotion that they give this child is second to none.

> Excellent placement. The carers have a high commitment to the children. They'd fight tooth and nail for them.

> It's amazing. It's really, really good.

They also described the sensitive ways in which kin carers dealt with the children, including undertaking Life Story work and helping a behaviourally difficult boy, who could not talk about his feelings, to express them on paper and so share them with his carer. There were few complaints about difficulties arising from the generation gap between grandparents and their grandchildren.

There were just two placements in this group of 16 about which the workers had concerns. In one, the grandmother who was the carer and another relative who lived nearby were very hostile to the children's mother. They would shout, use bad language and 'slag her off' in front of the children. The grandmother also restricted the children's contact with their mother unnecessarily. Things the social worker said would be misinterpreted in the struggle between the grandmother and the mother and both would criticise the worker. In addition, the mother would sometimes condone behaviour of which the grandmother disapproved. The social worker considered that the children would have been better off placed elsewhere:

> The dysfunctional situation that exists has just been carried on from generation to generation and that's where I would feel that it is not the best thing for them to remain within this home.

At the same time, the worker acknowledged the positives in this placement:

> [The grandmother] genuinely cares about Matt and Jo and has got their best interests at heart and that's the good thing about children staying with their own family. She's persevered and she's carried on and she doesn't give up easily.

This case illustrates how difficult it is to work in such entrenched family situations:

> Out of all my cases, I found the Chatwin family the most difficult family to work with because of all the dynamics going on between the adults. And the children were sort of stuck in the middle. It was a huge problem.

A second social worker had concerns that the child was receiving too little one-to-one attention from a friend carer who was seen as looking after the child mainly to meet her own emotional needs.

Now that the views of the social workers have been considered, we turn to those of the children.

The children

We conducted interviews with 16 of the children who lived with kin. Eleven were living with their grandparents (eight couples and three single grandparents), three with an aunt and uncle and two with friends (one with his step-mother and the other with the parents of a school friend). All but two were still living with their carers. One young man aged 19 had just moved to his own flat with the assistance of his Leaving Care team social worker, because his aunt and uncle, who had brought him up since the age of five, were moving out of the city. One young woman of 13 had returned to live with her parents. The children were divided fairly evenly between the age groups 7–10 (5), 11–15 (5) and 16–20 (6). Nine were girls and seven were boys.

How the children had come to live with their relatives or friends

When asked how they had come to live with kin, some children were too young to recall the event or recalled just that it was 'scary' going somewhere new. A few recalled elements of the events, such as 17-year-old Jason who knew that he was about to go on holiday abroad with his mother when he ended up staying with his grandparents, but he did not know why this had happened. Tim, aged 19, explained that his mother had found it hard to look after him, that her marriage had broken up and that his aunt and uncle had taken him under their wing and been just like a mum and dad to him. An 18-year-old girl said that at the social worker's suggestion she had been placed with the parents of her friend, initially for a couple of days but she had stayed five years. A 10-year-old girl gave a vivid account:

> Researcher: Can you remember, did your social worker ask you where you wanted to live?
>
> Child: No, she just knocked on everyone's door. They goes 'No', and finally my Gramp said, 'Yes,' in his house. I felt really relieved 'cos I wanted to live with someone. So I felt really relieved.

One 12-year-old boy, who four years previously had left a foster family to live with his grandparents, saw the move as 'Nan's idea' but had no understanding of the reason: 'It's my Nan's idea – let me live here and all that'.

A 15-year-old girl said that she had very recently been told why she was living with her grandfather, after her lack of understanding had emerged at a statutory review:

> Young person: All I remember is just going through social services with my mum first off, and just coming here to live and I've only just found out the reason why I come to live here.
>
> Researcher: Right, so what was the reason?
>
> Young person: Something to do with my mum couldn't cope or something and that's all they keep telling me. Just she can't cope because she was on her own and she was looking after me and my little sister and everything, and so I came to live with Nan and Grandad, and that's all I really know.

A small number of children mentioned some of the difficulties at home that were connected with their placement, although most did not. For example, one young man recalled the violence of his mother's partner and how he had tried to intervene by attacking him with a fork and a 17-year-old girl spoke of her mother's mental health problems.

The two children whose main parent had died (one a father, the other a mother) knew that this was the reason they had been looked after by their grandparents and two other children gave a reason for their need for care. Most children, though, either came up with no reason or said explicitly that they did not understand what had led them to leave their parents. For example, a 14-year-old girl explained it as follows:

Researcher: So what did you tell your friends and so on, about where you were living?

Child: Well I tried to explain to them, like, everything what was going on, where I was living, because I just reckon that they'd ask me a question which would... so I just told them the whole story so that they wouldn't keep on asking. But then they'd always ask why I went into care, and I don't know. I just don't know.

Researcher: So that's not something anybody's ever talked to you about?

Child: No, no one's ever told me.

Researcher: Is that something you'd want to know more about?

Child: I did want to know. I don't care now because it doesn't particularly affect me. It affects Judy [younger sister] though. I know she still wants to know.

Similarly, a boy of 16 said that 'a load of people that I know, friends and at school' ask him why he lives with his grandparents. He had asked his grandmother to explain but 'She said I'm not old enough to find out yet.'

When asked where they had wanted to live at the time, some children said that they had partly wanted to live with their parents and partly with the kin carers; or looking back they thought that probably they had wanted to be with the kin carers with whom they were living. One girl who had subsequently returned to her father said that she had wanted to be with him but at the same time had not wanted to leave her aunt and uncle.

A few young people compared their circumstances with their current kin carers with their previous experiences. One boy of 10 said there were fewer rules with his friend carer than with his previous foster carers; whilst a 15-year-old boy said that he preferred his grandmother's disciplinary methods to his mother's.

Relationships with their carers

Most of the children had close relationships with their carers and said, when asked to whom they felt closest, that it was to one or both of them. One girl of 10 said that she was closest to her five-year-old sister with whom she shared the placement, whilst others included a cousin or brother as well as their carers. One boy of 10, who was close to his friend carer, mentioned that he did not get on with her 13-year-old daughter. A girl of 18 who was living with her school friend's parents said:

> I get on really brilliant with them. Oh, she's lovely; she really is! She treats me like one of her own daughters. She's a lovely woman.

Just one boy of 12, who said that he got on with his grandparents but that they sometimes argued about his brother, added a caveat:

> They are OK – not as good as Mum. I want to go and live with Mum again but she is going to move to Greentown and then I would miss my friends here. I miss living with Mum. I've got the smallest room in the house.

A teenage girl who had returned to her father said that her aunt and uncle had yelled at her, favoured her younger sister and in the end had 'chucked her out' as the placement was not working. However, she said that when it was good it had been 'really nice' living there. She added that even so, she would have liked her own room and more money. This 14-year-old complained about having to economise:

> It was really annoying because she used to drag me in and out of charity shops, and I'd be like, why are we doing this? We can afford normal stuff.

This girl and another 17-year-old both mentioned financial issues. The 17-year-old explained that since her grandmother had died she had had a number of arguments about money and that she was always asking her grandfather for pocket money. She said that she was worried that she would 'go down the wrong path' like her mother. It appeared that the family had functioned better when her grandmother was alive and some of the difficulties had become focused around money. Another young person had also had worries about money since his grandfather had been in hospital and the arrangements for his pocket money were no longer working. Given the financial difficulties of many carers it is not surprising that this can become an issue, particularly with teenagers (see also Broad *et al.* 2001; Daly and Leonard 2002; Doolan *et al.* 2004; Middleton *et al.* 1994).

Confidantes

We asked the children and young people who they would talk to if something was worrying them. Of the ten who answered this question, six mentioned their kin carers and sometimes others as well, such as other relatives. The other four named other confidantes who were generally other family members. For example, one boy of 15 who was living with his grandparents chose his aunt and an older sister, while another boy who had left his aunt and uncle chose his grandmother and his cousins, and a 17-year-old living with grandparents confided in her friends or her aunt. Two children mentioned their social worker, one mentioned a child psychiatrist she was seeing and two children said they would talk to their mothers as well as their grandparent carers.

Contact with parents and other relatives

The children were asked if they saw their parents or other relatives. Their replies emphasised the importance to them of their relationships with parents and the wide range of relatives with whom many maintained links. One boy of 17, whose file had shown that he had been affected by his parents' lack of interest in him, now had regular visits from his mother and his half-sister, because his grandmother had made the arrangements and provided transport, but he had no contact with his father:

> Ever since I was four my dad asked my mum to marry him and move to London, and she said no, so he just moved. And if he was that worried or bothered about me, he could have kept in contact just to make sure or something, but he obviously wasn't worried…but that doesn't mean that I've got to have the same attitude.

In contrast, in two cases children's fathers (and in one case also the uncle) lived with the carers' families, so the children saw them frequently. One was a seven-year-old who said that she did not like her father's method of discipline, which was shouting at them. She also saw her mother monthly and found this contact 'a bit funny' but 'quite nice.' A variation on this situation of regular contact with family members was that of a 14-year-old girl who had lived with her aunt and uncle and seen her grandmother daily as she took her to school and met her afterwards to allow her carers to work. In addition, regular contact with her parents had gradually led to weekends and she later returned to them. A quite common situation (as noted earlier) was for children to see their aunts, uncles and cousins frequently as part of the day-to-day contact with the extended family.

Other children saw their parents less frequently, for example one boy only saw his mother three times a year. He wanted to see more of his sister and his former foster carers, with whom he had lived before moving to his grandparents. Some children wanted to see more of their parents. Nine-year-old Marie lived with her separated grandmother, saw her father three times a week and her grandfather and his new partner on some weekends. However, she had not seen her mother for three years because she was in a psychiatric hospital and her social worker thought it would upset her. She disagreed.

One girl of 10, who saw her mother weekly, expressed a longing to be closer to her mother when she said that she would like to see her every day:

> 'Cos I love her so much. And I don't want to lose her for all the rest of my life.

When asked where she would really like to live she said with both her grand-mother and her mother.

Sophie, a girl of 11, saw her mother regularly and said that she was lovely and 'one of the best.' She did not see her sister who was in foster care, nor her violent father, who social workers believed had probably sexually abused her. She declared: 'I absolutely hate my Dad…he's nasty.'

As they grew older, some young people had formed rather closer relation-ships with a parent by making their own arrangements to see them or had started to want to get to know a parent who had been out of contact. For example, the young man who had just moved to his own flat was seeing more of his mother who had learning difficulties, now he could come and go as he pleased. A 17-year-old girl living with her grandfather had become closer to her mother after her grandmother died and she now saw her father regularly too. Carl, a 16-year-old boy wanted to see his mother whom he did not know and his grand-mother was making arrangements for this to happen.

Only one child (a boy of 10) who was living with a family friend had no contact with his parents or other relatives. He said he would like to see his father, whom he had not seen since he was a baby.

Two children expressed real sadness about never having had contact with a sibling. Sixteen-year-old Carl did not want to see his father who frightened him but he said that he thought all the time about a younger brother, who had been adopted years earlier and whom he had never known. A boy of 12, who was lonely and bored living with his grandparents, regularly saw his siblings who were in foster care and his mother monthly. He talked in an idealising way about returning to live with his mother, who he thought was looking for a bigger house so they could all get back together. He had an idea of 'things being back to normal,' which included his older brother who had died in infancy being part of the family. Both of these children were somewhat isolated and seemed to be expressing a longing for closer connection to their birth family and to have more friends.

The children's overall relationships with others

We asked children to fill in an ecomap. The child was in the centre and they wrote the names of other people in their lives, placing those who were closest or most important in the inner circles and others in the outer circles. We did this to help to explore children's relationships and particularly how they saw those with their parents and kin carers.

Four of the ten children who did this placed both their current carers and a parent in the innermost circle – often adding to the same circle siblings who lived with them or elsewhere. Two of these children started by placing their carers closest to them and only added a parent equally close as an afterthought later in the exercise. Four of the children placed their carers closest to them and a parent further away.

The girl who had expressed a longing for her mother placed her mother and partner closest to her, with her grandparent carers and siblings a little further away. The teenage girl who had returned to her parents placed them closest to her and put the carers, with whom she had previously lived, some distance away.

Relationships with social workers

The children were mostly very enthusiastic about their current or former social workers (see also Aldgate and McIntosh 2006; Altshuler 1999). One young man of mixed ethnicity now had a black Leaving Care worker who had helped him in planning his career and had previously had an African-Caribbean social worker who had seen him fortnightly and undertaken activities to connect him to his heritage. Another Leaving Care team worker had been very helpful in finding a flat for a young person. Children recalled social workers to whom they could talk, whom they could ring if they were worried and who took them out to do activities. One young woman was very pleased because the social worker had organised contact with her brother and often telephoned her, whilst another child recalled two social workers she had not liked and two who had been 'OK'.

However, one young woman was concerned that her separated grandfather had been trying to ring the social worker for two weeks without success and added 'nobody's bothered.' She wanted to see her social worker more often and talk to her about her arguments with her grandfather. In addition, one girl was very concerned that her social worker was planning to move her from her kin placement when she did not want to leave.

Seven children had no memories of having a social worker although one spoke of seeing a counsellor in the early days of the placement but had felt like it was 'telling tales about Mum.'

The children's friendships and bullying

Most of the children had plenty of friends but a few seemed rather isolated. For example, one boy of 16 had just left school and none of his school friends lived nearby, so that he mostly stayed in. He was waiting for his exam results and had not succeeded in finding any work. Another boy of 12, who lived alone with his grandparents, said he did not have many friends to play with near him and contrasted this with the large foster family where he had lived previously in which there were a lot of other children. Similarly, a 12-year-old boy who lived with his grandparents and younger brother and who felt lonely, looked back wistfully to the foster placement he had left at the age of four where there were many other children and he had had plenty of friends.

A number of the children said that they had been bullied (see also Broad *et al.* 2001). One boy had been bullied at school because he was black but this had been stopped. A teenage girl had been so badly bullied, with name calling and attempts to trip her on the stairs, that she had been moved to a Tuition Centre. She put it down to her family's reputation going before her. The isolated school leaver also spoke of severe bullying which had been reported to the police. The lonely 12-year-old also recalled being bullied when he was younger.

A few children described bullying arising because other children had discovered that relatives were bringing them up. One young woman said that her brother's friends had taunted him with living with 'old fogeys' who expected him to return home early in the evenings.

Activities and exams

Seven of the younger children mentioned clubs and activities that they attended. These included playing football, body-popping (dancing) at clubs, helping the local rugby team, playing in the school basketball team, fishing with a grandfather, making model cars and attending a church youth club. Another two young people had part-time jobs and one was learning to drive. The other seven young people did not tell us about any activities or hobbies.

One young man had achieved seven GCSEs and another was awaiting the results of his six exams. Three of the young people had left school and were attending college, one after being Head Girl. Two others were planning to go to college or university to study vocational subjects. One young man had a steady job even though his abilities were limited. These findings are similar to those of Broad and his colleagues (2001), who found that young people living with kin were keen to get qualifications and had a clear idea about future employment.

The children's views of their placement

Most of the children were positive about their placements. One 17-year-old put it this way:

Researcher: Where would you like to be living? What do you think you would have said at that point [when you moved to your grandparents]?

Young person: I think I would have said, I would like to be living with my mum, but I'm glad that I'm with my nan and granddad because I know that I'm not going to be going anywhere, because as they're getting on, old and that, and they're settled down, and they're happily married, and they've got a home and they've got money to pay for it, and they've got cars. And they bought a lot of stuff for me, because I left all my stuff over my mum's flat.

This young man added that living with his grandparents had helped him to grow up and that he had learned a lot from them. Similarly, the young man who had moved into his own flat said of living with his aunt and uncle 'It was really good, I really enjoyed it there.'

When asked, if they could choose, where they would most like to be living, most named the kin carers with whom they were living. Even the young person who was having arguments with her grandfather and missing her grandmother who had died, was nonetheless positive about her current living arrangements.

Two children however were less positive. Simon who had gone to live with his grandparents after his mother died said that it was 'Sometimes good and sometimes not so good' and spoke of having arguments with his younger sister. Nonetheless, he said he was quite happy where he was. Julian who was 12 said that he had been living with his grandparents since he was four and so was used to it. However, he thought it got worse as he got older. There were no other children in the area and nothing to do so he was very bored. Julian seemed somewhat depressed and anxious. He was the boy who idealised his mother and imagined going to live with her. He had started seeing a worker at the local CAMHS, so it appeared that his unhappiness was being addressed.

Depression

Fourteen out of the 16 children completed a depression questionnaire (Kovacs and Beck 1977). Most of the children (8) showed no signs of depression but six did. Three showed some signs (scores of 9 to 18) and another three showed significant depression at the level that requires intervention (scores of 19 and over).

The young people who were somewhat depressed included one young woman who had separated from her husband leaving her in limbo and somewhat socially isolated, although still living with relatives; a boy who had been rather friendless since leaving school and a child who was very lonely. Those who were more severely depressed included a young woman who had returned to a parent but who felt that her kin carers had favoured her sister. When asked what advice she would give to another child who was going to live with relatives, she said:

But I would just say, learn from everything that you do, anything that goes wrong, don't think of it as a bad thing, think of it as a lesson. It is going to be really hard but at least you're not in care. The only thing is, some people, certain people, I happen to be one of them, can't help it that they just generally do look on the bad things and always worry about it. The thing is I know I'm doing it and I really try to look at the good things but all the bad thoughts always come floating through my head.

The second was a child who had gone to live with his relatives who were still grieving the loss of one of their adult children. The third was a girl who had been singled out for rejection before she moved to her carers.

Three wishes

At the end of the interviews the children were asked what they would wish for if they had three wishes. Three mentioned having no money problems or having more money whilst many mentioned issues concerning their families. For example, one 10-year-old girl said: 'I wish I had all my family living with me.' another wished for her mother who had mental health difficulties to get better, to see her half-brother and for her separated grandparents to get back together. Another girl wanted her grandmother to be alive again and to be reunited with her family; a boy wanted to stay living with his grandparents and for his sister to join them; whilst another teenage boy wanted his mother to be alive again. Julian who was particularly lonely and lacking in friends wanted to see his father again and for his long deceased brother to be alive.

The parents

In addition to these interviews with children, we conducted interviews with six parents (three fathers and three mothers). Three were parents whose children were living with relatives. The children of the other three parents had been returned to them (or the parent was living with the relatives with whom the children were placed). The kin carers were mostly grandparents, aunts and uncles. It was not easy to interview parents as many kin carers preferred that we did not contact them. In a few cases, although the carers gave permission for us to contact parents, they had proved elusive or made arrangements to meet the researchers that were not kept. Although we only managed to speak to a very small group of parents, their views nonetheless proved interesting.

How the placements were made

Parents were frank about the difficulties that had led to their children moving to relatives. One mother described the domestic violence the children had witnessed and her own drink problem, whilst another talked about her 11-year dependence on drugs and the violence that she had endured from her husband, including stabbings and beatings. A mother who had learning difficulties admitted frankly that she had not been coping with her two small children and that one had been losing weight. One father had been instrumental in having the children removed from their mother after discovering their injuries during a contact visit, whilst two parents had been the subject of allegations of abuse.

Some mothers had suggested the placement with their parents and this had been followed up by social workers. In one case the move to relatives had occurred after a mother's complaint about ill treatment in foster care had led to placement breakdown. In another case, the mother had left her children with her parents when escaping from her violent partner and they had remained there when she returned to him. Two of the parents had fairly good relationships with the current kin carers but one mother's relationship with them was 'up and down'.

Two parents in contrast had objected to their children being placed with these particular relatives. After allegations of abuse against a father the children were placed with relatives. He said:

> We never agreed to any of it. Well number one, which is a very bad thing to do with kids, is me and the [relatives], never got on. And number two, we knew factually that the [female carer] herself, being in a barren marriage wanted our youngest daughter for herself. They don't realise that it's abusive to treat one as a favourite and the other not. And that happened a lot.

One couple explained that their children were moved to a relative once care proceedings were instigated after a series of allegations. However, children's services had then made plans for this relative to keep the children without involving the parents:

> And initially we felt betrayed by [my relative], even though we realised that she was only doing it for Stuart's sake, not obviously for anything against us. But it's almost as if you felt betrayed, because you know these people have obviously arranged this beforehand, and just not said anything to you.

The parents' views of the placements

In spite of these misgivings the parents felt that their relatives had provided good care for the children. Those who had asked for relatives to have the children, in particular, often saw the arrangements as beneficial both for the children and themselves:

> At that time it was brilliant 'cos Jan and Sophie was together. So at least she was with family and all that lot, so yes it was fine. I'd rather them be with family than strangers.

> I ain't lost nothing – not really. I still see them. I still get involved with their upbringing. I ain't really lost nothing, I'm lucky I didn't lose everything altogether 'cos they could have adopted them to other people and I'd never seen

them, and that's why I'm happy for them to stay here. I'd rather they stayed in the family.

Contributions to the kin carers

The parents did not contribute financially to their children, except in one case to give pocket money and in another to help the grandparents if they were in particular need. One mother bought the children videos, crayons and sweets when she could afford it: 'It ain't contributing, but it's doing something.'

Relationships between the parents and kin carers

Four of the parents had good relationships with the carers. A mother who was grateful for what her parents were giving her children said:

> I think they're better off here, I can't give them what my mum and dad give them. I know my mum and dad wouldn't do nothing to hurt them or nothing. They brought us up, there's nothing wrong with us, except I just went a bit off the rails.

One father had remained hostile to the placement and had only spoken to the carers through the children. He felt that his dislike was returned by the male carer who would say 'Oh God, it's him on the phone again' when he rang the house. Another mother explained that she had always had a difficult relationship with her mother, the children's grandmother who was their carer, and as a result this mother had stayed out of the children's lives for long periods.

Contact

Contact levels also varied. One mother saw her older daughter daily as she would drop in to see her on the way back from school but contact with the younger daughter had remained at six-weekly intervals, which she was hoping would be increased. A second parent saw her children all day on Saturdays at the grandparents, an arrangement which worked well. Another mother was devoting herself to her new baby and would have been happy to have less contact than had been arranged.

Two parents had had supervised contact because of the allegations made against them and these had changed to unsupervised visits, overnight stays and eventually the children had been returned. For the father who lived with his children and carers, all his time with the children had been supervised by the carers for the first year and this condition had subsequently been relaxed.

The parents' views of social workers

The parents' experiences of social workers ranged from the good to the bad. One father was very bitter at the way the allegations against him had been handled, that the children were removed and then placed with an aunt with whom he did not get on. He complained that none of his extended family was approached to look after the children, even though some of them knew the children better than the aunt to whom they went. He acknowledged that his family might not have been approached because of the allegations against him. He said: 'Our lives have been wrecked by the social services. My children aren't like family any more, really.'

He felt that his children would have made better educational progress if they had stayed with him and children's services had not interfered. Nonetheless, his current social worker was seen as acceptable:

> I've never really had any trouble with the present social worker. She's been the social worker for four or five years now, and she's always been fairly fair. But she's still the social worker. I think she still lies, and she still doesn't do what she says she's going to do, but she hasn't really picked on us as such.

Two other parents were either angry about the arrangements for their children to be placed with the relative carers or felt upset by the restrictions placed on contact with their children. One mother was critical of the social worker who, she said, rarely visited and did not involve her enough in her children's lives nor offer their grandmother sufficient help.

Two other parents recognised their difficulties in looking after their children and were positive about the assistance that had been provided. One had been referred by social workers to a hostel and had given up drugs and the other had received intensive residential help in order to help her to learn how to care for a subsequent baby.

Almost all the parents had been offered help with their own problems. Two had used the services of Alcoholics Anonymous to overcome their alcohol problems, one had received help with anger management and another was offered counselling by his GP and had later paid for counselling for himself. Two mothers had received assistance in leaving their violent partners.

The future

All of the parents who had their children living with them saw this as a stable arrangement. Two of the other parents were quite content for their relatives to bring up their children, either feeling that they themselves would not be able to do so or having moved their focus onto a younger child whom they had been able to parent more successfully. One mother, on the other hand, was hoping to get her children back one at a time.

Advice to others

When asked what advice they would give to someone else in the same situation, their answers reflected their rather different situations. One commented:

> Just basically work with your family and try and be involved as much as you can and also never give up, because you could turn round and land up retrieving your family that you once had and you lost.

A parent who thought that the children should never have been removed said:

> If you can take it then fight – fight tooth and nail. But if you can't take it – and I was very close to it – then cower down and if the social worker says, 'Jump,' just say, 'How high?' And I have fought, and it's lengthened the time that the kids have been away from us, no doubt, without a shred of a doubt. But my children should never have been taken.

Summary

The interviews with the social workers showed that they had strong views on both the advantages and disadvantages of kinship care. However, their views on the reality of kin carers' situations were strongly polarised. Those who considered that kinship carers received similar levels of service to other carers often did not know the levels of allowance they received and waited until asked for help, unaware of how difficult some carers found it to request assistance. They were also sometimes unaware of the extent of difficulties revealed in the interviews with the carers. In contrast, some social workers were very alive to the inequities in allowances and services provided to kin carers, did what they could to assist them and appreciated the quality of the kin placements. Whilst on the whole, involvement with kin carers was low key, in a few cases there were significant challenges to face where the family dynamics made intervention difficult.

The children's interviews revealed that some children did not understand why they were living with kin but nonetheless most felt settled and close to their kin carers. Two children were less happy about living with kin partly because there were no children their age in the area and they were lonely. There was a great variety of contact arrangements with most children seeing a number of relatives and often at least one parent regularly. A number of children wanted to see a parent (or sibling) more often or wanted to make contact with a parent who had lost touch with them, so issues about contact did not disappear simply because children were living with family or friends. Kin carers, especially grandparents, are sometimes in a position to help to trace a child's parent and re-establish contact, but this may not be possible for carers who are friends. The children who had social workers were generally very positive about them. A number of children described being bullied, sometimes about living with kin.

In the small group of parents whom we interviewed, half were pleased that the kin carers were looking after their children and about their own access to them but the others either objected to the children being placed with those particular relatives or had a poor relationship with them. Nonetheless, they all thought that the children were well cared for.

Now that the views of the social workers, children and their parents have been considered, we turn to examine in the next chapter the implications of the study's findings for policy and practice.

Chapter 10

Implications for Policy and Practice

In the context of placement shortages and concerns about the quality of care provided by local authorities for children living away from home, the issue of care by family and friends has become increasingly salient. There is very little research on kin placements in the UK, although the small-scale studies that have been undertaken by pioneers in this area have laid an important foundation of knowledge (see e.g. Broad *et al.* 2001; Doolan *et al.* 2004; Flynn 2002; Pitcher 1999). This study was undertaken to provide information about the characteristics, progress and outcomes of children placed with family and friends, to compare these with a similar group of children placed with unrelated foster carers and to consider the factors that contributed to success in kin placements. Through intensive interviews with sub-samples of the children placed with kin, their parents, kin carers and social workers, we aimed to shed light on the needs of these children and their carers.

The study deliberately set out to examine not only placements with relatives but also those with friends, unlike much of the research in other countries. Since the sample was drawn from family and friends carers known to children's services it does not include what is likely to be the much larger group of kin who bring up children under informal arrangements where children's services are not involved (Tapsfield and Richards 2003).

This chapter draws together the key findings from the study. First, differences in the outcomes of kin care placements in our four local authorities will be considered. Second, placements with kin will be compared with those with unrelated foster carers. The third section focuses on the outcomes of the two kinds of placements and considers which factors are related to 'success' in kin care. Throughout the chapter, attention will be drawn to some of the implications of our findings for policy and practice. The use of the words 'statistically significant', have been used sparingly in this chapter, but it should generally be assumed unless stated otherwise.

The kin carers

Amongst the kin carers, grandparents were the largest group (45%), followed by aunts and uncles (32%), who often considerably increased their family size in order to take the children, with much smaller numbers of older siblings and cousins providing care. A substantial number of friends of the family, neighbours, ex-residential workers, former step-parents, teachers and others also stepped in to care for the children when they needed a stable home, accounting for almost one in five (18%) of these carers. Excluding friend carers, two-thirds of the children were placed with maternal relatives and a third with those on the father's side of the family.

Differences between the authorities in the study

At the beginning of the study, policies on kinship care were being developed in a mostly *ad hoc* way in our four local authorities, often in response to shortages of unrelated foster care placements. Some emphasised the use of particular legal arrangements such as residence orders or Regulation 38 placements more than others. All the authorities struggled to decide whether the standard of care at assessment should be the same as for other foster carers or whether it only needed to be 'good enough'.

The use of kin placements varied from a high of 41 per cent of all foster care placements in one authority to a low of 14 per cent in another. The proportion of poorer quality kin placements was considerably higher in the high-using authority (49%) than in the others (where the proportion varied from 8% to 38%). This authority had the highest levels of deprivation and of drug-using parents and it may be that more placements of a lower standard had been approved or that their monitoring arrangements were weaker. In addition, it was notable that in the authority with the lowest disruption rate and the highest proportion of good quality kin placements, most kin carers had been approved as foster carers.

How the placements with kin compared with those with unrelated foster carers

Making the placements

PREVIOUS TIME IN CARE

Children who were placed with non-related foster carers had spent significantly more time in care prior to the study placement (mean 16 months) than had children cared for by family and friends (mean 10 months). On the other hand, two-fifths (42%) of the children placed with kin has spent most of their childhood with a relative, (compared with only 2% of children in unrelated care). It seems likely therefore that children in the two groups shared the experience of prior separations from their parents, but that those who were later placed with kin had more often lived for at least part of that time with a relative. These earlier periods with relatives may well protect children from some of the discontinuities associated with going in and out of care.

HOW THE PLACEMENTS WERE MADE

Most (86%) of the placements with kin were made because relatives or friends came forward to offer to look after children or were already caring for them. In addition, a small number of children initiated the placement themselves (9%), as did one parent. It was interesting to note how rarely social workers appeared to have initiated kin placements (4%) (see also Doolan *et al.* 2004), although it is possible that the case files under-reported their efforts. Social workers were generally reactive to offers of help from the extended family or friends, although they sought out and assessed relatives more actively during care proceedings, sometimes specifically on the advice of children's guardians.

Given how rarely it appeared that social workers had made the first move to instigate kin placements, it was not surprising to find that for the majority of children with unrelated foster carers (57%) a kin placement had apparently not been considered. However, previous research has noted that family and friends placements are poorly served by current children's services structures, where there may be a built-in disincentive to make such placements if the burden of locating and approving caregivers falls on overworked field workers (Waterhouse and Brocklesby 1999) and this issue was raised by social workers in the interviews. Indeed, some social workers considered that family placement workers should undertake assessments of kin because they are time-consuming, and the family placement workers have more experience of this work and are independent of the kin family, who are often already known to the children's social workers. Using specialist kin workers is another option. One of our authorities was employing specialist kin workers at the start of the study but later withdrew them. A second authority recruited two specialist kin workers after the fieldwork took place, although recruitment for these positions proved difficult.

None of the authorities in the study used voluntary agencies to assess or support placements, although this is an area where practice is developing (see e.g. Broad 2001; Thomas-Peters 2004). Nor did our authorities use family group conferences or family network meetings to make or sustain kin placements, although some researchers advocate this approach (see e.g. Broad and Skinner 2005; O'Brien 2001). Research suggests that family group conferences are more successful in activating the family network than more traditional decision-making processes, so that children are more likely to be placed with kin and extended family resources are harnessed (Hamilton 2004; Lupton and Nixon 1999; Marsh and Crow 1998; Ryburn 1998). However, they incur costs to run and their use is very variable around the country. There is now government encouragement to increase the use of family group conferences (DfES 2007) and they are likely to be especially useful in making or sustaining kin placements when more than one family member offers to look after a child or when relationships between kin carers and the parents or other family members are strained.

PLACEMENT PATTERNS AND SCOPE FOR MAKING MORE KIN PLACEMENTS

The placement patterns were rather different for the two groups of children. When the study placement was with a relative, the children were significantly more likely to have had previous kin placements (with this or another relative) and if the placement ended they were more likely to move to another relative. (Indeed, quite often the family had made contingency plans as to which relative would take over care if this was needed.) Similarly, those with non-related carers were more likely to experience a previous or subsequent non-related foster placement. While this might well mean that some children have fewer available relatives, it may also mean that less effort is made for children placed with unrelated foster carers to locate relatives if the placement ends.

Given this evidence that children who are established in unrelated foster care rarely later go to relatives, that family and friends care is generally initiated by kin and the variability of kin placement rates nationally, there may well be more scope for making kin placements (see also Sinclair 2005b). Of course, if kin placement rates were to rise sharply, standards might fall and more difficulties become apparent, as has occurred in the US. Less committed kin carers might also be recruited. However, at present we are likely to be some way from this situation in the UK.

PLACEMENT WITH SIBLINGS

Although it has been argued that one advantage of kin placements is that siblings can be placed together, in practice similar proportions of children were placed with siblings in the two groups (53% v. 52%). Slightly but not significantly more kin carers took large sibling groups of three to five siblings.

Whilst very often a relative or friend took all or most of whole sibling groups, sometimes a sibling group was shared out amongst extended family members. For example in one case, a six-year-old went to the maternal aunt, the eight-year-old to his paternal grandparents and the 12-year-old sister to the maternal grandparents, whilst the two-year-old was adopted by strangers. Contact between siblings (other than those who were adopted) was generally well maintained when such arrangements were made.

RELATIONSHIPS WITH OTHER CHILDREN IN THE PLACEMENTS

Whilst the carers' children had to readjust when their relatives joined the family, this was often made easier as the newly arrived children often already knew them quite well. Nonetheless, some children were jealous when their relatives came to live with them, feeling that they had lost out on their parents' attention (see also Farmer *et al.* 2004; Sinclair 2005b). This was particularly a problem when the new children were attention-seeking or showed difficult behaviour, or if bedrooms had to be shared with children of very different ages. Even when the children of the family had felt a little pushed out at first, they often became protective of their relatives.

PLACEMENTS WITH NO OTHER CHILDREN

More children who went to live with family and friends than those in unrelated foster care were the only child in the home. This was true for 22 per cent of children with kin but only 6 per cent of those with unrelated foster carers. The placements of these lone children in kin care had an increased tendency to disrupt as compared with those where there were other children in the household, although the difference was not significant. The interviews revealed some loneliness amongst lone children, especially if they lived with elderly relatives with few other children in the locality and little contact with the extended family. This would suggest the importance of providing opportunities, and if necessary funding, for such children to take part in activities outside school hours and to mix with their peers.

ETHNICITY

Significantly more black and minority ethnic children (60%) were placed with unrelated foster carers than were living with kin (40%). This is different to the situation in the US where African-American children are disproportionately represented among children cared for by kin, and this finding is contrary to what has sometimes been assumed to be the case in the UK. It may be that black and minority ethnic parents are less successful in coming to the attention of social workers when decisions about care are being made or that fewer are in a position to provide care. Indeed, Ince (2001) argues for the importance of black and minority ethnic families being encouraged to take a more participatory role in decision-making processes when their children face the prospect of being looked after.

On the other hand, those children who were placed with kin were significantly more likely than those in non-related foster care to be placed with carers who had the same ethnic background as the children. Nevertheless, 11 per cent of kin carers and 12 per cent of unrelated foster carers represented only part of the child's ethnic background, for example a child of mixed ethnicity placed with white grandparents.

These findings about ethnicity and placement are of particular interest because of the desire to maintain children's cultural identity and to match children to carers in terms of ethnicity (see for example Thoburn, Norford and Rashid 2000; Thoburn, Chand and Procter 2005). There is a need for more research on kinship care and ethnicity, particularly as there might be a considerable proportion of black and minority ethnic kin carers in the community who are in difficulty and have no contact with services (see Broad, Hayes and Rushforth 2001; Richards 2001). A good start would be made if there was fuller recording of kin placements in national statistics to ensure that children's ethnicity is recorded as well as information on the numbers of placements made and/or supported under residence or special guardianship orders, Section 17 payments as well as under foster care arrangements.

ARRANGEMENTS FOR APPROVING AND REGULATING THE PLACEMENTS

Over half of the family and friends placements were initially made under what is now Regulation 38 of the Fostering Regulations 2002; a provision that allows emergency placements to be supervised and assessed for a period not exceeding six weeks before other placement arrangements are made. Although the intention of these provisions was to cover unforeseen circumstances, in practice only a quarter (22%) of these cases were not already known to children's services. Moreover, after the initial six-week period, no other arrangements had been made for two-fifths of the cases and some were not assessed for many months and even years, leaving children in placements that had not been subject to any formal approval or checks and carers in receipt of very low and sometimes unreliable payments.

When carers had been assessed as foster carers, over time social workers tried very hard to persuade them to apply for residence orders (see also Broad *et al.* 2001). The impetus for this was sometimes a view that the care order could be discharged and appeared to be encouraged as a cost-saving initiative and to reduce the numbers of children in care. These approaches occurred even when carers clearly needed help with parents who were undermining the placement or with contact difficulties. The effect would be to end social work visits and to move carers to a payment system that was discretionary and set at lower rates than the fostering allowances. This was not always made clear to kin carers. Some carers resisted residence orders because they felt the need to maintain children's services involvement in disputes with the children's parents and to ensure adequate financial support. For other carers the attraction of residence orders was that it was thought to normalise the family situation.

When carers had agreed to take on a relative's child without children's services involvement, local authorities generally took the view that the children were not their responsibility and refused payment if the carers later requested help (see also Doolan *et al.* 2004). There was considerable confusion about the legal arrangements for family and friends placements and particular variation in relation to the arrangements made for placements with friends, which might be considered as private fostering arrangements, supported under the Section 17 children in need budget or approved as foster placements. There was also variation in how local authorities used the legal provisions.

There is clearly a need for explicit information about the legal and financial provision available to family and friends to be provided from the outset. This should outline the advantages and disadvantages of the various options available (Broad and Skinner 2005). Indeed, it is planned that local authorities will now be required to develop transparent policies on the support they offer to kin carers, which will be formally assessed by Ofsted (DfES 2007) and this provides an opportunity for more openness and clarity with kinship carers. It is also important that decisions to suggest that kin carers apply for residence and special guardianship orders should only be taken when placements are free from serious difficulties requiring children's services involvement and that carers should understand the implications of making this move.

ASSESSMENT

In two-thirds (65%) of the kin placements, carers were assessed when the child was already living with them. This has the potential advantage that the children's progress and attachment to the carers can be assessed. On the other hand, social workers highlighted the fact that it could be harder to deal with shortcomings or to withhold approval from an ongoing placement. The third of cases where family and friends carers were assessed before placement included those that arose during care proceedings, when children were often placed with unrelated foster carers until kin carers had been assessed. These cases were also assessed most quickly. Others took as long as three years before an assessment was conducted.

If the proposed carers were considered as not meeting the standards for approval as foster carers because of their past difficulties or current health problems they were sometimes advised to pursue a residence order. The paradox of this policy was that children placed with kin where there was greatest need or risk were further disadvantaged by residence orders, since social work support and monitoring ceased and payments were discretionary. Certainly, some family and friends carers with quite serious health conditions, or whose past parenting had not been optimal, cared for children very well.

A number of carers had been reassured during the assessment that their standard of living would not change if they took on the children because of the financial allowance they would receive. In practice these reassurances had proved hollow and left kin carers disillusioned. It became clear during the interviews that some workers did not know what allowances were paid to kin carers. Social workers clearly need to be able to provide full information about the different legal arrangements and the allowances paid by their authorities, so that they are well informed when these issues are discussed with family and friends.

Most kin carers understood the need for assessment, but some questioned the appropriateness of prolonged in-depth assessment when they had already cared for the children for considerable periods. A number of carers felt that the assessment approach for non-related foster carers did not fit their circumstances very well and would have liked a keener appreciation of the service they were providing for the children and of their need for information about the relevant systems and services. If practitioners were using the same assessment approach as for new unrelated foster carers it may well have fitted the circumstances of such carers rather poorly (see e.g. Broad and Skinner 2005; Thomas-Peters 2004). One experienced practitioner suggests that a hybrid of the BAAF Form F (which is an assessment tool used with foster carers and adopters) and aspects of the Framework for Assessment (Department of Health, Department for Education and Employment and Home Office 2000) may be most suitable for assessing kin carers and weighing up any potential risks (Thomas-Peters 2004) and there is some literature to assist practitioners undertaking assessment (see, for example, Broad and Skinner 2005; Crumbley and Little 1997; Jackson 1999; Pitcher 1999; Talbot and Calder 2006). Nonetheless, there is a need for further development of a suitable assessment approach for kin carers (see e.g. FRG 2007) and this appears to have been recognised by government (DfES 2007).

Most commentators recommend using a strengths-based model focusing on the family in its particular context in order to help families to identify their strengths and resources and to investigate, in partnership with them, what supports would be needed to enable them to care (see e.g. Aldgate and McIntosh 2006; Broad and Skinner 2005; Doolan *et al.* 2004; Greef 2001; Pitcher 1999; Portengen and van der Neut 1999; Waterhouse 2001). This would be a major improvement as long as needed services are actually then provided.

A small proportion (13%) of kin carers in the study received regular support from family members, others had none at all (see also Richards 2001), whilst a few had met opposition from the wider family. It is therefore important that an evaluation of the family's social support systems is undertaken during assessment, so that those with low levels of informal support can be offered higher levels of services if they are needed (see also Farmer *et al.* 2004; Quinton 2004).

Further consideration also needs to be given to the thresholds to be used for approving kin carers (see also Flynn 2002). Carers who would not have been approved as non-relative foster carers because of health, age, accommodation or past offences[26] were nonetheless able to provide a good standard of care. It is important that kin with high levels of need or background difficulty are not too readily excluded from being approved as foster carers and from being assisted financially and practically.

Assessments of parenting need to explore whether adults whose own parenting had shortcomings have now progressed and it should not be assumed that the presence of difficulties in their adult children, such as substance misuse, are necessarily related to deficient parenting (see also Hegar and Scannapieco 1995). A range of issues particular to kinship care also need to be addressed (see e.g. Crumbley and Little 1997), including the carers' ability to protect children from their parents when necessary and to manage contact with family members. At the same time the quality of relationships between the child and carers and other members of their family needs careful consideration so that lower standards are not accepted for kin placements (see also Thomas-Peters 2004).

In addition, it may be that either specialised placement panels are needed or that existing panels need some training about the distinctive features of kinship care if they are to facilitate these placements without compromising on assessing risk. Such training needs to ensure that normative assumptions based on the characteristics of non-relative foster carers or adoptive parents do not become a barrier to a full understanding of the strengths and potential of kin carers.

The characteristics of the carers and children

Carer characteristics

The characteristics of kin carers were different from those of unrelated foster carers in a number of ways. Significantly more were lone carers (27% v. 14%); the majority of whom were lone women (although a few were single men) and they lived, at least initially, in overcrowded conditions (35% v. 4%). In addition, many more kin carers had a disability or chronic illness (31% v. 17%) and experienced financial hardship (75% v. 13%). The average age of the 32 kin carers we interviewed was 57 with a range of 35–82 years.

OVERCROWDING

Kin carers were much more likely to be living in overcrowded conditions and often they could not afford to remedy this situation without help. Many took on the care of sibling groups and although a few managed to convert rooms or extend their houses to accommodate the children, others had to manage by using living space for sleeping or by means of bedroom sharing. This could put pressure on the older children of the carers who lost the privacy of having their own bedrooms and whose belongings were readily accessible to younger children who might disrupt or destroy them. In some cases families were living in extremely overcrowded conditions and, in a number, lack of space contributed to mounting tensions and made the placement untenable. In two cases, the local authority had paid for an extension to a relative's council house in order to accommodate a very large sibling group but in other similar cases such help had not been forthcoming. This is an area in which housing departments could facilitate placements by arranging for exchanges to more suitable accommodation, especially if senior managers in children's services work with housing departments to ensure that kin carers are made a priority group for re-housing.

HEALTH DIFFICULTIES

As kin carers got older, and sometimes from the onset of caring, at least a third experienced disability or health difficulties, although such difficulties rarely triggered additional services. They had to make their own arrangements to care for the children when these problems were severe and sometimes only managed because of daily support from their other adult children. There was little evidence that children were adversely affected by their carers' health difficulties and on the few occasions when these became severe or life-threatening, other relatives generally stepped in and assumed care of the children. Nonetheless, the older carers did find that they had less energy for child care than they had enjoyed when bringing up their own children.

FINANCIAL CIRCUMSTANCES

Most but not all the kin carers in the study received some financial help from children's services but the allowances they received were usually lower than those for unrelated foster carers. After the Munby judgement (FLR 2002), which clearly stated that local authorities should not discriminate against family and friends by paying lower fostering allowances, local authorities tended to pay kin foster carers the fostering allowance only, but without the additional payments for clothing, holidays, birthdays and Christmas that are routinely paid to unrelated foster carers. Kin carers looking after children who were subject to residence orders were often paid still less.

Some kin carers had had to reduce their income by giving up work or reducing their hours of employment in order to care for the children. Some managed financially, whilst others were in straitened circumstances, particularly when they cared for sibling groups, when children had special needs that made caring expensive or when payments were low or unreliable. Indeed, a few carers had only received full payments after they had involved others as advocates.

Some carers were also in debt because of court costs for residence order hearings or care proceedings (see also Richards 2001). Others were extremely hard up and struggled to make ends meet; they could not afford school uniforms, activities for the children, school trips or holidays (see also Aldgate and McIntosh 2006). It was quite common for kin carers to become socially isolated and some had not been out in the evening for years as they could not afford the expense of child sitters. In some of the families, the carers' own children were also disadvantaged and had to forego pocket money, activities, holidays and other treats.

As children reached adolescence, they were particularly aware of financial pressures that set them apart from their peers. From the perspective of kin carers, local authorities were short-changing them by not paying them at exactly the same rates as non-related foster carers when their expenses were the same. Indeed, if payments had been based on children's needs, these lower payments could not have been justified.

Thus, in a number of ways family and friend carers turned out to be considerably more disadvantaged than unrelated foster carers.

Children's characteristics

In contrast, the children in the two kinds of placements were remarkably similar in terms of their characteristics and the kinds of adversities, including child abuse and neglect that they had experienced prior to placement. They also had similar levels of emotional and behavioural difficulties overall, although children in unrelated foster placements were significantly more likely to have been recorded as having experienced emotional difficulties, such as anxiety and depression, before the study placement. Children with multiple health problems were more often placed with unrelated foster carers (43%) than with family or friends (21%), so it may be that children's services more often look for stranger foster carers when they need to place children with a range of health difficulties or that fewer kin feel able to undertake the care of such children.

The parental difficulties that had led to children being cared for away from home were also very similar. Similar proportions of the children had a parent who had died (11% v. 12%), experienced domestic violence (52% both), had mental health difficulties (44% v. 45%) or had misused drugs or alcohol (60% v. 51%). However, the children who had a parent who had been looked after by the state during childhood were more likely to be placed with unrelated foster carers than with kin. This suggests that professionals may exercise particular caution in placing children with relatives who experienced sufficient difficulty with their own children to necessitate substitute care.

Nonetheless, placements *were* made with relatives whose own parenting had shown some shortcomings, such as kin who had maltreated their children or who had had alcohol misuse problems. In spite of widespread concerns amongst practitioners about the transmission of dysfunctional parenting, on the whole these relatives had been able to parent the children adequately. On the other hand, in the very small number of cases where the children of mothers who had been (or were highly likely to have been) sexually abused by their fathers or stepfathers were placed with these men, these children were not successfully safeguarded (see also Margolin 1992).

In summary, there were few differences between the children who were placed with family and friends and those who went to unrelated foster carers. In contrast, the kin carers were considerably more disadvantaged in terms of their financial position, housing and health.

Contact

More of the kin placements were close to the child's family home and as a result fewer of these children changed school after the placement. Such proximity was however a double-edged sword, as when contact was problematic, such ease of access to the child was difficult for kin carers to control.

Children who were placed with relatives had higher levels of contact with aunts, uncles and cousins and, when they were living with paternal relatives, also with their fathers. Unsurprisingly, children placed with paternal relatives were more likely to maintain contact with their fathers and those placed with maternal relatives with their mothers. More children with unrelated foster carers (38%) than with kin (18%) had no contact with either parent.

Social workers have to assess whether relatives can protect children from their parents when necessary, and it is often assumed that this is a considerable challenge for kin, especially given such high-profile cases as that of Tyra Henry and Toni-Ann Byfield where children died because kin failed to do so. We found that children had not been protected from their parents or other relatives in just nine kin cases (6%). In most cases, kin managed the tricky business of putting the children's needs first very well.

However, difficult relationships between kin carers and the children's parents or other family members emerged for over half (54%) of the family and friends carers but for far fewer (16%) unrelated foster carers. Some parents were resentful that a relative had taken over the care of their children, other parents were actively hostile to the kin carers and a few made threats or actually attacked them, whilst others made false allegations against the carers or undermined the placement in other ways. Occasionally, two sides of the extended family were in conflict about who should be caring for the children. Work with the families as a whole was rare, even when conflicts between the kinship carers and the parents and other family members were acute, although it would have been helpful in some of these situations (Doolan *et al.* 2004; O'Brien 1999, 2000).

In such situations of conflict, family and friends carers often wanted the protection of care orders and the involvement of children's services in order to maintain adequate boundaries around contact between the children, their parents and/or other members of the family. In practice, social work staff supervised contact in far fewer kin carer placements (25%) than was the case in unrelated care (55%). Instead, kin carers supervised contact in two-fifths of the placements with supervised contact, something that unrelated foster carers undertook more rarely. They managed this difficult task very well and with considerable sensitivity to how parents were feeling. Indeed, it is notable that there were significantly more disruptions in kin care when contact was not supervised at all.

Some children were distressed and confused after contact with their parents, sometimes accompanied by deterioration in their behaviour (see also Farmer *et al.* 2004; Sinclair *et al.* 2004; Sinclair 2005b). The only time when contact with parents was terminated was as a result of advice from psychiatrists or other specialists. In many other cases more active management of contact by social workers was needed so that children did not receive confusing messages from parents about their ability to care for them and so that placements were not undermined. It is important that consideration is given to limiting or terminating contact when it is clearly detrimental to children.

The interviews with children revealed that whilst they often had a great deal of contact with extended family members, a few wished to see more of their parents, siblings or other relatives. Occasionally, kin carers were in a position to facilitate contact with a parent or siblings with whom the child had lost contact. When asked what they would wish for if they had three wishes, many of the children who were interviewed mentioned issues concerning their families. It is tempting to imagine that children living with relatives will not be subject to the preoccupations with birth families that characterise many children in care (see e.g. Ward 1995) but it appears that for some, at least, this is not entirely the case.

The impact of the children on the kin carers

Many of the carers had the satisfaction of seeing children flourish and thrive in their care. They also felt secure in the knowledge that they were providing an essential service to their family or friends and that they had obviated the need for the children to go into care and face an uncertain future (see also Broad *et al.* 2001). However, the positives in caring for these children were bought at a high cost for many carers.

Whilst ordinary foster carers plan to foster and this suits their life stage, for kin the idea of looking after someone else's children is neither planned nor expected. As a result, they made sacrifices and incurred losses to take the children (see also Young and Smith 2000). Several relatives gave up their jobs to look after the children, reducing their income and their pension entitlement. Ten per cent of the carers found that their marriage came under severe strain as a result of these abrupt changes in their circumstances and the complications of an 'interrupted life cycle' (Burnette 1999; Crumbley and Little 1997), in which retirement was indefinitely postponed and the task of child rearing taken up again. All but two of these marriages broke down (see also Jendrek 1994).

Moreover, older relative carers could feel socially dislocated as they did not fit with parents of the child's age or with their own friends who no longer looked after dependent children. Another big loss was the ability to go out in the evenings. Many had limited financial resources and found looking after children tiring when they were older and had less energy. Some too had other caring responsibilities for their own elderly parents or a sick partner (see also Pitcher 2002).

Some carers found that the time they were giving to the placed children lessened the time they could spend with their adult children, other grandchildren and partners. They also lost out on the pleasures of being grandparents as they had to take on the parenting role with its requirement to be the disciplinarian.

Grandparent carers were sometimes struggling with feelings of loss, shame or guilt about the difficulties of their adult children that had necessitated the children being removed from them or because they had been unable to take on a full sibling group and one or more of the children had been adopted by strangers (see also Minkler, Roe and Price 1992; Strawbridge *et al.* 1997). They sometimes also provided a great deal of support to one of the parents but knew that ultimately they had to put the children first. Others were still grieving for the death of the children's parents, and this could interfere with their capacity to parent effectively. Tensions with the children's parents and members of the extended family made caring for the children considerably more difficult. In many of these areas social workers or other professionals could assist carers.

Kin carers' views of the difference between kinship care and unrelated foster care

Several kin carers explained that being a kin carer was harder than being an ordinary unrelated foster carer because of hostility from the child's parents and lack of assistance with this. Those kin carers who knew foster carers were well aware that fewer services were provided and lower allowances paid to support kin placements. Unlike experienced non-relative foster carers who become adept at eliciting services (Farmer *et al.* 2004), many kin carers did not know what services existed, were reluctant to ask for help and when they did so were often told that as relatives they were not entitled to help, which effectively disarmed them. Indeed, it could be argued that whilst being a non-related foster carer is a source of pride, being a kin carer may be experienced as occupying a rather more ambiguous status (Crumbley and Little 1997).

There could also be the problem of being open about difficulties in review meetings when the children's parents, to whom they were related, were attending. Being honest in these meetings about the difficulties caused by the child or parent, carried the risk of heightening conflicts with the parents. This highlights the importance of discussing with kin before reviews how raising difficult issues will be handled at review meetings which the parents will attend.

Placement support services

Services

Social work visits to the children and the carers in kin placements were at slightly but not significantly lower levels than in unrelated foster care. In terms of overall levels of services and support from children's services, however, significantly more kin carers received low levels of service (69%) as compared with unrelated foster carers (47%). Particularly high levels of support had sometimes been needed at the start of the kin placements (see also Pitcher 2002).

Mental health services (28% kin v. 29% unrelated foster care) and statements of special educational need (22% kin v. 26% unrelated foster care) were provided for similar proportions of children in each group, whilst additional educational help was provided at only a slightly higher rate for children with non-related foster carers (31% kin v. 38% unrelated foster care).

Two-thirds of the children in each group had emotional and behavioural difficulties that ranged from minor to severe. For kin carers this presented particular challenges as they had neither been prepared nor trained to cope with children with such severe difficulties. Many kin carers struggled valiantly to bring order to these children's fragmented lives. Two-fifths of the children who showed any emotional or behavioural problems received some assistance, with similar levels of help provided to the children in the two groups. However, between a third (38% in unrelated care) and almost half (47% with kin) of the children with the most serious difficulties were not receiving any intervention.

Both groups of carers therefore lacked services. However, a major difference between the two groups was that very few of the kin carers had a family placement worker, whilst almost all the unrelated foster carers had the benefit of this second worker. In addition, few had access to training or to foster carer groups, which provide the additional benefit of enabling unrelated foster carers to give individual support and advice to each other.

Unmet needs

Given their backgrounds, it was not surprising that both groups of children often arrived in the placements with a legacy of behavioural and emotional difficulties. Parenting children whose previous experiences included domestic violence, parental conflict, abuse, neglect, mental health problems and substance misuse was very different from bringing up their own children

The many gaps in services for the children with kin carers no doubt in part reflects the paucity of specialist provision in some areas and the difficulty that kin carers have in gaining access to scarce resources. It also emerged that children's social workers (unlike family placement workers) were often unaware of the range of placement resources that existed for carers.

The most pressing need was for counselling and specialist help for children with severe and persistent behavioural and emotional difficulties. Kin carers also required adequate financial payments to cover the costs of caring for the children, including assistance with exceptional costs such as school uniforms or caring for children with acute health or behavioural problems. In the absence of such help, some carers were in situations of severe financial hardship. In addition, a few children clearly did not understand why they were living with family or friends and not with their parents and blamed either the kin carer or social worker. It is important that professionals ensure that clear explanations have been given to children about the reasons for the placement and that kin carers are given advice on how to address this issue with children as the placement progresses. In many cases, kin carers appeared to have avoided dealing with this question. It is likely to be considerably more difficult for family or friends carers to explain to children why they are not living with their parents than for unrelated foster carers, since kin sometimes have strong feelings about the reasons for care and may feel responsible for these difficulties (Crumbley and Little 1997). For a few children Life Story Work (see e.g. Shah and Argent 2006) was needed to help them to come to terms with their past.

At the same time, it appeared that not all the parents had either been clearly told or had accepted that they would not be able to resume care of the children and a number of children too lacked a clear understanding of the plans for their future (see also Aldgate and McIntosh 2006). Work with parents and children, to ensure that they are clear about future plans, is clearly vital. This might also go some way towards dealing with the fear of many kin carers that the children will be taken from them. Some children would also have benefited from advice about how to explain to their friends that they lived with kin. Whilst many children welcomed living with a relative as more normal and less stigmatising than being in care, a few were taunted by other children about their birth family or experienced bullying because they lived with relatives. These are areas of practice with family and friends that would benefit from more attention.

A range of services would have assisted kin carers. There was a clear need for assistance with contact issues when there were high levels of conflict or parents were undermining the placement. Many carers would have welcomed help or training to understand and manage the behaviours of the children they were looking after. Whilst the idea of training may lack appeal for some kin carers, they might be engaged by building on their desire to develop their skills and knowledge in the rather different situation of bringing up someone else's children (Doolan et al. 2004; Flynn 2001; NFCA 2000). Practical help with the caring task was also needed. Only 8 per cent of the kin carers received regular respite care. There were a good number of situations where regular support care or respite care might have provided a much-needed break for the carers and lessened some of the stress of caring (see DfES 2007).

Access to groups of kin carers would have been welcomed by some carers and might have lessened their sense of isolation and enabled links to be made with other kin carers (see e.g. Pitcher 2002). Financial help for activities for the children, for school uniforms and for child sitting to allow for occasional evenings out, was also often needed. A few kin carers clearly needed counselling in their own right, especially in coming to terms with unresolved issues of loss and guilt related to the difficulties of their adult children that had led to the children requiring their care. Carers with health problems or who had caring responsibilities for their elderly relatives sometimes also needed help from adult services, a link that was often lacking.

It did not appear that many kin carers were using services for parents in the community, such as parenting training and Sure Start, but this may have been because of the ages of the children when we interviewed kin. It is also possible that family and friends carers do not see such services as readily accessible or particularly suitable for them.

Relationships with social workers

Some kin carers praised the children's social workers highly and many were anxious to retain their involvement. Others were concerned about the lack of priority given to their cases. Whilst their comments have similarities to the views of non-relative foster carers from other studies (see e.g. Farmer *et al.* 2004; Sinclair 2005b), in other ways their experiences had been rather different. The kin carers had not infrequently had to battle to receive adequate payments or to resist pressure to apply for residence orders, situations that unrelated foster carers had not faced. They were also more likely to resent the specific restrictions that accompanied fostering children (such as seeking permissions for certain activities) which experienced unrelated foster carers take for granted.

The small number of children, who were interviewed, were mostly very enthusiastic about contact with social workers. Whilst social workers themselves generally saw involvement with kin carers as satisfying work, they sometimes faced kin carers who were far from acquiescent and were not in agreement with their views.

The difficulties posed by some kin carers

There were specific difficulties in helping a few family and friends carers. In these situations, the family dynamics served to keep the social worker on the periphery of events (see also O'Brien 1999). For example, a few social workers felt that a mother was playing off the carer against children's services so that both parent and carer became hostile to the social worker. At other times, extended family members colluded with the parents against the caring relatives. When the extended family was locked in conflict, intervention was particularly difficult and skills in mediation or family work were needed. In addition, there were particular difficulties if practitioners entertained doubts about the quality of an ongoing placement and had to balance the disadvantages to the child of a move away from kin against those of continuing in a placement of poor quality.

A small number of carers were openly hostile to the parents and restricted their contact or blocked help for the children. Overall, when we looked at the cases where carers were exceptionally uncooperative or resentful of children's services, these were often families that later emerged as having provided a particularly poor standard of care.

The outcomes of the placements
Children's well-being and progress in the placements

Having established that broadly similar children were placed in kin and unrelated foster care placements, we investigated how the outcomes for the two groups of children compared. We found that children showed similar levels of general health and school attendance in the two types of placement and more than three-quarters of the children (77%) in both types of placement also showed improved behaviour in their placements. Ratings on other dimensions of well-being were also very similar, as was the overall rating of the quality of the placements. Sixty-six per cent of the kin placements and 73 per cent of those with unrelated foster carers were considered to be positive placements in which the children were happy and developing well. Thirty-four per cent of those with kin and 27 per cent with unrelated foster carers were less satisfactory, including 10 per cent with kin and 6 per cent with unrelated foster carers that were highly unsatisfactory.

Duration of placements and why placements ended

The quality of the placements was therefore similar in the two groups. A major difference, however, was that by follow-up the placements with kin had lasted on average longer (4 years 9 months) than those with unrelated foster carers (3 years 11 months). Looked at another way, almost three quarters (72%) of the children with family and friends were still in the study placement two years from the date the sample was drawn, as compared with only 55 per cent of those with unrelated foster carers.

The higher rate of placement endings from unrelated foster care was principally because of planned moves to other placements, reflecting the much higher numbers of unrelated foster placements that were from the outset intended to be short-term. Disruption rates as a proportion of all the placements were very similar in the two types of placement (18% with kin and 17% with unrelated carers). Only five of the kin and two of the unrelated placements ended because of the carer's poor health or death.

Poor standards in placement

In most cases family and friends, like unrelated foster carers, provided excellent care for the children. The files contained many accounts of children with difficult backgrounds thriving once they moved to these placements. There were, however, 10 per cent of cases in kin care and 6 per cent in unrelated foster placements where the children's care was of a very poor standard. They included children who were singled out for rejection, bullied, beaten and neglected. There was no significant difference between the rates of poor placements in the two kinds of care.

However, the very unsatisfactory placements with family and friends lasted significantly longer than those in unrelated care. There seemed to be two reasons for this. Some placements continued because there was little or no social work monitoring and any referrals about difficulty (often from family members) were disregarded. In other situations, social workers had allowed standards to fall considerably below those that would have been accepted for other children, either feeling that they could not readily intervene in ongoing kin placements or thinking that, for children, being with family trumped other difficulties. It is never easy to move to end placements that have been implicitly approved for long periods (see e.g. Farmer and Parker 1991) and the fact that children were living with family members seemed to heighten this dilemma for practitioners. Since, in more than half of these cases kin had been approved as foster carers, foster carer approval did not of itself distinguish between these very unsatisfactory cases and others.

Allegations that appeared well founded were made against similar proportions of carers in both groups (4%). However, kin carers experienced more unsubstantiated allegations (4%) than unrelated foster carers (1%), most of which appeared to have been made maliciously by parents intent on undermining the placements. This could make it difficult for practitioners to distinguish between mischievous allegations from family members and those which expressed well-founded concerns about children's care.

These findings suggest that there needs to be improved review and monitoring of kin placements so that earlier, more decisive action can be taken in those few placements where care is clearly unsatisfactory for the child. There may also need to be an emphasis in training, at reviews and during supervision on the importance of maintaining adequate standards of care and not allowing thresholds for intervention to be set too high in kin placements. In addition, skilled communication with children is needed to assist them to voice any reservations they have about their kin placements without feeling that they are betraying their loyalty to family members. This is especially important when professionals or family members have reported concerns about the placement.

Factors that were related to placement outcome

Children placed with grandparents were the least likely to experience disruption (8%), as compared with 27 per cent of those with aunts and uncles and 30 per cent with other family or friends. This compares with 23 per cent of placement disruptions for children with unrelated foster carers. The lower likelihood of placement disruption with grandparents as compared with aunts and uncles may be because grandparents less often had their other children living in the family (11% of grandparent and 63% of aunt and uncle placements) and research has shown the link between placed children having a negative impact on other children in the family and placement disruption (see e.g. Farmer *et al* 2004; Sinclair 2005b). It is also possible that grandparents, more than other relatives, had cared for their grandchildren from early on in their lives. There was no difference in the quality of placements as between different relatives.

In addition, when kin carers had been approved as foster carers the placements were significantly less likely to disrupt than when they had not. This could be because the approval process had excluded kin carers with greater difficulties and/or because approved kin carers received more support. However, there were considerably higher levels of disruption in kin than in non-relative care when young people were aged over ten at placement. This would suggest the need for good assessment and more intensive support when older children are placed with kin.

Indeed, both types of placement were more likely to disrupt when children had behavioural problems or poor school attendance. Over half the children in both settings had emotional or behavioural difficulties that were sufficiently serious to require some help or remedial action. Kin carers were much more likely than unrelated foster carers to be struggling to cope with these difficulties (45% kin v. 30% unrelated foster carers). There were many reports on file of family and friends who were close to breaking point and worn down by the child's behaviour. Sometimes, additional difficulties were caused by one of the children's parents living in the home with the carers or the carers providing considerable assistance to parents who lived elsewhere. These findings echo those from other research that has shown that kin carers, especially grandparents, tend to be in poorer physical and mental health than unrelated foster carers (e.g. Hegar and Scannapieco 1999; Minkler *et al.* 2000) and experience considerable stress (Fuller-Thompson *et al.* 1997).

When carers showed signs of strain, significantly more placements in both groups disrupted but the disruption rates were higher in unrelated care (52% of strained unrelated placements disrupted as compared with 29% of strained kin placements). As a result, by follow-up, when carers were under strain, far more of the kin (71%) than unrelated placements (48%) were continuing. Similarly, when children's behaviour changed for the worse, both types of placement were more liable to disrupt, although in this situation considerably more of the kin placements continued in spite of this difficulty (56%) than did so in unrelated care (27%). In addition, the placements of children with particularly high levels of previous adverse experiences or of previous difficult behaviour significantly less often disrupted when they were with kin than when children were living with stranger foster carers.

As might be expected, the kin carers showed considerably higher levels of exceptional commitment (65% v. 31%) to the children they were looking after and many persevered under very challenging circumstances. Indeed, kin carers tended to treat the children they looked after like their own children (and the extended family generally also treated them as members of the family). In kinship care significantly fewer placements disrupted when carers were highly committed to the children, but this was not true in unrelated care. These findings together suggest that kin carers were more likely to persevere beyond the point at which unrelated foster carers conceded defeat, even when they were under considerable strain.

Return to a parent

Children returned more often to a parent from unrelated foster carers (13% of cases) than from kin (6% of cases). This was partly because the placements with kin in our sample were more often intended to provide a long-term home than an interim placement from which return could be affected. It may be that relatives do provide interim care more often than appears here, but that these arrangements are often informal and so would not appear in our sample (Brandon *et al.* 1999; Packman and Hall 1998).

Further areas for research

Much of the research on kinship care has been conducted in the US. However, this study suggests that American research in this field should be used with some caution since the profiles of children and carers in the two countries are rather different. The majority of kin carers in the US are elderly single African-American grandmothers, whilst most kin carers in the UK are white couples. Moreover, whilst kinship care in the US is disproportionately used for African-American children, in our study black and minority ethnic children were more likely to be placed with unrelated foster carers than with relatives. On the other hand, the kin carers in the two countries are alike in that they experience financial hardship, overcrowding and health problems.

In view of the paucity of research on family and friends placements in the UK, there are a considerable numbers of areas that would benefit from further research. Importantly, there is a need to examine how placements are made, the circumstances in which decisions are made not to use such placements and the interaction of these factors with ethnicity.

There is also a need for a scoping study to consider the organisational arrangements that best initiate and sustain kinship placements. This might assist in considering whether there would be advantages if kinship care was be treated as a different service from foster care (e.g. O'Brien 2000; Ryburn 1998) or whether there is more to commend bringing the two groups of carers under the same management and support structure (Flynn 2001; NFCA 2000). The use of alternative models where local authorities commission a voluntary agency to undertake kinship assessment and/or support work should also be considered.

Further research on assessments in kin placements is also very much needed, as is focused research on which interventions or support are most effective (see, for example, Kelley *et al.* 2001; Stozier *et al.* 2004). Studies should ideally include measures of strain and of the psychological well-being of kin carers so that these can be compared to those of other caregivers. It would be useful if research could include substantial proportions of black and minority ethnic kin carers to examine their situation and needs for service.

There is also a need for better information about the many family and friends who bring up children without making contact with children's services.

Attitudes to placements with family and friends

The social workers who were interviewed considered that care by family and friends conferred major benefits on children in terms of continuity, identity and feelings of belonging. However, the views of social workers on the reality of kin carers' situations were strongly polarised. Some considered that family and friends carers received similar levels of service and offered little themselves, whilst others were very alive to the inequities in allowances and services provided to kin and sometimes battled with their own managers to secure resources. This latter group of practitioners was also sensitive to the reluctance of many kin carers to ask for help, even when in considerable difficulty.

We detected a general attitude amongst social workers that kin should be able to manage without help (see also Stogdon 1999), which may in part be fuelled by ideas about the strengths of relative placements where children are already known to the carers, as well as by attempts to contain the costs of these placements. Such attitudes are probably also underpinned by a reluctance to assist family members to do what many think should be done out of a sense of kinship affection and obligation (O'Brien 2000). There may also be issues about giving more to relatives to support children than is given to parents; whilst relatives may be viewed more as service users than as people who are providing a valuable service. In addition, policy-makers and managers often have concerns that providing adequate support or recompense to kin will open the floodgates and be unmanageable (Tapsfield 2001). These attitudes are in urgent need of wider debate since it seems unlikely that adequate services will be provided to family and friends without a major change in such attitudes.

Conclusion

In the UK, in the absence of a strong policy steer at the national level on family and friends care, individual local authorities have developed policy and practice in a variety of ways and in response to varying pressures (Flynn 2001; Greef 1999; Tapsfield 2001). Some authorities have developed well articulated policies and practice, using research evidence and promoting a holistic, strengths-based approach (see e.g. Doolan et al. 2004), whilst others have moved to employ specialist kinship care workers, generally located in family support or family placement teams. However, those authorities that have not developed strong policies to enable and support carers are likely to be vulnerable to particularly variable practice on the ground. Indeed, a recent study (Sinclair et al. 2007) has found large differences between local authorities in their use of kin care and even greater differences between teams within individual authorities.

Special guardianship was introduced after the completion of this study and local authorities committed to enabling practice with kin carers may use it well, whilst other authorities could use it to restrict the services they provide to kin placements. Concerns about inter-generational dysfunction (see e.g. Flynn 2001; Ryburn 1998; Tan 2000) are often uppermost in the minds of practitioners and in a situation of resource constraint, kinship placements are readily targeted as an area of practice where cost savings can be made. The uneasy position of kinship care on the boundary between the public and private spheres of caring, leads to a situation where some kin carers struggle to care for needy children with low levels of support and financial help.

This situation mirrors that in the US where, without federal guidance, and despite considerable academic and political attention, there is confusion, uncertainty and variation by state (US DHSS 2000). However, an opportunity exists in this country to guide the development of kinship care before any steep upward growth emerges.

Commentators have called for an authoritative national policy and practice framework and guidance to improve the situation of kin carers and the children they look after (e.g. Blaiklock 2005; Broad and Skinner 2005; Farmer and Moyers 2005; FRG *et al.* 2007; Hunt 2003; Hunt *et al.* 2007; Sinclair *et al.* 2006). In response, the government has signalled its clear intention to provide a 'new framework for family and friends' (DfES 2007). This is intended to ensure that the option of kinship care is considered from the first stages of decision-making about children's placement needs and local authorities will also be required to consider kin as potential carers as part of the care plan lodged at the outset of care proceedings. This, together with the duty in the Children and Adoption Act 2002 to consider relatives when decisions are being taken about adoption, should help to ensure that kinship care is explored from an early stage. It is planned that local authorities will also be required to have transparent policies about the support they offer to kin carers, in line with a set of expectations of what an effective service should be, and these policies will be subject to inspection. In addition, kin carers will be entitled to apply for residence orders after children have lived with them for a year and the orders will continue until young people reach the age of 18. These policy changes are a welcome start and it is to be hoped that once the details of the new framework have been developed it will ensure that substantial improvements are made.

These developments will need to be underpinned by changes in social work education, post-qualifying and in-service training to highlight the contribution and particular needs of kinship carers and the approaches to them that are most beneficial (see e.g. Flynn 2001; NFCA 2000; Waldman and Wheal 1999). Training in ways of working with family networks and in mediation would also be useful (see e.g. O'Brien 2000, 2001), as would the further development of social work approaches that build on kin families' strengths and work in partnership with them. In addition, there might be advantages if work with kinship carers becomes a fully recognised practice area, but only if the status of workers is on a par with other specialist practitioners, such as those in the area of adoption and family placement.

There is already much that authorities can learn from each other about policies and arrangements that appear to facilitate good practice (see e.g. Ainsworth and Maluccio 1998; Beeman and Boisen 1999; Tapsfield 2001; Wheal 2001). It would therefore be helpful if the forthcoming changes were to be accompanied by a strong national initiative, building on the available research, which would encourage the development and sharing of good and innovative policy and practice throughout the country. However, such developments are only likely to have an impact if family and friends care is steered and prioritised at the highest levels within each local authority.

This study shows that children placed with family and friends do as well as those with unrelated foster carers but have the important advantage that their placements last longer. Placements with kin generally ensure that children thrive, are well nurtured and remain connected to their roots. These placements therefore deliver good quality and make a major contribution to stability for children who cannot live with their parents. This is a real achievement given the disadvantages faced by kinship carers. At present kin carers' commitment and willingness to continue against the odds benefits the children they look after, but the good outcomes for these children are sometimes achieved at the expense of the kin carers themselves. In addition, the recovery of some of the children with kin is being compromised by lack of services.

The challenge for children's services is therefore to build on good practice around the country and the emerging research evidence to develop and implement positive policies and practice in kinship care. We are at a crossroads where there is a real opportunity to ensure that kin carers do receive adequate remuneration and support and the needs of the children they look after are met so that they can recover from their past experiences and reach their full potential.

Variables Used
in the Regression Analyses

Note: A number of variables were excluded from each regression analysis because the numbers were small or there was too much missing data.

Variables used in the regression analyses for predicting disruption in kin placements

Prior to placement: Local authority, child's health problems, past behaviours (stealing or damaging property, truanting, school exclusion, offending), age when the placement was made, which relative placed with (e.g. grandparents or aunts and uncles), siblings still living with parents.

During the placement: School attendance, child being beyond control, whether contact was supervised, carer commitment, carer struggling to cope/strained.

Variables used in the regression analyses for predicting quality in kin placements

Prior to placement: Local authority, child's health problems, past behaviours (defiance at home or school, truanting, fighting other children, being fearful, bedwetting), levels of previous difficult behaviour, parental drugs misuse.

During the placement: School attendance, carer commitment, carer struggling to cope/strained.

Variables used in the regression analyses for predicting disruption in non-related foster care placements

Prior to placement: Age when the placement was made, high number of child adversities or separations from parents, past behaviours (defiance at school, stealing or damaging property, fighting with peers, truanting, school exclusion, bullying others, bedwetting, eating problems, depressed, self-harming, over-suspicious, number of emotional difficulties, overfriendly, inappropriate sexualised behaviour, sexually abusing/inappropriate behaviour, total numbers of behaviour difficulties), statement of special educational needs, with siblings in placement, siblings still living with parents.

During the placement: school attendance, educational performance below ability, emotional/behavioural problems requiring help, being beyond control, improvements in the child's emotional/behavioural development, carer struggling to cope/strained, mental health services offered to the child.

Variables used in the regression analyses for predicting quality in non-related foster care placements

Prior to placement: Parental drugs misuse, past behaviours (defiance at home and school, truanting, fighting other children, being fearful, bedwetting, history of poor appetite or emotional distress or lack of confidence, restless, lacking concentration, high levels of previous difficult behaviour).

During the placement: School attendance, emotional/behavioural problems requiring help, carer commitment, carer struggling to cope/strained.

References

Ainsworth, F. and Maluccio, A.N. (1998) 'Kinship care: False dawn or new hope?' *Australian Social Work December, 51,* 4.

Aldgate, j. and Bradley, M. (1999) "Supporting Families through Short-term Fostering." London: The Stationery Office.

Aldgate, J. and McIntosh, M. (2006) *Looking After the Family: A Study of Children Looked After in Kinship Care in Scotland.* Edinburgh: Social Work Inspection Agency.

Altshuler, S.J. (1998) 'Child well-being in kinship foster care: Similar to, or different from, non-related foster care.' *Children and Youth Services Review 20,* 5, 369–88.

Altshuler, S.J. (1999) 'The Well-being of Children in Kinship Foster Care.' In J.P. Gleeson and C.F. Hairston (eds) *Kinship Care: Improving Practice Through Research.* Washington DC: CWLA Press.

Australian Institute of Health and Welfare (AIHW) (2007) *Child Protection Australia 2005–2006.* Child Welfare Series No. 40, Cat. No. cws28, Canberra, AIHW.

Beeman, S., Kim, H. and Bullerdick, S. (2000) 'Factors affecting placement of children in kinship and non-kinship foster care.' *Children and Youth Services Review 22.*

Beeman, S. and Boisen, L. (1999) 'Child welfare professionals' attitudes towards kinship foster care.' *Child Welfare 78,* 3, 315–30.

Benedict, M., Zuravin S. and Stallings, R. (1996) 'Adult functioning of children who lived in kin versus non-kin family foster homes.' *Child Welfare LXXV,* 5, 529–49.

Berrick, J.D., Barth, R.P. and Needell, B. (1994) 'A comparison of kinship foster homes and foster family homes: implications for kinship foster care as family preservation.' *Children and Youth Services Review 16,* 1/2, 33–63.

Berridge, D. and Brodie, I. (1998) *Children's Homes Revisited.* London: Jessica Kingsley Publishers.

Berridge, D. and Cleaver, H. (1987) *Foster Home Breakdown.* Oxford: Blackwell Publishers.

Birmingham Area Child Protection Committee (2004) *Chapter 8 Case Review. Toni-Ann Byfield.* Birmingham ACPC Special Cases Review Group.

Blaiklock, O. (2005) *Britain's Pensioner Parents: The Quandary of Parenting Your Grandchildren.* A Report from the office of the Rt. Hon. Frank Field MP.

Brandon, M., Thoburn, J., Lewis, A. and Way, A. (1999) *Safeguarding Children with the Children Act 1989.* London: The Stationery Office.

Broad, B. (1999) 'Kinship care: Enabling and supporting child placements with kin.' In *Assessment, Preparation and Support: Messages from Research.* London: British Agencies for Adoption and Fostering.

Broad, B. (2001) (ed.) *Kinship Care: The Placement Choice for Children and Young People.* Lyme Regis: Russell House Publishing.

Broad, B., Hayes, R. and Rushforth, C. (2001) *Kith and Kin: Kinship Care for Vulnerable Young People.* London: National Children's Bureau.

Broad, B. and Skinner, A. (2005) *Relative Benefits: Placing Children in Kinship Care.* London: British Association for Adoption and Fostering.

Brooks, D. and Barth, R. (1998) 'Characteristics and outcomes of drug-exposed and non-drug-exposed children in kinship and relative foster care.' *Children and Youth Services Review 20,* 6, 475–501.

Brown, S., Cohon, D. and Wheeler, R. (2002) 'African American extended families and kinship care: How relevant is the foster care model for kinship care?' *Children and Youth Services Review 24,* 1, 53–77.

Burnette, D. (1999) 'Social relationships of Latino grandparent caregivers: A role theory perspective.' *The Gerontologist 39,* 1, 49–58.

Child Welfare League of America (2005 updated) *Kinship Care: Fact Sheet.* Available at www.cwla.org/programs/kinship/factsheet.htm (accessed on 9 April 2007).

Chipungu, S. and Everett, J. (1998) *Children Placed in Foster Care with Relatives: A Multi-State Study.* Washington, DC: Department of Health and Human Services.

Cleaver, H. (2000) *Fostering Family Contact.* London: The Stationery Office.

Connolly, M. (2003) *Kinship Care: A Selected Literature Review.* Auckland: Department of Child, Youth and Family. Available at www.cyf.govt.nz/documents/KinshipCare.pdf (accessed on 9 April 2007).

Crumbley, J. and Little, R.L. (eds) (1997) *Relatives Raising Children: An Overview of Kinship Care.* Washington, DC: Child Welfare League of America.

Cullen, D. and Lane, M. (2003) *Child Care Law: A Summary of the Law in England and Wales.* London: British Association of Adoption and Fostering.

Daly, M. and Leonard, M. (2002) *Against All Odds: Family Life on a Low Income in Ireland.* Dublin: Combat Poverty Agency.

Department for Education and Employment Literacy Task Force (1997) *The Implementation of the National Literacy Strategy.* London: Department for Education and Employment.

Department for Education and Skills (2000) *The Children Act.* London.

Department for Education and Skills (2006) *Statistics for Education: Children Looked After by Local Authroities Year Ending 31 March 2005,* vol. 1. London: Department for Education and Skills.

Department for Education and Skills (June 2007) *Care Matters: Time for Change.* Cm. 7137, Secretary of State for Education and Skills.

Department of Health (1995) *Looking After Children: Assessment and Action Records.* London: The Stationery Office.

Department of Health (1998) *The Quality Protects Programme: Transforming Children's Services* (LAC (98) 28).

Department of Health (1999a) *Children Looked After by Local Authorities, Year Ending 31 March 1989, England.* London: Department of Health.

Department of Health (1999b) *Children Looked After by Local Authorities, Year Ending 31 March 1998, England.* London: Department of Health.

Department of Health (2000) *The Quality Protects Programme: Transforming Children's Services 2000/01: District Council's Role* (LAC (2000) 15).

Department of Health (2001) *Children Act Report 2000.* London: Department of Health.

Department of Health (2003) *The Integrated Children's System.* Exemplars.

Department of Health, Department for Education and Employment and Home Office (2000) *Framework for the Assessment of Children in Need and their Families.* London: The Stationery Office.

Doolan, M., Nixon, P. and Lawrence, P. (2004) *Growing Up in the Care of Relatives or Friends: Delivering Best Practice for Children in Family and Friends Care.* London: Family Rights Group.

Dubowitz, H. (1994) 'Suggestions for future research. Special Issue: A research agenda for child welfare.' *Child Welfare 73,* 553–64.

Dubowitz, H., Feigelman, S. and Zuravin, S. (1993) 'A profile of kinship care.' *Child Welfare 72,* 153–69.

Family Rights Group (2007) *Pilot Assessment Template for Family and Friends Carers* (Unpublished) London: Family Rights Group.

Family Rights Group *et al.* (2007) *The Role of the State in Supporting Families and Friends Raising Children Who Cannot Live with Their Parents. A Policy Response to the Care Matters Green Paper.* London: FRG.

Farmer, E. and Parker, R. (1991) *Trials and Tribulations: Returning Children from Care to Their Families.* London: HMSO.

Farmer, E. and Owen, M. (1995) *Child Protection Practice: Private Risks and Public Remedies.* London: HMSO.

Farmer, E. and Pollock, S. (1998) *Sexually Abused and Abusing Children in Substitute Care.* Chichester: Wiley.

Farmer, E., Moyers, S. and Lipscombe, J. (2004) *Fostering Adolescents.* London: Jessica Kingsley Publishers.

Farmer, E. and Moyers, S. (2005) *Children Placed with Family and Friends: Placement Patterns and Outcomes.* Report to the Department for Education and Skills. Bristol: University of Bristol.

Flynn, R. (2000) 'Family and friends as foster carers: Briefing paper.' In *Family and Friends Carers: Social Workers' Training Guide.* London: National Foster Care Association.

Flynn, R. (2001) 'Training Materials for Kinship Foster Care.' In B. Broad (ed.) *Kinship Care: The Placement Choice for Children and Young People.* Lyme Regis: Russell House Publishing.

Flynn, R. (2002) 'Kinship care: Research review.' *Child and Family Social Work 7,* 311–21.

FLR (2002) Case Reference R. (L and Others) v. Manchester City Council, R (R and Another) v. Manchester City Council 1 FLR 43.

Fuller-Thompson, E., Minkler, M. and Driver, D. (1997) 'A profile of grandparents raising grandchildren in the United States.' *The Gerontologist 37*, 3, 406–11.

Goldberg, D.P. and Hiller, V.F. (1979) 'A scaled version of the General Health Questionnaire.' *Psychological Medicine 9*, 139–45.

Goodman, R. (1994) A modified version of the Rutter Parent Questionnaire including extra items on children's strengths – a research note.' *Journal of Child Psychology and Psychiatry 35*, 8, 1483–94.

Grandparents Plus and Adfam (2006) *Forgotten Families: Needs and Experiences of Grandparents Who Care for Children Whose Parents Misuse Drugs and Alcohol.* London: Grandparents Plus and Adfam.

Greef, R. (ed.) (1999) *Fostering Kinship: An International Perspective on Kinship Care.* Aldershot: Ashgate.

Greef, R. (2001) 'Family dynamics in kinship foster care.' In B. Broad (ed.) *Kinship Care: The Placement Choice for Children and Young People.* Lyme Regis: Russell House Publishing.

Greenfields, M. and Statham, J. (2004) *Support Foster Care: Developing a Short-break Service for Children in Need.* London: Institute of Education, University of London.

Grogan-Kaylor, A. (2000): 'Who goes into kinship care? The relationship of child and family characteristics to placement into kinship foster care.' *Social Work Research 24*, 3, 132–41.

Hamilton, A. (2004) *Rewarding the Family.* Edinburgh: Children First.

Hannah, L. and Pitman, S. (2000) *Oz child's Kith and Kin program.* Melbourne: Oz Child.

Harwin, J., Owen, M., Locke, R., Forrester, D. (2003) *Making Care Orders Work: A Study of Care Plans and Their Implementation.* London: The Stationery Office.

Hegar, R. and Scannapieco, M. (1995) 'From family duty to family foster care: The evolution of kinship care.' *Child Welfare 64*, 200–216.

Hegar, R. and Scannapieco, M. (eds) (1999) *Kinship Foster Care: Policy, Practice and Research.* Oxford: Oxford University Press.

Hunt, J. (2001) 'Kinship Care, Child Protection and the Courts.' In B. Broad (ed.) *Kinship Care: The Placement Choice for Children and Young People.* Lyme Regis: Russell House Publishing.

Hunt, J. (2003) *Family and Friends Carers: Scoping Paper Prepared for the Department of Health.* London: Department of Health.

Hunt, J., Waterhouse, S. and Lutman, E. (2007) *Keeping Them in the Family: Outcomes for Abused and Neglected Children Placed with Family or Friends Carers through Care Proceedings.* Draft Report to the Department for Education and Skills. University of Oxford.

HMSO (2002a) *The Fostering Services Regulations 2002.* Statutory Instrument 2002, 57, London: HMSO.

HMSO (2002b) *National Minimum Fostering Standards.* London: HMSO.

Iglehart, A. (1994) 'Kinship foster care: Placement, service and outcome issues.' *Social Service Review 16*, 107–122.

Iglehart, A.P. (1995) 'Readiness for independence: Comparison of foster-care, kinship care and non-foster care adolescents.' *Children and Youth Services Review 17*, 3, 412–32.

Ince, L. (2001) 'Promoting Kinship Foster Care: Preserving Family Networks for Black Children of African Origins.' In B. Broad (ed.) *Kinship Care: The Placement Choice for Children and Young People.* Lyme Regis: Russell House Publishing.

Jackson, S. (1999) 'Paradigm Shift: Training Staff to Provide Services to the Kinship Triad.' In R. Hegar and M. Scannapieco (eds) *Kinship Foster Care: Policy, Practice and Research.* Oxford: Oxford University Press.

Jendrek, M.P. (1994) 'Grandparents who parent their grandchildren: Circumstances and decisions.' *The Gerontologist 34*, 2.

Jordan, L. and Lindley, B. (eds) (2006) *Special Guardianship: What Does it Offer Children Who Cannot Live with Their Parents?* London: Family Rights Group.

Kelley, S.J., Whitley, D., Yorker, B.C. and Sipe, T.A. (2001) 'A multi-modal intervention for grandparents raising grandchildren: Results of an exploratory study.' *Child Welfare LXXX*, 1.

Kosonen, M. (1993) 'Descriptive study of foster and adoptive care services in a Scottish agency'. *Community Alternative 5*, 2, 126–8.

Kovacs, M. and Beck, A.T. (1977) 'An Empirical Clinical Approach Towards a Definition of Childhood Depression.' In J.G. Schulterbrandt and A. Raskin (eds) *Depression in Children: Diagnosis, Treatment and Conceptual Models*. New York: Raven.

Kroll, B. (2007) 'A family affair? Kinship care and parental substance misuse: Some dilemmas explored.' *Child and Family Social Work 12*, 1, 84–93.

Laws, S. (2001) 'Looking after Children within the Extended Family: Carers' Views.' In B. Broad (ed.) *Kinship Care: The Placement Choice for Children and Young People*. Lyme Regis: Russell House Publishing.

Lernihan, U. and Kelly, G. (2006) 'Kinship Care as a Route to Permanent Placement.' In D. Iwaniec (ed.) *The Child's Journey Through Care: Placement Stability, Care Planning, and Achieving Permanency*. Chichester: Wiley.

Lindheim, O. and Dozier, M. (2007) 'Caregiver commitment to foster children: The role of child behavior.' *Child Abuse and Neglect 31*, 361–74.

London Borough of Lambeth (1987) *Whose Child? The Report of the Panel Appointed to Inquire into the Death of Tyra Henry*. London: London Borough of Lambeth.

Lupton, C. and Nixon, P. (1999) *Empowering Practice? A Critical Appraisal of the Family Group Conference Approach*. Bristol: Policy Press.

Malos, E. and Bullard, E. (1991) *Custodianship: The Care of Other People's Children*. London: HMSO.

Margolin, L. (1992) 'Sexual abuse by grandparents.' *Child Abuse and Neglect 16*, 735–41.

Marsh, P. and Crow, G. (1998) *Family Group Conferences in Child Welfare*. Oxford: Blackwell Science.

Mason, J., Falloon, J., Gibbons, L., Spence, N. and Scott, E. (2002) *Understanding Kinship Care*. Sydney: NSW Association of Children's Welfare Agencies Inc. and the University of Western Sydney.

McFadden, E.J. (1998) 'Kinship Care in the United States.' *Adoption and Fostering 22*, 3, 7–15.

Messing, J.T. (2005) *From the Child's Perspective: A Qualitative Analysis of Kinship Care Placements*. Berkeley, CA: National Abandoned Infants Assistance Resource Center, School of Social Welfare, University of California at Berkeley.

Middleton, S., Ashworth, K. and Walker, R. (1994) *Family Fortunes: Pressures on Parents and Children in the 1990s*. London: Child Poverty Action Group.

Minkler, M., Roe, K.M. and Price, M. (1992) 'The physical and emotional health of grandmothers raising grandchildren in the crack cocaine epidemic.' *The Gerontologist 32*, 752–61.

Minkler, M., Fuller-Thompson, E., Miller, D. and Driver, D. (2000) 'Grandparent Caregiving and Depression.' In B. Hayslip and R. Goldberg-Glen (eds) *Grandparents Raising Grandchildren*. New York: Springer Publishing.

Morgan, A. (2004) *A Survival Guide for Family and Friends Carers*. London: Family Rights Group.

Mosek, A. and Adler, L. (2001) 'The self-concept of adolescent girls in non-relative versus kin foster care.' *International Social Work 44*, 2, 149–62.

National Foster Care Association (1999) *Survey of Young People's Views of the Fostering Service to Inform the National Standards for Foster Care*. London: NFCA.

National Foster Care Association (2000) *Family and Friends Carers: Social Workers' Training Guide*. London: National Foster Care Association.

O'Brien, V. (1999) 'Evolving Networks in Relative Care – Alliance and Exclusion.' In R. Greef (ed.) *Fostering Kinship: An International Perspective on Kinship Care*. Aldershot: Ashgate.

O'Brien, V. (2000) 'Relative Care: A Different Type of Foster Care – Implications for Practice'. In G. Kelly and R. Gilligan *Issues in Foster Care: Policy, Practice and Research*. London: Jessica Kingsley Publishers.

O'Brien, V. (2001) 'Contributions from an Irish Study: Understanding and Managing Relative Care.' In B. Broad (ed.) *Kinship Care: The Placement Choice for Children and Young people*. Lyme Regis: Russell House Publishing.

Packman, J. and Hall, C. (1998) *From Care to Accommodation: Support, Protection and Control in Child Care Services*. London: The Stationery Office.

Parker, R. Ward, H., Jackson, S., Aldgate, J. and Wedge, P. (1991) *Looking After Children. Assessing Outcomes in Child Care*. London: HMSO.

Patton, N. (2003) *The Effects of Parental Drug Use – Children in Kinship Care: A Review of the Literature*. The Mirabel Foundation.

Pitcher, D. (1999) *When Grandparents Care*. Plymouth City Council Social Services Department.

Pitcher, D. (2002) 'Placement with grandparents: the issues for grandparents who care for their grandchildren.' *Adoption and Fostering 26*, 1, 6–14.

Portengen, R. and van der Neut, B. (1999) 'Assessing Family Strengths – A Family Systems Approach.' In R. Greef (ed.) *Fostering Kinship, An International Perspective on Kinship Care*. Aldershot: Ashgate.

Quinton, D. (2004) *Supporting Parents: Messages from Research*. London: Jessica Kingsley Publishers.

Quinton, D., Rushton, A., Dance, C. and Mayes, D. (1998) *Joining New Families: Adoption and Fostering in Middle Childhood*. Chichester: Wiley.

R. *(ota) L.* v. *Manchester City Council* (2002) 1 FLR 43, QBD.

Richards, A. (2001) *Second Time Around – A Survey of Grandparents Raising their Grandchildren*. London: Family Rights Group.

Roskill, C. (2007) *Wider Family Matters: A Guide for Family and Friends Raising Children Who Cannot Live With Their Parents*. London: Family Rights Group.

Rowe, J., Caine, H., Hundleby, M. and Keane, A. (1984) *Long-Term Foster Care*. London: Batsford.

Rowe, J., Hundley, M. and Garnett, L. (1989) *Child Care Now: A Survey of Placement Patterns*. London: British Agencies for Adoption and Fostering.

Rushton, A. and Dance, C. (2003) 'Preferentially rejected children and their development in permanent family placements.' *Child and Family Social Work 8*, 4, 257–67.

Russell, C. (1995) *Parenting the Second Time Around: Grandparents as Carers of Young Relatives in Child Protection Cases*. Unpublished dissertation, University of East Anglia.

Ryburn, M. (1998) 'A new model of welfare: Re-asserting the value of kinship for children in state care.' *Social Policy and Administration 32*, 1, 28–45.

Scannapieco, M. and Jackson, S. (1996) 'Kinship care: The African American response to family preservation.' *Social Work 41*, 2, 190–96.

Selwyn, J. and Saunders, H. (2006) *Greenwich Kinship Care Team: An Evaluation of the Team's Work*. Report to Greenwich Council, The Hadley Centre, School for Policy Studies, University of Bristol.

Shah, S. and Argent, H. (2006) *Life Story Work: What it is and What it Means*. London: British Association of Adoption and Fostering.

Shlonsky, A.R. and Berrick, J.D. (2001) 'Assessing and promoting quality in kin and nonkin foster-care.' *Social Service Review 75*, 60–83.

Sinclair, I., Gibbs, I. and Wilson, K. (2004) *Foster Carers: Why They Stay and Why They Leave*. London: Jessica Kingsley Publishers.

Sinclair, I., Gibbs, I. and Wilson, K. (2005a) *Foster Placements: Why They Succeed and Why They Fail*. London: Jessica Kingsley Publishers.

Sinclair, I. (2005b) *Fostering Now: Messages from Research*. London: Jessica Kingsley Publishers.

Sinclair, I., Baker, C., Lee, J. and Gibbs, I. (2007) *The Pursuit of Permanence: A Study of the English Care System*. London: Jessica Kingsley Publishers.

Skuse, T., Macdonald, I. and Ward H. (1999) *Looking After Children: Transforming Data into Management Information: Third Interim Report to the Department of Health*. Loughborough: Centre for Child and Family Research, University of Loughborough.

Smith, A.B., Gollop, M.M., Taylor, N.J. and Atwool, N.R. (1999) *Children in Kinship and Foster Care*. Research Report. Children's Issues Centre, University of Otago, Dunedin, New Zealand.

Spence, N. (2004) 'Kinship care in Australia.' *Child Abuse Review 13*, 4, 263–76.

Stallard, P. (2002) *Think Good: Feel Good: A Cognitive Behavioural Therapy Workbook for Children and Young People*. Chichester: John Wiley and Sons.

Stokes, J. and Greenstone, J. (1981) 'Helping black grandmothers and older parents cope with child rearing: A group method.' *Child Welfare 60*, 691–701.

Stozier, A.L., Elrod, B., Beiler, P. Smith, A. and Carter, K. (2004) 'Developing a network of support for relative caregivers.' *Children and Youth Services Review 26*, 641–56.

Stogdon, J. (1999) *A Report to the Winston Churchill Memorial Trust: An Account of My Journey to the United States of America to Explore the Role of Grandparents and Kinship Care*. Unpublished report.

Strawbridge, W.J., Wallhagen, M.I., Shema, S.J. and Kaplan, G.A. (1997) 'New burdens or more of the same? Comparing grandparent, spouse and adult child caregivers.' *The Gerontologist 37*, 4, 505–10.

Strijker, J., Zandberg, T. and ven der Meulen, B. (2003) 'Kinship foster care and foster care in the Netherlands.' *Children and Youth Services Review 25*, 11, 843–62.

Sykes, J., Sinclair, I., Gibbs, I. and Wilson, K. (2002) 'Kinship and stranger foster carers: How do they compare?' *Adoption and Fostering 26*, 2, 38–48.

Talbot, C. and Calder, M.C. (2006) *Assessment in Kinship Care.* Lyme Regis: Russell House Publishing.

Tan, S. (2000) *Friends and Relative Care: The Neglected Carers.* Unpublished PQ in Social Work Dissertation, Brunel University.

Tanner, K. and Turney, D. (2003) 'What do we know about child neglect? A critical review of the literature and its application to social work practice.' *Child and Family Social Work 8*, 25–34.

Tapsfield, R. (2001) 'Kinship Care: A Family Rights Group Perspective.' In B. Broad (ed.) *Kinship Care: The Placement Choice for Children and Young People.* Lyme Regis: Russell House Publishing.

Tapsfield, R. and Richards, A. (2003) *Family and Friends Care: The Way Forward.* London: Family Rights Group.

Terling-Watt, T. (2001) 'Permanency in kinship care: An exploration of disruption rates and factors associated with placement disruption.' *Children and Youth Services Review 23*, 2, 111–26.

Thoburn, J., Norford, L. and Rashid, S. (2000) *Permanent Family Placement for Children of Minority Ethnic Origin.* London: Jessica Kingsley Publishers.

Thoburn, J., Chand, A. and Procter, J. (2005) *Child Welfare Services for Minority Ethnic Families: The Research Reviewed.* London: Jessica Kingsley Publishers.

Thomas-Peters, K. (2004) 'Assessment of kinship carers – Some key issues.' *Representing Children 17*, 2, 96–106.

Thornton, J. (1987) *An Investigation into the Nature of Kinship Foster Care.* Unpublished Doctoral Dissertation. New York: Yeshiva University.

Thornton, J.L. (1991) 'Permanency planning for children in kinship foster homes.' *Child Welfare 70*, 593–601.

United States Department of Health and Human Services (2000) *Report to the Congress on Kinship Foster Care.* United States Department of Health and Human Services, June.

Waldman, J. and Wheal, A. (1999) 'Training Needs of Friends and Families Who are Foster Carers.' In R. Greef (ed.) *Fostering Kinship.* Aldershot: Ashgate.

Ward, H. (ed.) (1995) *Looking After Children: Research into Practice.* London: HMSO.

Ward, H., Jones, H., Lynch, M. and Skuse, T. (2002) 'Issues concerning the health of looked after children.' *Adoption and Fostering 26*, 4, 1–11.

Ward, H., Munro, E.R. and Dearden, C. (2006) *Babies and Young Children in Care: Life Pathways, Decision-Making and Practice.* London: Jessica Kingsley Publishers.

Waterhouse, S. and Brocklesby, E. (1998) 'Kinship Placement in the United Kingdom.' In *Placement Choices for Children in Temporary Foster Care.* London: National Foster Care Association.

Waterhouse, S. and Brocklesby, E. (1999) 'Placement Choices for Children – Giving More Priority to Kinship Placements?' In R. Greef (ed.) *Fostering Kinship: An International Perspective on Kinship Care.* Aldershot: Ashgate.

Waterhouse, S. (2001) 'Keeping Children in Kinship Placements within Court Proceedings.' In B. Broad (ed.) *Kinship Care: The Placement Choice for Children and Young People.* Lyme Regis: Russell House Publishing.

Webster, D., Barth, R.P. and Needell, B. (2000) 'Placement stability for children in out-of-home care: A longitudinal analysis.' *Child Welfare 79*, 5, 614.

Wheal, A. (2001) 'Family and Friends Who are Carers: A Framework for Success.' In B. Broad (ed.) *Kinship Care: The Placement Choice for Children and Young People. Lyme Regis: Russell House Publishing.*

Wulczyn, F.H. and Goerge, R.M. (1992) 'Foster care in New York and Illinois: the challenge of rapid change.' *Social Service Review 66*, 278–94.

Young, D. and Smith, C.J. (2000) 'When Moms are incarcerated: The needs of children, mothers and caregivers.' *Families in Society: the Journal of Contemporary Human Services 81*, 2, 130–41.

Notes

1   July 2000.

2   To July 2002.

3   These figures show some differences between the local authority returns to the DoH (now to the Department of Children, Schools and Families) and their own statistics.

4   *The Integrated Children's System (ICS)* was developed to improve outcomes for children and is a practice and case record keeping framework for working with children and their families introduced by the government in the UK. It provides forms supported by information technology for recording assessments, plans and reviews on children and their families. It is based on an understanding of children's developmental needs in the context of parental capacity and wider family and environmental factors. *The Looking After Children* dimensions relate to children's progress on the dimensions of health, education, emotional and behavioural development, family and peer relationships, self-care and competence, identity and social presentation (see Parker et al 1991).

5   The Foster Placement (Children) and Adoption Agencies amendment (England) Regulations 2001 allowed authorities to approve a person as a foster carer or prospective adoptive parent where they or a member of the household have been convicted of or cautioned for a specified offence which was committed while under the age of 18 or was of a relatively minor nature. In 2002 the Fostering Services Regulations 2002 (HMSO 2002a) and the National Minimum Standards for Fostering (HMSO 2002b) were introduced. These regulations now require the same standards for family and friends foster carers as they do for unrelated carers (and see note 23).

6   In November 2001, Mr Justice Munby ruled in an administrative court case – *R.* v. *Manchester Council, ex parte L and Others and ex parte R and Others* – that the local authority was wrong to pay kinship foster carers less than other foster carers. The case concerned two applications for judicial review of Manchester's policy regarding foster payments for children in care. In one case the maternal grandparents of three children were made the long-term foster carers after care orders had been issued and in the other the children were placed with their older half-sister on care orders after an independent social work assessment – meaning the children were looked after within the terms of Sections 22 and 23 of the Children Act 1989. Munby ruled that the council's policy was in breach of the European Convention on Human Rights. It does not mean that local authorities have to pay all carers the same amount, but any difference in allowances has to take into account the needs of the individual child and not the status of the carer (Community Care 4 2004).

7   Regulation 38 of the Fostering Services Regulations 2002, which is intended to be used in unforeseen circumstances and may not last for more than six weeks. This replaced Regulation 11, which was used at the time of the study but we use the more up-to-date terminology for the sake of simplicity.

8   The fieldwork took place before the introduction of special guardianship orders (see e.g. Jordan and Lindley 2006; Roskill 2007 for details about these).

9   There was information on only 38 per cent of files about the financial circumstances of the carers (45% of kin and 30% of non-related foster carers).

10   A researcher rating of 'definitely overcrowded' was made if there was evidence on the file of overcrowding (e.g. social workers actively seeking alternative housing for families because the families needed more room after they had taken the child or children to live with them or if overcrowding was mentioned in the review minutes). This applied to 22 per cent of kin carer families but to only 3 per cent of non-related carers. A rating of 'probable overcrowding' was made when information on the file suggested over-crowding but no specific reference was made to this (e.g. a grandmother living in a two-bedroom flat who was taking care of two of her grandchildren) and this was true for 13 per cent of kin carers but only 1 per cent of stranger foster carers. There was no evidence of overcrowding on the file for 65 per cent of kin carers but almost all (96%) of the non-related carers.

11   The information from the case files about the health difficulties related to 65 per cent of kin carers and 32 per cent of the non-related foster carers.

12   In particular, in relation to schooling, these children were much more likely to be defiant or uncooperative at school (Fisher's exact test, $p = 0.000$), fight with their peers (Fisher's exact test, $p = 0.000$), bully other children (Fisher's exact test, $p = 0.000$), steal or break the property of others (Fisher's exact test, $p = 0.000$) and were much more likely to have been suspended or excluded from school before the study placement (Fisher's exact test, $p = 0.000$). Furthermore, they were more likely to have a history of self-harm (Fisher's exact test, $p = 0.002$), over-friendly behaviour with strangers (Fisher's exact test, $p = 0.001$), wetting the bed (Fisher's exact test, $p = 0.000$), soiling (Fisher's exact test, $p = 0.000$), being psychologically distressed (Fisher's exact test, $p = 0.000$), being miserable or depressed (Fisher's exact test, $p = 0.001$), having particular fears (Fisher's exact test, $p = 0.000$), displaying inappropriate sexual behaviour (Fisher's exact test, $p = 0.030$) and being over-friendly with strangers (Fisher's exact test, $p = 0.001$). There were no differences in these behaviours between the children in the two groups.

13   Regulation 38 of the Fostering Services Regulations 2002.

14   Part II of the Children Act 1989, Section 8, Residence Orders.

15   Private fostering regulations concern those children who are fostered privately under the age of 16 (or under 18 for young people with disabilities) who are cared for by someone other than a parent, relative, person with parental responsibility or an approved foster carer, for 28 days or more, whether or not any payment is made (Children Act 1989, Section 66) (Cullen and Lane 2003.) The Children (Private Arrangements for Fostering) Regulations 2005 revoke and replace the Children (Private Arrangements for Fostering) Regulations 1991 (SI 1991/2050). Measures in section 44 of the Children Act 2004 and the Children (Private Arrangements for Fostering) Regulations 2005 are expected to strengthen the private fostering notification scheme under the Children Act 1989 and provide additional safeguards for privately fostered children.

16   Information about family placement workers was mentioned on the case files of 45 per cent of the kin-placed children and 38 per cent of the children placed with unrelated foster carers.

17   The rating had four levels, as follows. In 'well-supported' placements children had an allocated social worker; carers generally received support from a family placement worker and had access to training and carer support groups. Children had access to help if they needed and wanted it (e.g. psychological help, Life Story work, keeping safe courses). If there were difficulties in the placement for whatever reason (e.g. illness in the family), extra help was provided (e.g. respite care, nursery places, supervision of contact). In 'fairly well-supported' placements, children and carers received many, but not all, of the support services detailed above. A rating of 'little support' was made when children and carers received few of these services and of 'no support' when none of these support services were provided.

18   Some carers with serious health difficulties were young, but grandparents more often suffered from heart disease and other serious illness, as would be expected.

19   Our approach to health was derived from the 'Looking After Children: Assessment and Action Records' and children were classified as being 'normally well' if they were unwell for less than a week in the previous six months. Children who were 'sometimes ill' were unwell for between 8 and 14 days in the previous six months; 'often ill' meant that they were unwell between 15 and 28 days in the previous six months and 'frequently ill' was recorded for children who had been ill for more than 28 days in the previous six months. This measure was about the general health of the child and even when children had a long-term health condition, it gave an indication of how frequently this affected their daily lives.

20   By 2002, DfES guidelines suggested that 80 per cent of children would reach the expected SATS levels (Level 2 at age 7; Level 4 at age 11 and Level 5 at age 14), (see DfEE 1997).

21   It will be recalled from Chapter 2 that children had already been in placement for varying lengths of time before the date on which we selected the sample but these durations were fairly similar for the two groups.

22   Children were selected for the study if they were in placement on 31 July 2000 and if their placements were still continuing on 31 July 2002 the placement was rated as having survived.

23   Since the numbers of disruptions were small we used statistical tests that allowed for this.

24   The subsequent introduction of the Fostering Services Regulations 2002 (Regulations 27 (5) and (6)) does allow the local authority to approve someone with specific offences as a relative carer. The specified offences are set out at 27 (7) and amplified by the Criminal Justice and Court Services Act 2000 Section 26 (1). The approval of a very senior manager would be required.

25   In practice, parental responsibility remains with the birth parents and is shared with the holder of a residence order. However, the holder of a residence order has the advantage of the 'status quo' if there is a challenge to the residence order.

26   The question of offences is now covered under Regulation 27 (6) of the Fostering Services Regulations 2002 (see note 24 above).

Subject Index

Author Index